Plotting the News in the Victorian Novel

Edinburgh Critical Studies in Victorian Culture
Series Editor: Julian Wolfreys

Recent books in the series:

Rudyard Kipling's Fiction: Mapping Psychic Spaces
Lizzy Welby

The Decadent Image: The Poetry of Wilde, Symons and Dowson
Kostas Boyiopoulos

British India and Victorian Literary Culture
Máire ní Fhlathúin

Anthony Trollope's Late Style: Victorian Liberalism and Literary Form
Frederik Van Dam

Dark Paradise: Pacific Islands in the Nineteenth-Century British Imagination
Jenn Fuller

Twentieth-Century Victorian: Arthur Conan Doyle and the Strand Magazine, 1891–1930
Jonathan Cranfield

The Lyric Poem and Aestheticism: Forms of Modernity
Marion Thain

Gender, Technology and the New Woman
Lena Wånggren

Self-Harm in New Woman Writing
Alexandra Gray

Suffragist Artists in Partnership: Gender, Word and Image
Lucy Ella Rose

Victorian Liberalism and Material Culture: Synergies of Thought and Place
Kevin A. Morrison

The Victorian Male Body
Joanne-Ella Parsons and Ruth Heholt

Nineteenth-Century Settler Emigration in British Literature and Art
Fariha Shaikh

The Pre-Raphaelites and Orientalism
Eleonora Sasso

The Late-Victorian Little Magazine
Koenraad Claes

Coastal Cultures of the Long Nineteenth Century
Matthew Ingleby and Matt P. M. Kerr

Dickens and Demolition: Literary Afterlives and Mid-Nineteenth-Century Urban Development
Joanna Hofer-Robinson

Artful Experiments: Ways of Knowing in Victorian Literature and Science
Philipp Erchinger

Victorian Poetry and the Poetics of the Literary Periodical
Caley Ehnes

The Victorian Actress in the Novel and on the Stage
Renata Kobetts Miller

Dickens's Clowns: Charles Dickens, Joseph Grimaldi and the Pantomime of Life
Jonathan Buckmaster

Italian Politics and Nineteenth-Century British Literature and Culture
Patricia Cove

Cultural Encounters with the Arabian Nights in Nineteenth-Century Britain
Melissa Dickson

Novel Institutions: Anachronism, Irish Novels and Nineteenth-Century Realism
Mary L. Mullen

The Fin-de-Siècle Scottish Revival: Romance, Decadence and Celtic Identity
Michael Shaw

Contested Liberalisms: Martineau, Dickens and the Victorian Press
Iain Crawford

Plotting Disability in the Nineteenth-Century Novel
Clare Walker Gore

The Aesthetics of Space in Nineteenth-Century British Literature, 1843–1907
Giles Whiteley

The Persian Presence in Victorian Poetry
Reza Taher-Kermani

Rereading Orphanhood: Texts, Inheritance, Kin
Diane Warren and Laura Peters

Plotting the News in the Victorian Novel
Jessica R. Valdez

Forthcoming volumes:

Her Father's Name: Gender, Theatricality and Spiritualism in Florence Marryat's Fiction
Tatiana Kontou

The Sculptural Body in Victorian Literature: Encrypted Sexualities
Patricia Pulham

Olive Schreiner and the Politics of Print Culture, 1883–1920
Clare Gill

Victorian Auto/Biography: Problems in Genre and Subject
Amber Regis

Gissing, Shakespeare and the Life of Writing
Thomas Ue

Women's Mobility in Henry James
Anna Despotopoulou

Michael Field's Revisionary Poetics
Jill Ehnenn

The Americanisation of W. T. Stead
Helena Goodwyn

Literary Illusions: Performance Magic and Victorian Literature
Christopher Pittard

The Ideas in Stories: Intellectual Content as Aesthetic Experience in Victorian Literature
Patrick Fessenbecker

Pastoral in Early-Victorian Fiction: Environment and Modernity
Mark Frost

Edmund Yates and Victorian Periodicals: Gossip, Celebrity and Gendered Spaces
Kathryn Ledbetter

Literature, Architecture and Perversion: Building Sexual Culture in Europe, 1850–1930
Aina Marti

Oscar Wilde and the Radical Politics of the Fin de Siècle
Deaglán Ó Donghaile

Home and Identity in Nineteenth-Century Literary London
Lisa Robertson

Manufacturing Female Beauty in British Literature and Periodicals, 1850–1914
Michelle Smith

New Media and the Rise of the Popular Woman Writer, 1820–1860
Alexis Easley

For a complete list of titles published visit the Edinburgh Critical Studies in Victorian Culture web page at www.edinburghuniversitypress.com/series/ECVC

Also Available:
Victoriographies – A Journal of Nineteenth-Century Writing, 1790–1914, edited by Diane Piccitto and Patricia Pulham
ISSN: 2044-2416
www.eupjournals.com/vic

Plotting the News in the Victorian Novel

Jessica R. Valdez

EDINBURGH
University Press

For Baltimore and Hong Kong

Edinburgh University Press is one of the leading university presses in the UK. We publish academic books and journals in our selected subject areas across the humanities and social sciences, combining cutting-edge scholarship with high editorial and production values to produce academic works of lasting importance. For more information visit our website: edinburghuniversitypress.com

© Jessica R. Valdez, 2020, 2022

Edinburgh University Press Ltd
The Tun – Holyrood Road, 12(2f) Jackson's Entry, Edinburgh EH8 8PJ

First published in hardback by Edinburgh University Press 2020

Typeset in 11/13 Adobe Sabon by
IDSUK (DataConnection) Ltd,

A CIP record for this book is available from the British Library

ISBN 978 1 4744 7434 4 (hardback)
ISBN 978 1 4744 7435 1 (paperback)
ISBN 978 1 4744 7436 8 (webready PDF)
ISBN 978 1 4744 7437 5 (epub)

The right of Jessica R. Valdez to be identified as the author of this work has been asserted in accordance with the Copyright, Designs and Patents Act 1988, and the Copyright and Related Rights Regulations 2003 (SI No. 2498).

Contents

Acknowledgements	vi
Series Editor's Preface	x
Introduction	1
1. 'These Acres of Print': Charles Dickens, the News and the Novel as Pattern	26
2. Arrested Development: Characterisation, the Newspaper and Anthony Trollope	59
3. 'The End is No Longer Hidden': News, Fate and the Sensation Novel	93
4. Israel Zangwill, or 'The Jewish Dickens': Representing Minority Communities in the Novel and Newspaper	124
Postscript	167
Bibliography	170
Index	186

Acknowledgements

Many have contributed to the eventual shape this book has taken. First, I want to acknowledge the support of various institutions that made this monograph possible. I am thankful for the financial support of the Early Career Scheme Fellowship, awarded by the Research Grants Council of Hong Kong. I received four courses of teaching relief as well as funding for a research assistant and conference travel. The Doris Zimmern HKU-Cambridge Hughes Hall Fellowship allowed me to work on the monograph in Cambridge and to share my research with scholars in the UK and Europe. A Visiting Research Fellowship with the School of Literature, Art and Media at the University of Sydney gave me time to complete revisions to the monograph and to share my research in Australia. Finally, the Faculty of Arts at HKU generously provided pre-tenure funding that assisted my revisions. While a graduate student at Johns Hopkins University, I received funding from the Johns Hopkins Program for the Study of Women, Gender and Sexuality which enabled me to visit Anthony Trollope's personal letters at Princeton University. The Johns Hopkins Program in Jewish Studies gave me the opportunity to teach the class, 'The Victorian Novel and the Jewish Question', which inspired the fourth chapter of this monograph. I am particularly indebted to my students in this class, whose discussion of Israel Zangwill's *Children of the Ghetto* enlivened my own research.

I also thank Edinburgh University Press, including Michelle Houston, Ersev Ersoy and Julian Wolfreys, for their help, support and efficiency. An earlier version of Chapter 1 was published in *Victorian Periodicals Review*, and a section of Chapter 4 appeared in *Studies in the Novel*. I thank the editors and reviewers of both journals for their helpful suggestions and permission to republish. Also, I thank the Lilly Library at Indiana University for giving me permission to publish an image from the Michael Sadler Collection of Ephemera.

I hired a team of undergraduate students to conduct online research for this project, and I want to thank them for their hard work: Chan Hiu Tung Samantha, Natalie Mo, Anne-Vivien Paris, Tan Hei Paul, Wong Jing Man Jessica, Olivia Xu Lingyi and Yuen Chi Heng Jason. While working on this monograph, I supervised three MPhil students, and our conversations indirectly contributed to the eventual book. These students are Olivia Xu Lingyi, Natalie Mo and Anneliese Ng Ka Man. Finally, I thank Niketa Gupte Narayan for her careful copyediting of the manuscript.

The Nineteenth-Century Seminar at Dickens Universe in 2016 was especially helpful in the transition from dissertation to monograph. I am indebted to Tricia Lootens and Sharon A. Weltman's leadership of our seminar and to the seminar participants for their community and feedback: Michelle Allen-Emerson, Alex Bove, Chelsea Bray, Dagni Bredesen, Benjamin Hudson, Rebecca Richardson, Jason Rudy, Tabitha Sparks and Lisa-Marie Teubler. I am so thankful to have been part of this seminar and to have formed lasting friendships as a result.

As a graduate student at Johns Hopkins University, I benefitted from the guidance, mentorship and training of Amanda Anderson, Sharon Cameron, Simon During, Douglas Mao, Chris Nealon and Jesse Rosenthal. I continue to benefit from the support of good friends from graduate school, including Elisha Cohn, Christiane Gannon, Jason Hoppe and Kara Wedekind. I am deeply appreciative of the support provided by the Gender History Workshop (fondly called the Geminar). This community of gender historians was essential to my Hopkins experience. They provided insightful feedback on early drafts of the chapters in this monograph as well as a rigorous but supportive academic community. In particular, I want to thank Claire Cage, Jessica Clark, Sara Damiano, Toby Ditz, Rob Gamble, Stephanie Gamble, Claire Gherini, Katie Jorgenson Gray, Katie Hemphill, Amanda Herbert, Katie Hindmarch-Watson, Elizabeth Imber, Ren Pepitone and Rebecca Stoil.

I thank David Hershinow, Stephanie Hershinow and Maggie Vinter for keeping me accountable over the past decade. Our 'Accountability Project' has been a source of companionship throughout every step of our careers. During our dissertation years, we met every 'First Friday' in Hampden, Baltimore. Now that we are scattered across the globe, we are fortunate if we Skype twice per semester; but we continue to stay in touch and to celebrate each other's successes. I am thankful for their continued friendship, and I am excited to see all our books finally come into print.

Nan Zhang is an especially dear friend and intellectual companion. She has provided unflagging support throughout my writing of this monograph as well as insightful feedback on earlier versions of several chapters. She is also a source of constant debate and inquiry, and I deeply value her presence in my personal and academic life. Finally, I thank her for hosting me years ago in Shanghai and making my career at the University of Hong Kong a possibility.

In Hong Kong, Emily Ridge has been there every step of the way with friendship and feedback. She encouraged me when I felt that this book was impossible, and she provided incisive and pragmatic suggestions on several chapters. I also appreciate the support and mentorship of my former and current colleagues in the School of English at HKU, including Wendy Gan, Haewon Hwang, Otto Heim, Elaine Ho, Chris Hutton, Adam Jaworski, Kendall Johnson, Douglas Kerr, Janny Leung, Dirk Noël and Page Richards. I am also thankful for the community of my newer colleagues, including Anya Adair, Elizabeth Ho, Rashna Nicholson and Nicholas Luke, as well as the help of our current and former office staff, including Samantha Chan, Anny Hui, Franky Lau, Mandy Leung and Tamix Wong. Kitty Mak has been an especially helpful and supportive influence. In the last stages of the revision process, the Women's Studies Research Centre's Writing Group at HKU has been a supportive community, and I finished my introduction during one of their on-campus writing retreats. Special thanks to Urania Chiu, who organised the writing retreats, and also to Julia Bowes, Staci Ford, Puja Kapai, Elizabeth LaCouture, Sylvia J. Martin, Priscilla Song, Alicia Weisberg-Roberts and Lisa Yiu. Above all, at HKU, I am grateful to my mentor, colleague and friend, Julia Kuehn. When I was a fairly fresh PhD and a new hire at HKU, I found Julia's generosity, encouragement and feedback essential to my transition from graduate student to professional academic. She has read many drafts of chapters and grant applications, and she has been an important interlocutor for me when thinking through my research. I cannot thank Julia enough for her generous and thoughtful mentorship.

Frances Ferguson helped shape the early seeds of this project when it was just a dissertation; I am thankful for her generosity, patience and insight. Judith Walkowitz became an informal second supervisor to me, and I appreciate her willingness to take an extra student under her wing. Caroline Levine read an earlier draft of the monograph, and her feedback helped me to transform it to its current form. And finally, I am indebted to Vanessa Smith for sponsoring my visit to the University of Sydney.

Isobel Armstrong has been a source of strength and insight throughout my academic career, which began during my first semester of graduate school with her seminar 'Space, Place, and Boundary in the Nineteenth Century Novel'. With the support of pre-tenure funding from HKU, she traveled all the way to Hong Kong to read and workshop my manuscript. Her feedback was transformative, and she is an example of what I hope to be as an academic, mentor and colleague.

I should also thank my friends who are not academics but who have supported me along the way, including Diana Iskelov, Euna Lhee, Pam Lowry, Debbie Tang and Denise Terry.

I am especially indebted to my parents, Jerry and Kathy Valdez, for encouraging my love of literature at a young age and for their support throughout the years. My grandparents – Caroline McManus, Norris McManus (who passed away before I finished my PhD), and Elizabeth Tobin Valdez – also have been sources of love and support.

I couldn't have finished this book without the love of my immediate my family: my funny cats – Teddy, Emma, Mimi (who recently passed away) and our new addition, Calvin – and finally, my husband, partner and best friend, David Schley, who has read every chapter of this monograph multiple times, and who means more to me than anything (even Teddy).

This project germinated in my graduate years in Baltimore and reached its fruition in Hong Kong. The writing of this monograph is intertwined with my memories of these two cities. I hope for a better future for them both, and this is why I have dedicated my book to them.

I am writing in September 2019, so I'll conclude with my support for the Hong Kong people and pro-democracy protesters:

香港人加油! (Hong Kong People, Add Oil!)

Series Editor's Preface

'Victorian' is a term, at once indicative of a strongly determined concept and an often notoriously vague notion, emptied of all meaningful content by the many journalistic misconceptions that persist about the inhabitants and cultures of the British Isles and Victoria's Empire in the nineteenth century. As such, it has become a by-word for the assumption of various, often contradictory habits of thought, belief, behaviour and perceptions. Victorian studies and studies in nineteenth-century literature and culture have, from their institutional inception, questioned narrowness of presumption, pushed to the limits of the nominal definition, and have sought to question the very grounds on which the unreflective perception of the so-called Victorian has been built; and continue to do so. Victorian and nineteenth-century studies of literature and culture maintain a breadth and diversity of interest, of focus and inquiry, in an interrogative and intellectually open-minded and challenging manner, which are equal to the exploration and inquisitiveness of its subjects. Many of the questions asked by scholars and researchers of the innumerable productions of nineteenth-century society actively put into suspension the clichés and stereotypes of 'Victorianism', whether the approach has been sustained by historical, scientific, philosophical, empirical, ideological or theoretical concerns; indeed, it would be incorrect to assume that each of these approaches to the idea of the Victorian has been, or has remained, in the main exclusive, sealed off from the interests and engagements of other approaches. A vital interdisciplinarity has been pursued and embraced, for the most part, even as there has been contest and debate amongst Victorianists, pursued with as much fervour as the affirmative exploration between different disciplines and differing epistemologies put to work in the service of reading the nineteenth century.

Edinburgh Critical Studies in Victorian Culture aims to take up both the debates and the inventive approaches and departures from convention that studies in the nineteenth century have witnessed for the last half century at least. Aiming to maintain a 'Victorian' (in the most positive sense of that motif) spirit of inquiry, the purpose of the series is to continue and augment the cross-fertilisation of interdisciplinary approaches, and to offer, in addition, a number of timely and untimely revisions of Victorian literature, culture, history and identity. At the same time, the series will ask questions concerning what has been missed or improperly received, misread, or not read at all, in order to present a multi-faceted and heterogeneous kaleidoscope of representations. Drawing on the most provocative, thoughtful and original research, the series will seek to prod at the notion of the 'Victorian', and in so doing, principally through theoretically and epistemologically sophisticated close readings of the historicity of literature and culture in the nineteenth century, to offer the reader provocative insights into a world that is at once overly familiar, and irreducibly different, other and strange. Working from original sources, primary documents and recent interdisciplinary theoretical models, Edinburgh Critical Studies in Victorian Culture seeks not simply to push at the boundaries of research in the nineteenth century, but also to inaugurate the persistent erasure and provisional, strategic redrawing of those borders.

Julian Wolfreys

Introduction

After returning from Australia for the first time in three years, George Talboys joins his friend Robert Audley at a Westminster coffee house. There he picks up a 'greasy *Times* newspaper of the day before from a heap of journals on the table', only to confront the printed evidence of his wife's death: 'On the 24th inst., at Ventnor, Isle of Wight, Helen Talboys, aged 22.' Audley tries to comfort Talboys and assures him that 'there may be some other Helen Talboys' or it 'may be a misprint for Talbot'. Talboys, however, believes that his wife is dead: 'Yes, there it was in black and white – "Helen Talboys, aged 22."'[1]

Talboys marvels that 'one line in the *The Times* newspaper could have so horrible an effect upon him', and he sits 'rigid, white, and helpless, staring stupidly at the shocked face of his friend'. It later turns out that Helen is not dead but faked her death so as to marry the wealthy landowner Sir Michael Audley. While Talboys takes the newspaper's report as unimpeachable fact, the novel shows it to be a fraud authored by his wife. *Lady Audley's Secret* (1862) dramatises a contradiction inherent in news: the form and structure of the newspaper invite readers to apprehend it as a factual account of recent events, but its contents are often wrong or even fraudulent. The news of Helen's death instigates the plot of the novel as Robert Audley begins to suspect that his uncle's wife, Lady Audley, is in fact Helen Talboys. The newspaper, like the novel, might also be called 'Lady Audley's Secret'.

Newspapers are frequently wrong in the worlds of Victorian novels, from the mistaken report of John Harmon's death in *Our Mutual Friend* to allegations of extra-marital affairs in *Phineas Finn*. They titillate, disturb and torment their readers with allegations that appear unlikely but true, and they both propel and disrupt the progression of novelistic plots. This monograph is about the ways that nineteenth-century novels envision newspapers and incorporate, problematise, and transmute news stories into fictional narrative. By fictionalising a discourse that lays claim to factuality, the novels examined in this book interrogate the operations of 'narratives of the real' and their effects on a community of readers. Fictional narrative functions as a form of media theory; novelists deploy the news in varying ways in order to explore the types of individuation and communal formation enabled by an expanding and diversifying newspaper press. By experimenting with the narrative functioning of the newspaper, the novel also undergoes a process of formation as it tests out the ways that texts can function. Victorian novelists thus emerge as early media theorists, thinking through the contrasting (and sometimes overlapping) systems of reality offered by newspapers and novels.

This monograph is called 'Plotting the News' because it traces the ways that Victorian novels experimented with news discourse by injecting it into varying kinds of plots and modalities, from the *Bildungsroman* to melodrama to the Anglo-Jewish novel. However, it could also be titled 'Analogising the News' since these novelists conceived the news through metaphors and analogies as a means of theorising its formal and social workings. Novelists across the nineteenth century cultivated a variety of analogies for the newspaper press, including 'acres of print', a 'corps of scribblers', 'Mt. Olympus', an 'ever-whirling wheel', and, perhaps most familiar to readers today, 'the fourth estate'. Newspapers claimed, in some form, to represent the nation (or fragments of that nation), and novels interrogated this representative claim through metaphorical and narrative logic.

The novels in this monograph cover a period of transformation in both the novel and the newspaper press, beginning with Dickens's early work in the late 1830s and concluding briefly with *Dracula* in 1898. The nineteenth century witnessed changes in the circulation of information no less transformative than the rise of the twenty-four-hour news cycle and the spread of social media have been in our own. Rather than offering a stable analogue for a nation, newspapers saw dramatic shifts in form, genre and readership over the period, sometimes within a single decade. It makes sense, then, that the writers in this monograph sought to analyse the social workings of news through a shifting series of metaphors, analogies and plots.

Nineteenth-century newspapers frequently relied upon modalities and genres that were also common in novels, and thus their figuration within novels provides a site of generic and formal theorisation, a site of meta-fictional practice. Each chapter of this monograph addresses a different narrative modality and its relationship to the news. Charles Dickens interrogates the distinctions between fictional and journalistic storytelling, while Anthony Trollope explores novelistic *Bildung* in serial form; the sensation novels of Wilkie Collins and Mary Elizabeth Braddon locate melodrama in realist discourses, and Anglo-Jewish writer Israel Zangwill explores how best to represent and mediate a hybrid minority experience. At the core of these metaphors and narrative forms inheres a theorisation of the newspaper's influence on society. By integrating newspapers and news stories into their plots, novels teach readers to reflect self-consciously on the forms and practices of the narratives they consume.

Analogues For The Nation

This monograph gets to the heart of scholarly claims that the novel and the newspaper analogise the nation in parallel ways. For Franco Moretti, the novel is the symbolic form of the nation, a 'form that (unlike an anthem or a monument) not only does not conceal the nation's internal differences but *manages to turn them into a story*'.[2] Many critics have seen the novel's formal elements – its free indirect discourse, its need for closure, and its frequent reliance upon an omniscient narrator – as tools of discipline and social control.[3] Realism in particular is seen as an instantiation of middle-class ideology. The novels in this monograph, however, invite readers to re-examine the operations of realistic and realist narratives, thus interrupting the apparent immanence of nation and community.[4] They do so at the level of representation, in scenes of newspaper reading, writing and circulation, as well as at the level of style, metaphor, plot and characterisation. The novel both incarnates and represents ways of interrogating national affiliations, showing that an individual's connection to nation is one of constant self-examination and revision.[5] On the one hand, as I will show, novelistic form shares some of the paradoxes of journalism, making the depiction of news and newspapers an important site for self-reflexive formal experimentation. On the other hand, novels feature newspapers that restrict the social experiences of characters and communities. Fictional iterations of the newspaper and other print media create breakages in plot and narrative that then require the novel to rework itself into an adapted form. Thus, the novels in this monograph constantly interrogate the ways that print media shape communities.

Understandings of the relationship between the novel and the nation have been influenced by Benedict Anderson's *Imagined Communities*, which emphasises the role of print media in facilitating modern conceptions of nation.[6] Anderson's analysis of print media is a formal one, as he claims that novelistic and newspaper form causes readers to 'think nation'. The 'old-fashioned' novel creates a fictional world that analogises nation; the imagined community in the novel moves up and down history as it follows a 'solitary hero through a sociological landscape of a fixity that fuses the world inside the novel with the world outside'.[7] The 'simple novel-plot' thus functions as a 'device for the presentation of simultaneity', as readers encounter characters that act concurrently in the same community 'without ever meeting'.[8] The newspaper similarly juxtaposes people and events 'without the actors being aware of each other', thereby connecting them in the mind of its readers. Anderson calls the newspaper an '"extreme form" of the book', in that it becomes obsolete almost as soon as it is distributed; the daily circulation of the newspaper thus creates an 'extraordinary mass ceremony: the almost precisely simultaneous consumption ("imagining") of the newspaper-as-fiction'.[9] For Anderson, then, there is no substantial difference between the fictiveness of the novel and that of the newspaper. He merges the formal and material qualities of both kinds of print media and suggests that they work together to analogise community. As Jonathan Culler has argued, Anderson is not interested in the specific communities imagined by novels but in their formal analogy to 'a society conceived as national'.[10] Anderson's theory thus relies upon a holistic account of novelistic and journalistic form.

This monograph argues, however, that Anderson's thesis of print media falls short in two ways. First, his account is a simplistic and generalised understanding of the formal workings of news and novel, one that fails to attend to textual and generic specifics as well as theories of how these media work. Second, he collapses distinctions between the novel and the newspaper and treats them as stable categories, whereas the novels in this monograph experimentally work through the potentialities of their formal qualities and participate in the formation of the process of categories. The novels discussed here experiment with the ways that text and discourse shape community via narrative formations.

Anderson's inattention to the nuances of fiction and non-fiction becomes evident in his case study from the opening of the 1924 Indonesian novel, *Semarang Hitam*. In the passage quoted by Anderson, a young man reads in the newspaper about a vagrant who died alone on the roadside. For Anderson, this doubleness – our reading about the young man reading – affirms the national imaginary invoked by the novel. He invites us to perceive the young man as a national type who represents the countless other individuals that make up the nation. Certainly, this is how Anderson understands the young man's response to the vagrant's death. He argues that the young man does not 'care the slightest who the dead vagrant individually was: he thinks of the representative body, not the personal life'.[11] The scene of newspaper reading thus exemplifies for the novel reader the community invoked by the world of the novel. For Anderson, the novelistic embedment of the newspaper in *Semarang Hitam* seems simply to reaffirm their intertwined fictionality.

Yet while both the novel and the newspaper ask the reader to imagine others and thereby extrapolate a larger community, one is blatantly make-believe while the other lays claim to some semblance of reality. Anderson's understanding of fictiveness – that is, the fictive quality of imagining a nation composed of other like-minded people – is not exactly the same as a fiction that is known by reader and writer to be make-believe. In Anderson's passage from *Semarang Hitam*, the newspaper asks the young man to imagine the death of someone presumed to be real, while the novel as a novel reminds the reader of the young man's fictionality.[12] This is doubly complicated when the newspaper report is embedded in a novel: in this case, a fiction represents the story as non-fiction, but the novel reader is simultaneously aware of its fictional place within a novel. By asking readers to read about a young man reading, the novel enables them to recognise this resemblance and to reflect on their own practices of reading, possibly with more aesthetic and narratological self-consciousness than evinced by the young man in Anderson's account. Thus, the embedded newspaper does not simply provide an in-text replication of the analogisation of national community of the novel; rather it becomes a site of metafictional awareness. By blurring the distinctions between the novel as self-professed fiction and the newspaper as factual fiction, Anderson's formal analysis fails to acknowledge the extent to which the fictionality of the novel enables a self-avowed and self-critical engagement with nation that emerges in novels.

Anderson is also inattentive to the nuances and variations in novelistic and journalistic form; his analysis relies predominantly on formal generalisations rather than textual and generic specifics and practices of close reading. In his account, the newspaper is characterised by an overarching structure, and it relies upon readers to respond uniformly to modern print media, when in fact readers respond to texts in unpredictable ways.[13] Anderson's account overlooks the 'significant heterogeneity in a population'.[14] Readers do not always consume the newspaper in its daily or weekly format, or identify with the imagined audience of any particular newspaper. In his critique of Anderson, Pierre Bourdieu and Jürgen Habermas for their inattention to generic and textual specifics, Dallas Liddle advocates for a more careful treatment of nineteenth-century newspapers that 'engage particular periodical texts *as* texts' and attends to the various genres that make up a newspaper.[15] Liddle instead traces a dialogic relationship between the nineteenth-century novel and newspaper, one that takes journalistic genres into consideration rather than treating the newspaper as a uniform structure.

This monograph interrogates the nineteenth-century novel's varying approaches to conceiving the newspaper as a form, system, genre, or collection of genres. Rather than instilling a uniform response in nationally minded readers, these fictional newspapers act on their worlds in a variety of ways. By incorporating newspapers and news discourse into their framework, Victorian novelists experimented with the ways that generic and formal qualities might have real social traction. This book explores novelistic imaginings of the press and its varying social effects. Characters consume the news in widely diverse ways, some finding themselves at the mercy of tyrannical editors and others reading the news radically against the grain. Novels explore, theorise and experiment with the formal convergences and divergences between the newspaper and the novel, as the embedded newspaper becomes a means of testing out the social repercussions of text. The self-avowed fictionality of the novel enables a critical engagement with the kinds of realities constructed in and from texts. Novels were already engaged in the practice of theorising the newspaper long before contemporary intersections in media studies, novel theory and print culture. This means that, rather than reinforcing bourgeois ideology, these novels are constantly experimenting with form, media and society.

Novelistic Realisms and the Form of News

When nineteenth-century novels incorporate newspapers and news stories into their fictional narratives, they play with the lines between fact and fiction. This book suggests that novelistic depictions of newspapers represent a continued project of articulating and theorising narrative realisms.[16] Critics have long argued that the early novel distinguished itself from lies and frauds through its formal realism; it claimed to offer a greater truth because of its freedom from referential reality.[17] By contrast, the mid to late nineteenth century has been viewed as a period of high realism, in which it would seem the forms and justifications for realism are well entrenched. I argue, however, that these depictions of the news in the novels reveal a self-reflexive interrogation of novelistic realisms and other narratives of the real. I understand realism in terms of formal and narrative self-reflexivity, an exploration of how form shapes readers and their social worlds. In one sense, we might consider novelistic representations of the newspaper and news discourse as sites of experimentation, where novelists tested out and imagined different scenarios for how print media might enter real life. In *The Serious Pleasures of Suspense*, Caroline Levine identifies realism as a mid-century 'critical aesthetic project' with a 'serious emphasis on testing and the suspension of judgment', borrowing 'their model of perception from scientific experimentation'. This experimentation, for Levine, is embedded in narrative suspense; Levine believes that novelistic realism entails 'the activity of stopping to doubt our most entrenched beliefs'.[18] I argue that novelistic realisms are based in an interrogation of realist modes through figurations of the newspaper.[19] Thus, my understanding of realism involves not its referential quality but its interrogation of media and narrative practices.

To understand nineteenth-century novelistic explorations of the news, it helps to think first about the formal difference between fiction and non-fiction. Ralph Rader argues that readers believe non-fiction to be true not because of its referential accuracy but because of its formal claim to external reference. He writes:

> The true story invites us to believe it as an account of fact and makes sense only if we do think of it as referring beyond itself to what its author did not create; it presents itself as true – reality referring – and our assumption that it is true governs our entire imaginative participation in its meaning and value. . . . Both the intelligibility and the effect of the true story, then, depend on its factuality considered merely as form, quite independent of the actual connection with external reality which the form of course implies.[20]

The way that a reader imaginatively responds to a text depends upon its formal cues. A true story necessarily requires a reader to process it as fact; if it turns out to be wrong, then it is experienced as fraud, not fiction. Thus, for Rader, the claim of a story to factuality inheres in its form rather than any real reference to external reality. His distinction is helpful in thinking through the kinds of reading invited by newspapers. News stories – presented as true – act on readers and their subjects in tangible and real ways, whether factual or not. This means that, even when characters claim to be sceptical of a particular story or newspaper, they can't help but respond to the allegations as true.[21]

Yet news is also a unique kind of non-fiction, because of serial distribution and, as a result, the passing interest of each issue for readers. As soon as the day's newspaper comes out, yesterday's paper is no longer 'news'. This regular routine serves to construct readerly relationships to the everyday. Writing of the periodical press more broadly, Margaret Beetham defines the periodical form according to its deeply regular structure; it functions as a regulating mechanism of readers' lives because of its close connection to clock time. She argues that it is impossible to separate the periodical from the structures by which industrial societies regulated between work and leisure.[22] This is all the more true for the nineteenth-century newspaper press, which tended to come out more frequently than periodicals and addressed a larger swath of society. The serial structure of the newspaper, what Anderson has called a 'mass reading ceremony', facilitated its intersection with and construction of perceptions of everyday reality.

The newspaper is not only characterised by its serial publication; theorists also identify a style and tense peculiar to the newspaper. 'The news' as a construct valorises recentness, immediacy and proximity in its selection and writing. It creates a style that suggests that something only just happened, what Lennard Davis calls the 'median past tense', rather than 'the normal tenses of past or present'.[23] This means that the newspaper mediates between narratives of the past (that is history) and those of the present (that is spoken language), casting itself in terms of 'slightly deferred immediacy'.[24] In this sense, then, the newspaper lays claim to and constructs conceptions of both reality *and* relevance, insisting upon its immediate application to the reader's world.

In its claim to relevance and reality, the daily or weekly newspaper creates the appearance that events and 'news' happen according to serial time. In doing so, they restructure readers' understandings of what is probable and realistic. According to Niklas Luhmann, the 'serial production of news' requires a systemic 'deception' in making it appear that news occurs on a regular basis.[25] Yet 'news' in its original sense refers to happenings that are out of the ordinary. As a result, modern news reconfigures our sense of the everyday, introducing the sense that uncommon and outrageous happenings might actually be normal. Luhmann insists that the idea of daily news – or news on any regular interval – is an 'evolutionary improbability', but because news has become a codified form, the system fosters and creates a perception of reality such that infrequent events become regularised and common. Luhmann understands the mass media as a system that constructs its own reality, one regulated by an internal code that determines what counts as information rather than by external standards for truth or objectivity. The very structure of the newspaper stakes a claim to facticity, necessitating that readers believe it to be recent, relevant and true. The factuality of news is thus embedded not only in the formal qualities of its stories, as Rader suggests, but in the system as a whole. By juxtaposing a structural claim to reality alongside an inclination to the newsworthy, the newspaper makes uncommon events seem part of everyday reality, a fact that Victorian novelists bring to the fore in their depictions of the press.

This is not to say that nineteenth-century novels or novelists were media theorists in the style of Luhmann, or that we can ahistorically apply Luhmann's theories of the mass media onto these examples. The novels in this monograph, however, do represent and analyse news in ways that critique the operations of the press and the form of the newspaper. The claim of the newspaper to reality is multifaceted, both inherent to its generic and formal structure as well as the implication that it refers to external events. Yet it also varies across newspapers and even particular genres within the newspaper. I argue that novelistic realism emerges in tension with the own brands of the real of the newspaper. George Levine has called realism a 'process' rather than a concrete genre, and he claims that nineteenth-century novelists 'were already self-conscious about the nature of their medium'.[26] Realists were responding to changes in their environment and engaging with ways to 'reorganise experience and reinvest it with value'.[27] I argue that part of this process of realism entails a complication and, at times, dismantling of the newspaper's claims to the real. In this sense, these novelists are neither naïvely mimetic nor repressively totalising in their representation of a real world; instead, they narrativise competing discourses of the real as a means of evaluating these realist claims and encouraging readers to become similarly conscious readers. The preoccupation of the novel with news highlights its own formal tensions and processes.

The British Press and the Nation

The nineteenth-century press featured a wide variety of publications, styles, genres and imagined readerships, ones that shifted dramatically over the century with developments in technology, literacy and communications. It included daily and weekly newspapers ranging from the establishment *The Times* to the radical *Reynolds Weekly*;

periodicals like *Cornhill Magazine* and *Blackwoods*; and family-oriented periodicals like Charles Dickens's *Household Words*. This multiplicity means that it is impossible to talk about the nineteenth-century press as a single entity. And yet, nineteenth-century writers frequently sought ways to speak of the press (or at least segments of the press) in ways that would allow for systemic evaluation, drawing upon metaphors and analogies to examine the press's role in a liberal society undergoing gradual democratic reform.

One common metaphor for understanding the press was that of the 'fourth estate', the conceit that the press represented the national public and acted as a check on the power of the government. The term is frequently attributed to Edmund Burke, first in 1840 by Thomas Carlyle.[28] Frederick Knight Hunt's *The Fourth Estate* (1850) traced the nineteenth-century emergence of press freedom and argued that a free press was a bulwark of British democracy.[29] This metaphor for the informal responsibilities of the press to the public became part of a national story of liberty and freedom; some scholars argue that the idea continues to shape contemporary histories of the British press. However, understandings of the press and its responsibilities to a national public often were in tension with each other and varied across the nineteenth century as the press underwent substantial changes.

On the one hand, perceptions of the press were related to larger debates about democratic reform. Fears about the mass electorate connected up with anxieties about the penny press and the 'unknown public'. By mid-century, Britain saw growing divisions in the reading public, as newspapers and periodicals targeted more specific readerships based on class, gender and other categories. Famously, Wilkie Collins wondered about the 'unknown public' in his 1858 article in *Household Words*, evidenced by 'a new species of literary production' available in shop windows and railway stalls.[30] He called it 'a public to be counted in the millions; the mysterious, the unfathomable, the universal public'.[31] Many Victorians worried about the dangers of volatile, unreliable and uneducated readers. As the newspaper press came to be seen as the voice of the British public (or publics), it also became increasingly associated with the marketplace and a newly emerging mass culture.[32] Sally Ledger has argued that the period saw a larger shift from an eighteenth-century conception of the people as a political entity towards an understanding of the people, or populace, as a commercial entity, partly because of the rise of the mass-market commercial newspaper press in the 1840s. Drawing upon John Barrell, Ivan Kreilkamp writes, 'The word "public" now signified, not an ideal of civic life, but simply "the country as an aggregate" and thus "the members of a community."'[33] Elaine Hadley has argued that the new prominence of mediated mass publicity was perceived as a 'phantasmagoric threat' to liberal values.³⁴ Matthew Arnold worried that newspapers fragmented the public into self-interested groups incapable of abstract thought; each publication was too deeply grounded in the practical and commercial interests of its target readership. For John Stuart Mill, the newspaper press inhibited individuality and independent thinking, fostering instead 'collective mediocrity' and the 'tyranny of opinion'. In all these accounts, the modern newspaper heralded a new understanding of the public sphere.³⁵ Debates about the newspaper press also interrogated the exact nature of the relationship between a newspaper and the public. Was it the responsibility of the newspaper to mirror an existing public or contribute to the creation of a public (or publics)? Was its role to educate a rational populace? Or did it threaten to become tyrannical in its capacity to influence an unthinking mass of readers?³⁶ These questions get to the heart of the realist mode and also proffered novelists the opportunity to mediate the novel's relationship to a nation and public.

Two contradictory visions of the national press, published some twenty years apart, illustrate the ways in which understandings of the media transformed across the 1850s and 60s. In 1850, an article in Dickens's *Household Words* depicted the newspaper as a symbol of British identity. It playfully foregrounds the newspaper at a British breakfast table, mocking celebrated chef and food writer Alexis Soyer's failure to appreciate its importance:

> [W]hen – with the unction of a gastronome, and the thoughtful skill of an artist – [Alexis Soyer] marshals forth all the luxuries of the British breakfast-table, and forgets to mention its first necessity, he shows a sort of ignorance. We put it to his already extensive knowledge of English character, whether he thinks it possible for any English subject whose means bring him under the screw of the Income-tax, to break his fast without – a newspaper.³⁷

By ridiculing Soyer's lack of cultural insight, the narrator asserts the role of the periodical as national critic while simultaneously making the newspaper a regular part of the imagined Englishman's morning. The article at first focuses on the breakfast habits of the privileged landowner, but it later expands the newspaper's circle of influence to include the noble lord and his 'Morning Post'; the minister of state and the *The Times* and the *Globe*; the farmer and the *Herald* or *Standard*; the conservative and his *Chronicle*; and the financial reformer with the *Daily News* and the *Express*. While each type is categorised according to his or her particular newspaper, the regular habit of newspaper reading makes them all English. This inclusiveness extends to the provinces, which 'cannot – once a week at least – satisfy their digestive organs till their local organ has satisfied their minds'.[38] The sheer expanse of these newspapers stands in for and expands the geography of Britain: 'If to these are added all the papers printed weekly and fortnightly in London and the provinces, the whole amounts to 1,446,150,000 square feet of printed surface, which was, in 1849, placed before the comprehensive vision of John Bull'. The newspapers engulf the physical space of England and dominate the visual field of the average 'John Bull'. In this sense, the content, form and materiality of the newspaper stand in for the British nation. Yet the article's account of this cultural practice also importantly excludes someone like Soyer, 'a foreigner' who has made England his 'adopted nation' after immigrating from France. Even though he was a celebrity chef in England and helped supply food to British soldiers in the Crimean War, the article leaves him outside the national imaginary. 'The Appetite for News' came out in 1850 at a time when the Taxes on Knowledge were still in effect and the penny press had yet to become a marked influence on another subset of the British public that 'The Appetite for News' excludes. Instead, "The Appetite for News" optimistically touts the importance of a free press to "the freedom and prosperity of the people."'[39]

More than twenty years later, a different vision of a diverse but representative British press arises in the 1873 cartoon, 'Our National Press', in which the caricaturist Gegeef depicts twelve daily newspapers that make up the British public sphere (Fig. 1). Coming out after the end of the Taxes on Knowledge and the expansion of a cheap press, this cartoon depicts a debased public that unthinkingly consumes lies, fluff and fraud, reflecting Habermas's account of the decline of the public sphere. The cartoon is part of a series of cartoons depicting national institutions, including 'Our National Church', 'Our National Parliament' and 'Our National Law'. Each newspaper is associated with two illustrated readers caricatured as national types, ranging from No. 5, who 'is the amiable gentleman who likes the high-class sentiment which pervades the D. N. [*Daily News*]' to No. 13, who

> was a Radical when young and of a strong mind. Was once a gentleman, always rich, was crossed in love; lost his brain in the field (racing,) and his temper with the gout; is bilious, out of sorts with the world, has no one to love him, nor amuse him; no one to abuse, nor be abused by, so naturally reads the STANDARD to prevent himself becoming mouldy.[40]

These characters are rendered visually and textually; some are described in remarkably specific narrative detail while still invoked as a more general type. The logic of this cartoon is circular: the newspapers exist because of their readers, and their readers come into public existence because they are reflected in the press. The cartoon foregrounds newspaper readers and renders the production of news in terms of mechanistic input and output. The labour of writers is figured only as ink, quill and an eye and an ear. The central box, labelled 'NEWS', represents the press as sort of a mini factory that resembles a slot machine; the telegraph wires extend into the machine, where they are transformed into coins labelled 'Leader', 'Critique' and 'All about Everything'. This cartoon imagines 'news' in a broad sense to contain a range of content, including the leader (or editorial), foreign correspondence, fashion, obituaries, opinion, rubbish, 'all about everything', money to lend, policy births and multiple instances of 'Puff'. Individual newspapers include law reports, beer and religion (*The Morning Advertiser*); 'follow my leader' (*The Times*); and 'to be sold' and bargains (*The Clerkenwell News*). The cartoon suggests the sheer variety of news items and their imagined publics, yet each paper is presented within an identical box. The presumption here is that the variety of materials, readers and news items make up the larger system of 'Our National Press'. Whereas the 1850 depiction from *Household Words* imagines a national whole in the routine practice of breakfast, Gegeef renders the press into a vast machine that generates print that is unreflective, random and shamelessly churned out to appeal to the self-interest of each group. Each reading public does not build up into a larger public, except insofar as they are part of the same factory of news.

The slot machine contains a mini-newspaper in which fact and principle are opposed to fiction and interest. This tension is a theme continued throughout the commentary of the cartoon. Gegeef writes, 'Daily papers, unavoidably perhaps, contain about equal proportions of Fact and Fiction, (including advertisements;) and sometimes Interest gets the upper hand of Principle.' Thus, this mingling of fact and fiction, principle and interest, is not the ethical responsibility of an individual writer but rather a contradiction inherent to newspaper form itself. While the illustration of the slot machine suggests an even opposition between fact and fiction, some of the examples suggest that these features are not so evenly distributed across each individual newspaper. For instance, a caption under the *Globe* suggests that its readers 'see no difference between Romance and Reality'. The reader of the *Daily Telegraph* (founded 1855) is a 'worshipper

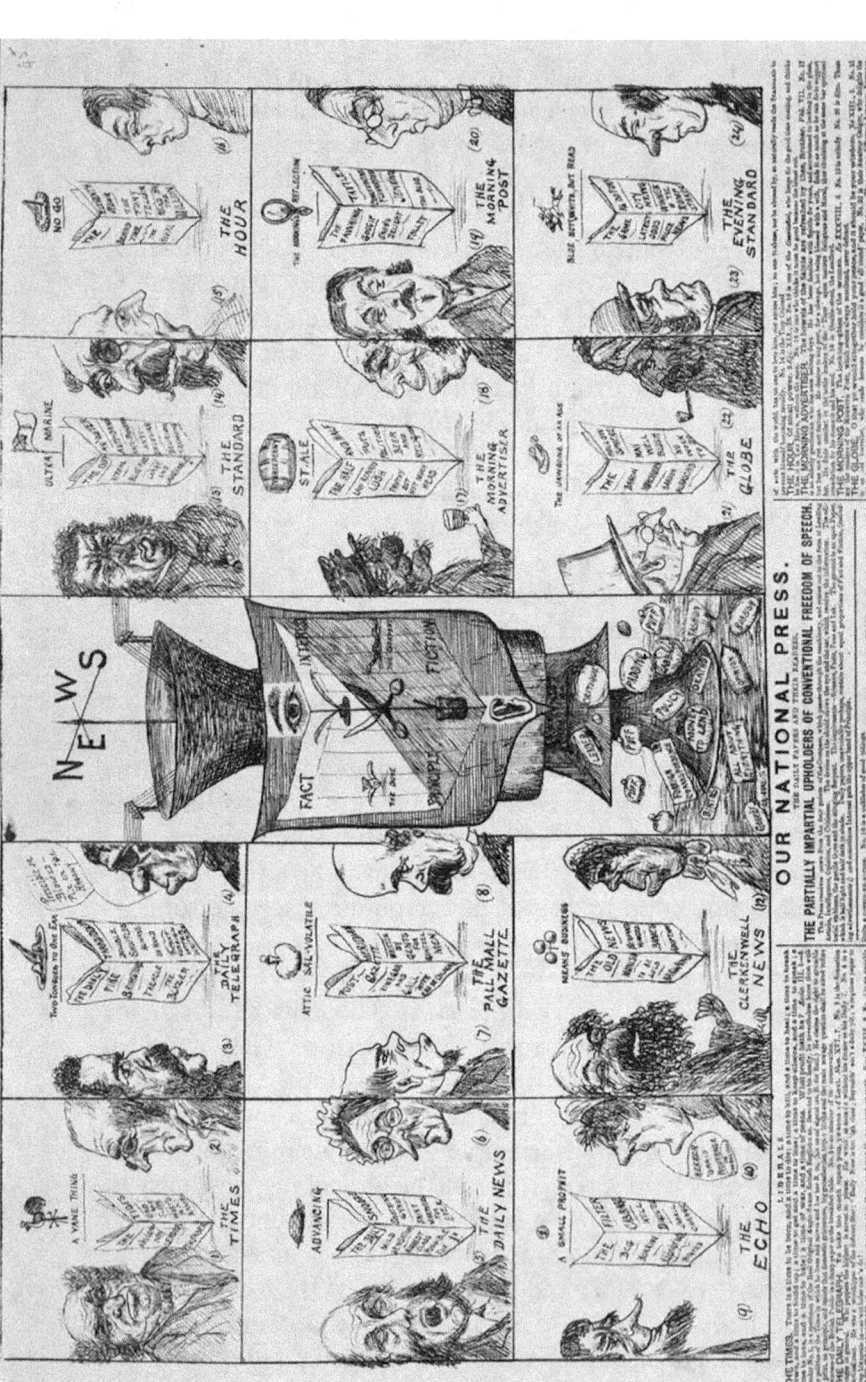

Figure I.1 Gegeef, 'Our National Press.' Courtesy Lilly Library, Indiana University, Bloomington, Indiana.

of the defunct *Star*', a newspaper that went out of business in 1852. This cartoon demonstrates the importance of metaphors, analogies and figurative models for thinking about the newspaper press, both in terms of how it represents the larger nation and also in terms of how it functions formally as a social text. Whereas Liddle emphasises the generic self-consciousness of nineteenth-century journalists, this cartoon renders the 'genres' of the newspaper – the leader, gossip and so on – as a random outcome of machinery.

This book focuses on the mid to late nineteenth century because this period witnessed a dramatic expansion in newspapers, periodicals and other print ephemera. *The Times* dominated the newspaper industry early in the Victorian era, but various developments contributed to the democratisation of newspapers over the second half of the century. These developments included new technologies fostering more efficient and cost-effective printing practices; a more connected network of nation and empire due to the railway, steamships and the telegraph; and the gradual removal of the so-called 'taxes on knowledge'.[41] These taxes were introduced over the course of the eighteenth century to restrict the circulation of cheap political papers. Stamped newspapers were accessible only to elite readers or were read collectively in public spaces.[42] The taxes inadvertently spawned an illegal trade in unstamped radical papers, which expanded in the 1830s as working-class radicals felt a sense of betrayal after the Reform Act 1832 failed to fulfil many of its promises.[43] They also contributed to the short-lived ascendancy of the *The Times*, which was exempt because of its high cost.[44] As the century went on, these taxes increasingly came under public protest, both by those advocating for a free press and by those who hoped to eradicate the radical press. Proponents of the 'respectable press' argued that tax reductions would eliminate the market for illegal radical newspapers. In 1836, the newspaper duty decreased from four pence to one penny per copy. The government repealed the advertisement duty in 1853 and the stamp duty in 1855. That same year, the *Daily Telegraph* became the first penny daily to be published in Britain. Some historians argue that 1855 was a watershed year in the liberalisation of the British free press. Others argue, however, that the British press encountered other kinds of restrictions, since the decreased regulation eradicated the unstamped radical press and made newspapers subject to the commercial marketplace. Regardless of one's outlook, 1855 is an important turning point in the history of the newspaper.[45]

With so many changes in the print marketplace, it is no wonder that the Victorian period witnessed a range of attempts to define and historicise the newspaper press. Before 1855, attempts to define the news were rooted in the legal discourse of the taxes on knowledge, as publishers and editors sought loopholes in tax law. Even after the duty on newspaper advertisements was lifted in 1853, the outstanding taxes still required papers published on a more frequent basis to pay a penny duty. When he launched a penny newspaper in West Sussex, William Woods Mitchell founded a monthly, rather than a weekly, to avoid the stamp tax. He wrote, 'I had hoped these little sheets would not have been recognised as newspapers, liable, under any circumstance of publication, to stamp duties . . . They contained no political articles or other elaborate reports, &c., which dignify a newspaper.'[46] He defines a newspaper in terms of its regularity (his 'little sheets' are published only on a monthly basis) and the political and elaborate quality of its content. Unfortunately, Inland Revenue did not buy his definition and forced him to pay the duty.

Attempts to pin down the exact qualities of the newspaper were anything but consistent. While some defined it as a broadsheet published at fixed intervals in sequential order, others used the terms journalism, the periodical press and newspapers interchangeably to describe the production of news.[47] The *Bradford Observer* defined the news in terms of its serial transience, arguing 'the news ceases to be news when the succeeding section of events gets into print. . .'[48] Charles Mitchell defined the news as 'events of recent recurrence' but also acknowledged that 'what is recent is relative' and arbitrary.[49] As a result, he defined the term, 'recent', according to the lunar month. Novelistic representations of the news, and their use of metaphors and analogies to do so, contributed to this multivalent effort to define and categorise the newspaper press and other serial modes of publication, particularly in their relationship to an expanding readership. The novels in this monograph register the shifting symbolic importance of the newspaper over the Victorian period. Dickens and Trollope grapple with a tyrannical press increasingly seen as the voice of the people, or even the 'fourth estate'. By 1892, however, Israel Zangwill's *Children of the Ghetto* problematises a capacity of the newspaper to speak on behalf of even a minor community.[50]

Overview of Monograph

This monograph traces novelistic accounts of news discourse, arguing that nineteenth-century novels represented the news and the newspaper in order to experiment with realist modes and novelistic form. This monograph is a story of the novel; it is not a history of the periodical or the newspaper. There already exists strong scholarship in periodical studies and the history of the press, including a rich emerging subfield in Victorian media studies. Work in this field by Laurel Brake and James Mussell, among others, examine the dramatic changes that took place in the production, dissemination and consumption of newspapers over the nineteenth century.[51] Because this book is concerned principally with the novel, I have organised the chapters not around shifts in the newspaper industry but around novelists, albeit in a loosely chronological order. Each chapter covers a period of time that saw significant changes in the media and historical landscape, which allows me to trace novelists' developing styles across their careers. Additionally, I selected nineteenth-century novelists who wrote for a wide range of outlets, from newspapers to periodicals to theatre. Charles Dickens famously started his career as a court reporter, and Anthony Trollope regularly wrote for *The Pall Mall Gazette*. Wilkie Collins and Mary Elizabeth Braddon tended to pull their stories from the news of the day, leading Victorians and contemporary critics alike to couple the sensation novel with crime news. And Anglo-Jewish writer Israel Zangwill started his career as a journalist in the English-language Jewish press of London. These diverse experiences, coupled with the fact that many of these writers published their novels serially, enabled them to reflect structurally and formally on the workings of news, newspapers, fiction and serial novels.

The first chapter, '"These Acres of Print": Charles Dickens, the News and the Novel as Pattern', argues that Dickens adapted his approach to novelistic form in response to problems posed by newspapers and the popular press. Early in his career, Dickens characterised the newspaper press as a meteorological force of destruction, a thunderstorm threatening to engulf the city of London yet continually produced to meet the endless public appetite for more news. As his career progressed, Dickens's novels increasingly valorised the artifice, or 'pattern', involved in narrative constructions of imagined worlds. In his postscript to his last complete novel, *Our Mutual Friend*, Dickens argues that the concealment of a major plot device in the novel was part of his 'design', comparing his work on the 'pattern' of the novel to 'the story-weaver at his loom'.[52]

The second chapter, 'Arrested Development: Characterisation, the Newspaper and Anthony Trollope', argues that Trollope's stories of development are continually interrupted and redirected by the newspaper. Characters encounter malicious and exaggerated depictions of themselves in the newspaper that are starkly at odds with their own self-conceptions and become paralysed by the disjunction between self and society. Yet Trollope draws upon the same tactics of his fictional journalists in his flattened account of the complex British news system. Newspaper editors like Quintus Slide of the Palliser novels and Tom Towers of the Barsetshire series are over-the-top caricatures; in doing so, Trollope conveys the distortion that he perceives in their construction of a national reading public. Trollope's journalists lay claim to representative reality, and yet they act out of malice, self-interest and self-deception. His journalists are caught between totalising claims (Quintus Slide, for example, claims to be the 'people's friend') and the restricted scope of journalistic practice. Trollope's novels imitate and rework journalistic writing practices to theorise the ethical and political effects of formal choices on public discourse.

Both Dickens and Trollope point to the specific modes and discourses that newspapers use to craft conceptions of nation. The second half of the book turns to novels that show how newspapers also perform powerful exclusions from the public sphere. In the sensation novels of Wilkie Collins and Mary Elizabeth Braddon, and in fiction about late-Victorian Anglo-Jewish communities by George Eliot and Israel Zangwill, we see how newspapers overlook, vilify and marginalise whole groups and ways of life.

The third chapter looks to the sensation novel, often called 'the newspaper novel', since it was associated with the newspaper and true crime.[53] This chapter, called '"The End is No Longer Hidden": News, Fate and the Sensation Novel', argues that the sensation novel converts the newspaper into a source of the superstition and 'atmospheric menace' for which the sensation novel is so famous. Rather than drawing upon newspapers for a sense of realism, as critics have argued, these novels make their newspapers integral to their providential plots. Wilkie Collins's *Armadale* amplifies this tension by transforming the newspaper into an agent of melodramatic fate, as its central female character, Lydia Gwilt, consults the newspaper for signs of her predetermined end. Because of her social marginality, Lydia cannot identify with newspaper readers nor aspire towards a plot of *Bildung*; instead, she imagines herself in the place of what theorist Niklas Luhmann calls 'norm violators'. Anderson's theory requires readers who can imagine themselves as interchangeable with other like-minded members of the reading community. In sensation novels, however, newspapers reinforce a social imaginary that alienates some characters and situates them within a predetermined destiny incapable of change. In doing so, these novels render anti-social and marginalised characters into melodramatic form. They also offer a means of thinking about how form and media necessitate some exclusionary practices.

In the final chapter, 'Israel Zangwill, or "The Jewish Dickens": Representing Minority Communities in Novel and Newspaper', I examine how the newspaper participates in novelistic depictions of late-nineteenth-century Anglo-Jewishness, with a focus on Israel Zangwill's 1892 novel, *Children of the Ghetto: A Study of a Peculiar People* (1892) and George Eliot's *Daniel Deronda* (1876). The dominant nineteenth-century Jewish newspaper, *The Jewish Chronicle*, sought to accommodate its readers and to represent a unified Jewish community to the larger national public; however, Jewish print culture more broadly was politically, culturally and linguistically diverse. Acknowledging the centrality of newspapers to the Jewish community, Zangwill dramatises the limitations of newspaper form and function to the cultivation of a broader affective attachment. In *Children of the Ghetto*, Zangwill contrasts the representative potential of novelistic realism with the English-language Orthodox newspaper, *The Flag of Judah*, which only imperfectly fosters an Anglo-Jewish community. The regularity and routinised labour of the newspaper dull its editor's sense of time and weakens his affective attachment to other members of his community. In contrast, novelistic realism enables Zangwill to convey the complex feelings that the Jewish ghetto elicits in the protagonist and novelist Esther Ansell, both when she resides there and later returns. The newspaper looks like a form conducive to affective connections only when it is repurposed by readers and made to work more like a novel.

This chapter also argues that Israel Zangwill reworks Eliot's novelistic approaches to community in *Children of the Ghetto*. Whereas *Daniel Deronda* concludes with Deronda's yearning towards Palestine and a nation for his people, *Children of the Ghetto* valorises the idea of the Jewish ghetto as a place of nostalgia, a setting that fosters affective attachment based not in anonymous communal imaginings but in lived and material proximity. Zangwill's novel dramatises the difficulties in creating a minor community within a larger national community, and the extent to which form matters in how that community is envisioned.

As this book shows, novelists often pointedly responded to newspapers by taking up well known events covered by Victorian newspapers and reworking them in their fictions. Each of the first three chapters features a news story adapted into fiction. The first chapter considers the influence of the Franz Müller trial on Dickens's *Our*

Mutual Friend; this transatlantic sensation featured a German immigrant who murdered a man on a British train and then fled to New York. The second chapter explores the ways Anthony Trollope's *The Warden* pointedly critiques *The Times*'s coverage of clerical corruption and the Crimean War. And in the third chapter, I consider what H. L. Mansel called the 'newspaper novel', specifically the similarities between Lydia Gwilt of Collins's sensation novel *Armadale* and Scottish heiress Madeleine Smith, who famously poisoned her lover in 1857. Rather than dealing with a particular news story, the fourth and final chapter deals with the representation of the Anglo-Jewish community to the broader public.

Rather than disciplining its characters into social conformity, these novels trace characters' struggles to create or restore form to their experiences. These struggles are dramatised in relationship to the newspaper, which often serves as a competing form or an agent of destabilisation. Thus, the serial form of the novel varies from the serial production of the newspaper, in that it constantly refers backwards and forwards, and it retains a sense of the formal whole it aspires towards, even if that whole is never achieved. While it is true that each issue of the newspaper forms the whole of *The Times*, and therefore gives a sense of a single entity moving across time, many novels suggest the harmful arbitrariness of newspaper form, whether structured by the need for financial support, a desire to titillate the reading public, or even the personal or public interest of the editor or writer. This is particularly true in the nineteenth century, when newspapers were less cognisant of how they structured the news. Indeed, novels by Wilkie Collins and others show the extent to which these motivations are concealed behind the final appearance of the newspaper, and therefore make an arbitrary outcome seem preordained or essential. I argue that many nineteenth-century novels explore the effects of form making on characters and communities and, in doing so, they seek to give aesthetic form to these individuals' experiences. Thus, while the newspaper seems to offer a representative reality in its text, the novels in this monograph show that form and experience are never fixed 'in black and white'.

Notes

1. Braddon, *Lady Audley's Secret*, p. 36.
2. Moretti, *The Way of the World*, p. 20. Similarly, Fredric Jameson argues that novelistic realism is committed to the status quo. Jameson, 'Afterword', pp. 279–89.

3. Examples include Miller, *The Novel and the Police*, 1988, and Finch and Bowen, 'The Tittle-Tattle of Highbury', pp. 1–18. Isobel Armstrong summarises this common understanding of the novel as a 'belief that the novel indelibly registers bourgeois ideology and morality ... [which] has meant that the novel's default position has been read as conservative and hegemonic'. She complicates this account by identifying a poetics of democratic imagination in the nineteenth-century novel, arguing that the novel incorporates generic innovation and formal experimentation as a means of democratic and even radical inquiry. Informed by Armstrong's account, this monograph identifies sites of novelistic formal self-reflexivity and experimentation in novelistic representation of newspapers and news discourse. Armstrong, *Novel Politics*, p. 3.
4. This book draws upon recent critical attention to the response of the novel to new media and technology in the nineteenth century. A recent example includes Anne Sullivan and Kate Flint's special issue on the technologies of fire for *Interdisciplinary Studies in the Long Nineteenth Century*, in which they explore 'fire as a visual and narrative technology in art, literature, and public displays by examining the ways in which it evoked competing symbolic values'. Sullivan and Flint, 'Introduction: Technologies of Fire'.
5. This book also argues that, partly in response to journalistic discourses of the real, novels experimented with ways of giving form to communal experiences. In this account, I am influenced by Isobel Armstrong's notion of a democratic and radical aesthetic. In both *Novel Politics* (2016) and *The Radical Aesthetic* (2000), Armstrong advocates for a cultural and theoretical re-imagining of the significance of the aesthetic, conceiving it instead as an inherent impulse towards form that locates art in everyday experience. In *Novel Politics*, she traces the 'self-conscious markers of a democratic imagination' throughout nineteenth-century novels, arguing that the genealogical imperative of the novel is a site of 'sharply critical self-consciousness where class and status are reimagined' (13). In *The Radical Aesthetic*, she argues, 'Art, that is, is a shaping of the *process* of shaping. It does not consist in achieved form, which would become finitude, but in the experience of making form, an experience distributed across makers and perceivers' (165). Isobel Armstrong, *The Radical Aesthetic*, p. 165.
6. Recently, however, a few critics have complicated this account; in particular, Nancy Armstrong and Leonard Tennenhouse argue that early America lacked 'the boundaries and the sovereignty that Anderson ascribes to nationhood', and thus novels of this period first had to 'imagine themselves as part of a very different form of social organization' before they could compose a national tradition. These novels, they argue 'could not make the experience of early America intelligible as a limited and sovereign people'. Armstrong and Tennenhouse, 'Novels before Nations', p. 355.
7. Anderson, *Imagined Communities*, p. 30.

8. Ibid. p. 25.
9. Ibid. p. 35.
10. Culler suggests that Anderson treats the world of the novel as 'an *analogue* of the nation'. Culler, 'Anderson and the Novel', p. 23.
11. Anderson, *Imagined Communities*, p. 32.
12. Pieter Vermeulen faults Anderson's failure to disentangle literature from the newspaper, arguing that '[l]iterature has the power to initiate the imagining of a non-national form of community'. Vermeulen, 'Community and Literary Experience', p. 103.
13. Patrick Brantlinger identifies in the Victorian era widespread fear about an unstable and expanding reading public, explaining that the 'underlying the inscription of anti-novel attitudes within novels is radical uncertainty all novelists share about how the reading public will interpret or misinterpret, use or abuse, the products of their imagination'. Brantlinger, *The Reading Lesson*, p. 3.
14. Liddle, *The Dynamics of Genre*, p. 145.
15. Ibid. p. 14.
16. Lennard Davis argues that the newspaper and novel emerged from the same news/novel matrix and that, as a result, novelistic discourse is not substantially different from other forms of discourse. Instead, they are all 'part of a general ideological system, a system, one might add, that was by and large unknowable to those within'. My account differs from his in my emphasis on the strategies of novelistic formal experimentation. Davis, *Factual Fictions*, p. 8.
17. According to Catherine Gallagher, 'until the mid-eighteenth century, there was no widely employed means of distinguishing between a fiction and a lie'. Gallagher, *Nobody's Story*, p. 163. Similarly, Ian Haywood argues that fiction and forgery (a kind of fraud) are 'blood relatives, even if they do not always choose to acknowledge each other'. Haywood, *Faking It*, p. 6. For more information on fraud and literature, see Russett, *Fictions and Fakes*.
18. Levine, *Serious Pleasures*, p. 10.
19. Isobel Armstrong makes a parallel argument in *Novel Politics*, when she argues that the mode of inquiry of the novel interrogates 'the realist mode *as* a mode', through ceaseless experiments 'with modes and idioms of narrative'. She calls these experiments 'the poetics of form that revise and rework realist modes'. Armstrong, *Novel Politics*, p. 86.
20. Rader, 'Defoe, Richardson, Joyce', p. 179.
21. I recognise that Rader's claim may not map perfectly onto all journalistic genres, including scandal news, yet even 'fake news' contains the possibility of truth. Scandal and gossip rely upon a muddying of the line between fact and fiction. This may be less true for nineteenth-century provincial newspapers, which tended to represent a particular political perspective and would appeal only to its side of the political spectrum. For a recent account of provincial newspapers, see Hobbs, *A Fleet Street in Every Town*.

22. Beetham, 'Towards a Theory', pp. 19–32.
23. Davis writes, 'The "median past tense" of the newspaper [mediates] between the past (reserved for narratives and history) and the present (which was most likely confined to spoken language, poetry, drama) – and this tense would be uniquely a journalistic one implying that what one was reading had only a slightly deferred immediacy.' Davis, *Factual Fictions*, p. 73.
24. Ibid. p. 73.
25. Luhmann, *The Reality of the Mass Media*, p. 25.
26. Levine, *The Realistic Imagination*, p. 4.
27. In his summary of Levine, Daniel Brown suggests that realism was 'a restorative method of representation, an attempt to bring about a sense of order to a generation of readers for whom the world seemed hopelessly fragmented and complex'. Brown, 'Realism and Sensation Fiction', p. 99.
28. Thomas Carlyle, *On Heroes*, pp. 98–122.
29. In this tradition, the *Leicester Chronicle* claimed in 1843 that its mission was 'to mirror the world as it is [rather] than to picture it as it should be' (as quoted in Barker). The *Leicester Chronicle* characterises its role as mimetic, as a mirror that reflects public opinion rather than contributes to its creation. Barker, *Newspapers, Politics and English Society*, p. 80.
30. Many middle-class writers and thinkers worried about the dangers of the cheap press and its potential influence on the working class. In the 1830s, the Utilitarians' answer to this problem was to provide cheap publications that aimed to improve the mental and moral condition of working and middle classes by counteracting the effects of the unstamped radical press, such as *The Political Register*, and of horror and crime fiction targeted at working-class readers. Charles Knight oversaw the Society for the Diffusion of Useful Knowledge, founded in 1827, and edited *Penny Magazine*, which sought to provide popular journalism that also instilled the virtues of industry, temperance and moderation in the working class.
31. Collins, 'The Unknown Public', p. 217.
32. Mary Poovey has argued that 1830–1864 saw the groundwork laid for what would eventually be a single 'mass' culture. She calls this a process of homogenisation, or the image of a single culture. Poovey, *Making the Social Body*, p. 2.
33. Kreilkamp, *Voice and the Victorian Storyteller*, p. 37.
34. Hadley, *Living Liberalism*, p. 41.
35. These accounts are in line with Jürgen Habermas's argument that the liberal public sphere of the eighteenth century gave way to a degraded commercial environment in the nineteenth century.
36. According to Mark Hampton, this conception of the role of the national press as mimetic rather than educative strengthened towards the end of the century, as writers became less confident in 'the idea of

rational persuasion of individuals' and in the educational potential of the news. He writes, 'the obvious answer was that if the press could not "influence" or "educate" public opinion, then it could "reflect", "express", or "mirror" it'. Hampton, *Visions of the Press in Britain*, p. 108. Yet mid-century writers also drew upon such language; after the lifting of the Taxes on Knowledge in the 1850s, the whole of the press was sometimes figured as representative of the nation.

37. [W. H. Wills], 'The Appetite for News', *Household Words* 10 (1 June 1850), p. 238.
38. Ibid. p. 239.
39. Ibid. p. 240.
40. Gegeef, 'Our National Press'.
41. The expanding reach and scope of the newspaper, facilitated by the railway, steamships and the telegraph, reconfigured how British citizens and imperial subjects thought about space. News agencies like Reuters were among the first trans-national corporations, and by the late nineteenth century, much of the world was united by an 'imperial press system'. Magee and Thompson, *Empire and Globalisation*, 28. Simon Potter argues that the imperial press system fostered a sense of 'diasporic Britishness' which he defines as 'an invented loyalty based not exclusively on ethnicity but rather developing aspects of a wider, shared high culture'. Rather than allowing for the fragmentation of ethnic, cultural, religious, or linguistic groups, the imperial press system fostered a 'superimposed Britishness' across a range of colonised peoples (p. 2). Reuters was established in 1851 as a nationalised wire service designed to provide copy for provincial papers, and its influence quickly expanded internationally. With its associations to London, Reuters participated in the construction of a sense of imperial belonging, as 'newspapers in Britain and across the white dominions of Australia, Canada, New Zealand, and South Africa labored to create and celebrate "Britishness"' (p. 115). Potter, *News and the British World*, 2, p. 115. For more information on the international news system, see Brennan, 'International News in the Age of Empire', pp. 107–32.
42. For more information, see 'Newspaper Taxes', *Dictionary of Nineteenth Century Journalism*, p. 454.
43. Hampton, *Visions of the Press in Britain*, p. 32.
44. This was an intended outcome, since *The Times* was not perceived as a radical threat to the government.
45. For a thorough account of the Victorian press, see Brown, *Victorian News and Newspapers*. She identifies two landmarks in newspaper history: first the repeal of the stamp duty which made the penny daily paper a commonplace, and secondly the formation of the Press Association in 1868.
46. Unfortunately, however, Mitchell was forced by the Inland Revenue to pay the duty. Martin Hewitt summarises this story in the prologue

to his recent monograph on the 'Taxes on Knowledge'. Hewitt, *The Dawn of the Cheap Press.*

47. [William Rathbone Greg], 'The Newspaper Press', *Edinburgh Review* 102 (October 1855), pp. 470–98.
48. *Bradford Observer*, p. 16. In 1865, *The Pall Mall Gazette* emphasised journalism's need to meet the demands of a fickle public: '[Journalism] is not a fine art, but the satisfaction of a great public want. . . . It must always be produced at a given moment and with very brief preparation.' '"The Times" and Constance Kent' *The Pall Mall Gazette* 70 (29 April 1865), p. 4.
49. Mitchell sought to provide an authoritative definition in *The Newspaper Press Director*, a publication targeted at commercial traders looking to place advertisements in appropriate publications. Mitchell's account shows that defining the newspaper press was not merely an esoteric practice; it was important for commercial and legal purposes as well.
50. The newspaper press was not depicted as the fourth estate until the 1820s. Barker, *Newspapers, Politics and English Society*, p. 24.
51. James Mussell's work in this area includes 'Cohering Knowledge in the Nineteenth Century: Form, Genre and Periodical Studies', 151–67 and 'Repetition: Or, "In Our Last"', 343–58. Brake's more recent work includes *Print in Transition*. Other work in this area includes the following: Alfano and Stauffer, *Virtual Victorians*; Galvan, *The Sympathetic Medium*; Menke, *Telegraphic Realism*; and Worth, *Imperial Media*. In 2015, *Victorian Periodicals Review* featured a special issue called, 'A Return to Theory', drawing upon media theory to understand Victorian periodicals and newspapers. Other contemporary work on Victorian media studies deals with the question of digitisation, including scholarship by Paul Fyfe. Other less recent work includes Brake and Codell, *Encounters in the Victorian Press*; Lyn Pykett's work, such as 'Reading the Victorian Periodical Press', pp. 100–8; Turner, *Trollope and the Magazines*; and Wynne, *The Sensation Novel*.
52. Dickens, *Our Mutual Friend*, p. 798.
53. [H. L. Manse], 'Sensation Novels', *Quarterly Review* 226 (1863): pp. 482–514.

Chapter 1

'These Acres of Print': Charles Dickens, the News and the Novel as Pattern

Over his career Charles Dickens concocted a range of metaphors for newspapers, calling them 'acres of print', 'a storm', a 'thunder-cloud', and (sarcastically) the 'master-spirits' of America.[1] In 1850, he co-wrote an article for *Household Words* that depicted London newspapers as a chaotic force of meteorological destruction:

> [T]he first black fringe of a thunder-cloud of newspapers impending over the Post-Office was discharging itself fitfully by fast degrees as the storm came on harder and harder, until it rained, hailed, snowed, newspapers threatening destruction to the miserable Post Office. All the history of the time, the chronicled births, deaths, and marriages, all the crimes, all the accidents, all the vanities, all the changes, all the realities, of all the civilised earth, heaped up, parceled out, carried about, knocked down, cut, shuffled, dealt, played, fathered up again, and passed from hand to hand, in an apparently interminable and hopeless confusion, but really in a system of admirable order, certainty and simplicity, pursued six nights every week, all through the rolling year![2]

The extended metaphor emphasises the sheer expansiveness of newspaper coverage, as the miscellaneous jumble threatens to engulf the city of London. The national post office, however, transforms the journalistic chaos into a system of serialised, daily distribution. The article ascribes an Andersonian understanding of serial national time not to the newspaper but to its distribution by the post office, which facilitates a national imaginary while also representing the body politic. The post office becomes a figurative body in its shuffling and knocking down and carrying about of the news.[3]

Dickens is famous for beginning his career as a reporter, so his metaphorical treatments of the newspaper press are telling in terms of his shifting attitudes towards print media. While Anderson has argued that newspapers enable readers to imagine national community, Dickens's writings are attentive to the varying ways that the newspaper press might shape, inhibit or fragment community through its uncontrolled production of miscellaneous content and matter. Just as the post office gives order to what appears to be an avalanche of newspapers and periodicals, Dickens's novels create the appearance of random contingency while also suggesting their patterned interconnection. Over the course of his career, Dickens increasingly valorised the artifice involved in narrative constructions of imagined worlds, asking readers to embark consciously on a make believe journey that enables them to envision alternative possibilities and to remake themselves in the process.[4] He suggests that fiction, on its re-entry into real life, has the potential to transform readers' relationship to the real. It occupies a middle space between news – which is largely random and contingent, and told before journalists know how to talk about events – and history, which is encountered retrospectively in the past tense.

I make this argument first through analysing the 'intangible creature' that narrates *Household Words*. This creature invites readers to imagine *Household Words* as an oral storyteller rather than an impersonal product of the print marketplace, while it also portrays the newspaper press as a chaotic explosion of texts produced in response to the public's insatiable craving for cheap print journalism. The intangible creature transforms into an authorial weaver in Dickens's last complete novel, *Our Mutual Friend*. By comparing the work of the novelist to the weaver at his loom, Dickens suggests that, even as readers experience the serial parts as random and contingent, the author imagines a larger pattern emerging from these pieces. He draws upon a real-life murder case at the time of the serialisation of the novel, and thus contrasts his novelistic devices to those he associates with the newspaper. This approach to novelistic fiction protects imaginative literature from fraudulent acts and reinvests it with the potential to transform the reader and his or her worlds.

Just as the post office organises the serial output of the daily press, Dickens experiments over his career with other metaphors for the working of serial narrative and its influence on a reading public. From an intangible creature telling stories to a weaver at his loom, Dickens encourages readers to see the instance of a particular serial output linked to its larger structure over time. In doing so, he privileges the power of fiction to cultivate new ways of envisioning community. This first chapter shows the growing distinction that Dickens drew between fiction and non-fiction in his communal visions for serial publication.[5] Fiction making enables alternative imaginings of reality in Dickens's novels, while also emphasising the constructed qualities of the real.

The 'Appetite for News' and *Household Words*

On 1 June 1850, *Household Words* published 'The Appetite for News', an essay, discussed in the introduction to this monograph, that characterised the public's 'constant craving' for cheap print materials as ravenous and insatiable. The article contended that 'these acres of print' are packaged to 'suit every appetite and every taste' with a barrage of miscellaneous events: 'of battle, murder, and sudden death; of lightning and tempest; of plague, pestilence, and famine'.[6] It concluded, 'good and evil [are] as broadly defined or as inextricably missed in the newspapers as they are over the great globe itself'. The extensive range of news does not make sense of these events but replicates the randomness of their occurrence. The goal of news, then, is not to organise but simply to produce enough to satisfy the public's craving 'every morning with as much as would fill about twelve hundred pages of an ordinary novel'. Although written anonymously by sub-editor W. H. Wills, 'The Appetite for News' is an unsigned article that maintains the central voice of *Household Words*. The article points to Dickens's concerns regarding the dangers of news information and opens up new questions about his relationship to journalism.

Widely recognised for his popularisation of serial publication, Dickens has long been associated with journalism and the popular press. His contemporary Walter Bagehot considered Dickens the quintessential reporter and writer of urban life, in which 'everything is there, and everything is disconnected'.[7] Bagehot wrote, 'His memory is full of instances of old buildings and curious people, and he does not care to piece them together', implicitly suggesting that Dickens's novels functioned in much the same way as the disorderly and chaotic newspapers. In his book, *Dickens the Journalist*, John M. L. Drew regards Bagehot's description as particularly resonant for Dickens's journalism, and he suggests that Dickens is in some ways a 'special correspondent for modernity' in helping us to make sense of his milieu.[8]

However, Dickens's treatment of the newspaper press in *Household Words* and his broader treatment of journalistic and novelistic forms suggest an alternative reading of Dickens's position in relationship to these genres. 'The Appetite for News', in particular, characterises the quantity and variety of newspapers, periodicals and other publications as chaotic discursive spaces. Generically distinct from the daily and weekly newspapers, as well as from other weekly periodicals, *Household Words* reflects upon the journalistic form – or rather, its miscellaneous form – both in its content and structure. By asking his readers to imagine a narrator at the centre of *Household Words*, Dickens openly reveals the artifice at the core of his journal.[9] Readers know that *Household Words* is only a mass produced journal, but Dickens asks readers to picture it at their hearth.[10] The journal relocates the figurative storyteller to the centre of communal imaginings, invoking Walter Benjamin's oral storyteller through the printed text.[11] This removes the periodical from the world of information and carries it into a space of accumulated experience and feeling. The storyteller crafts a pattern out of the seemingly disjointed articles that make up *Household Words*. It also construes development (moral and otherwise) partly as an act of imagination and storytelling, not an enforced conforming of the self to social norms. By inviting readers to participate in the construction of the journal's community, the journal encourages readers to think about how narratives imagine such communities.[12]

'A Preliminary Word', the article that opened the first issue of *Household Words* in 1850, introduces itself as an imaginative alternative to other newspapers and journals on the market.[13] The 1840s and 1850s saw a proliferation in periodicals targeted to increasingly specific demographics, partly as a means to avoid the taxes on knowledge. It had the effect of splintering the reading public into fragments. However, *Household Words* positioned itself as speaking to a larger readership, claiming that it would enter 'into innumerable homes' and reach 'the bosoms of young and old, of the well-to-do and poor . . .' It invites readers to envision themselves as part of a larger public, emphasising the artifice involved in this imaginary construction of community with the journal at its centre.[14]

Dickens sought to bring an unprecedented degree of cohesion to *Household Words* as a whole and to its separate parts, while also differentiating the journal from other publications. The weekly journal, published from 1850 to 1859, was a departure from the periodical norm both in terms of price and function. For the first time, a periodical read by the middle class was priced at the affordable sum of 2*d*. As Lorna Huett has pointed out, *Household Words* worked to invert and destabilise social views of the cheap press, so long associated with both political radicalism and sensationalism marketed to the lower classes. Consistent with this image, *Household Words* differentiated itself by creating at its centre a guiding authorial figure to provide a sense of unity. Newspapers and periodicals had long used an editorial 'we' to give coherence to their publications, but the use of the 'we' in *Household Words* functions differently from the more traditional journalistic 'we'. Whereas other publications, such as *The Times* or *Lloyd's Weekly Newspaper*, used the 'we' to create a house style and a distinct voice for the journal, Dickens's central voice functions as an actual character narrating the various discrete stories and essays. He had originally intended to fashion a 'kind of semi-omniscient, omnipresent, intangible creature' who could 'bind all this together, and [. . .] get a character established as it were which any of the writers may maintain without difficulty'.[15] Although this creature did not turn out to be quite as concrete as he had previously imagined, he sought to create the impression of one presiding author: a shadowy, disembodied persona who would give the publication a 'collective sympathy'.

These early descriptions of *Household Words* call attention to the organisation he hoped to impose upon the periodical, to give the publication a narrative voice that readers could rely upon to provide cohesiveness. This intangible creature emerges even in 'A Preliminary Word': 'the hand that writes these faltering lines, happily associated with *some* Household Words before to-day, has known enough of such experiences to enter an earnest spirit upon this new task, and with an awakened sense of all that it involves'. Here the 'intangible creature' suddenly becomes Dickens himself. Embodied character, narrator and author become intermingled in this portrayal and play a centring role in arranging the miscellaneous pieces into a pattern. This emphasis on fictional voice and narrative arises very clearly within particular articles and stories in *Household Words*, as well as across the journal as a whole.

By developing a central narrative voice that functions like a character, Dickens is able to shy away from the arbitrary and ephemeral structure characteristic of the newspaper press.[16] Newspapers rely on an arbitrary juxtaposition of stories on the broadsheet; the structure of the newspaper suggests the exchangeability and ephemerality of each story and each day's newspaper, which must give way to another edition that is both identical and different the next day. Dickens, however, envisioned *Household Words* as a family magazine that offered stability through a single 'conductor', or editor. In 1839, he resigned from the editorship of *Bentley's Miscellany*, after he clashed with Richard Bentley over how the periodical should be organised. According to Sabine Clemm, 'Bentley's view emphasised the multifarious nature of a periodical with several different contributors and potentially differing opinions, whereas Dickens privileged the unity of the whole product under his command.'[17] For *Household Words*, this practice was more abstract; but in *Master Humphrey's Clock* (1840–1), Dickens created a weekly periodical in which an embodied narrator, Master Humphrey, gathered his friends around his hearth to share stories.[18] Both *Master Humphrey's Clock* and *Household Words* cultivated a sense of domestic community situated around the conceit of oral storytelling.

This vision for his periodicals contrasts with his depiction of the American press in *Martin Chuzzlewit* (1840–1), published around the time of *Master Humphrey's Clock*. Whereas his periodicals cohere around a fictional persona, the American press, in Dickens's rendering, fraudulently claims to represent the nation. Here Dickens distinguishes between fiction and fraud, in the sense that his periodicals foreground their artifice. *Martin Chuzzlewit* satirises the American press through the fictional newspaper, the *Rowdy Journal*. Despite its pretentions to be the international voice of America, the newspaper office is located down a narrow street and up a 'dirty flight of stairs' in a room 'all littered and bestrewn with odds and ends of newspapers and other crumpled fragments, both in proof and manuscript'.[19] Here the newspaper is not only heterogeneous in content but also physically torn into parts. The only journalist in the room is 'a small young gentleman of very juvenile appearance', whom Martin assumes to be the editor's son but turns out to be the acclaimed 'war correspondent'. The entire newspaper functions on 'personal' gossip and 'forgery', publishing letters reputed to be written by leading figures but really made up by its own meagre staff. And yet the America of the novel relies upon the *Rowdy Journal* for its national culture. When young Martin Chuzzlewit asks about the role of 'the national poets, the theatre, literature, and the arts' in American culture, the Americans tout their journalistic 'master-spirits' who were 'renowned, as it appeared, for excellence in the achievement of a peculiar style of broad-side essay called "a screamer"'.[20] Indeed, one character appeared to 'grow quite faint at the bare thought of reading anything which was neither mercantile nor political, and was not in a newspaper', as he insisted, 'We are a busy people, sir, . . . and have no time for reading mere notions. We don't mind 'em if they come to us in newspapers along with almighty strong stuff of another sort, but darn your books.'[21] Dickens's satire of the American press ridicules its claim to stand in for national culture while predominantly preoccupied with economic self-interest. His worries about the American press continued nearly a decade later, when Dickens opposed the 1850–51 campaign to eliminate the taxes on knowledge. He felt that the taxes yielded some order to what otherwise might become a chaotic and perhaps tyrannical press. He wrote, 'if it were taken off, we might be deluged with a flood of piratical, ignorant and blackguard papers, something like that black deluge of Printer's Ink which blights America'.[22] Dickens attributed significance to both the taxes on knowledge and the post office in their curbing of a disorderly press. This anxiety about an unfettered and chaotic press continued throughout his career in dramatically shifting contexts.

The *Rowdy Journal* trades on exaggeration, lies and fraud to accomplish self-involved material interests, even as the editor insists on its representative significance. This satire contrasts with the 'intangible creature' that centres *Household Words*. Fiction and fraud look alike, but Dickens shows that they yield different critical and ethical outlooks on society. Whereas journalists and worldly characters make claims they know to be untrue for personal gain, Dickens imagines fictional narrative to offer a more generative pattern of sociability, particularly because it does not lay claim to facticity but rather openly announces its artifice.[23]

Dickens's journals cultivate a national imaginary through a centralised narrative persona akin to the post office that opened this chapter, but he envisions this communal creation to be in tension with the fraudulent and even destructive modes of community yielded by the newspaper press. Rather than working across print media in a fluid way, Dickens's journals suggest an early distinction between the potentialities of fiction and news. The 1840s and 1850s were a unique time in the history of the press, as the taxes on knowledge were campaigned against and gradually lifted. Dickens characterisation of the potential chaos of the press should be understood in light of this backdrop. Yet his writings continued to negotiate the blurred lines between novelistic narrative and the news into the 1860s, a decade characterised by sensational news and sensation novels and a rapid expansion in print materials available to readers. Dickens's last complete novel, *Our Mutual Friend*, interrogates the social ramifications of the ways that news and information circulate, suggesting the generative potential of fiction in shaping new communal and social visions.

The Writer as Weaver in *Our Mutual Friend*

In the postscript to his 1864 novel, *Our Mutual Friend*, Dickens compares his work as novelist to that of a weaver:

> Its difficulty was much enhanced by the mode of publication; for, it would be very unreasonable to expect that many readers, pursuing a story in portions from month to month through nineteen months will, until they have it before them complete, perceive the relations of its finer threads to the whole pattern which is always before the eyes of the story-weaver in his loom.[24]

In comparing himself to a weaver, Dickens suggests that he has crafted patterns across the serialised narrative of *Our Mutual Friend*, characterising the temporal movement of the serial novel in terms of the visual apprehension of a woven pattern. I want to make several points about this analogy. Dickens's imagined 'story-weaver' always retains the vision of the 'whole pattern' before his eyes, even as he weaves the threads of the novel slowly over time. This means that, like a weaver of a carpet or fabric, the writer must imagine a pattern before their labour brings it into reality, thereby recasting imagination as a kind of seeing. In contrast, Dickens's metaphor allows readers to see only a portion of the pattern at a time, because of the temporary concealment inherent to serial form. If readers encounter only bits and pieces each month, they cannot envision the whole and will experience the pattern as random and contingent miscellany. Thus, Dickens both instantiates the kind of imagination, or seeing, possessed by the creator and also the imaginative faith required in the reader, who must believe that the weaver has a 'larger pattern' always before his or her eyes.

In calling the novel a 'pattern', Dickens emphasises the repetitions involved in novel writing. This sounds rather like serial form, in the sense that it involves cycles and repetitions, but the difference is that a pattern incorporates these repetitions to create a greater arrangement. Dickens chooses a metaphor that is vague in generative ways. After all, a pattern can mean a set of instructions for a dressmaker; an exemplar or archetype to be imitated; a copy made from a prototype; or a decorative arrangement. Dickens's analogy works at the level of all these definitions, suggesting that repetitions across his novel serve as an arrangement that can also provide a model for the reader. The serialisation of the novel develops repetitions that build, retrospectively, into patterns, while less coherent or patterned serial forms – the newspaper, the penny dreadful and other publications – do not. This becomes evident in the way that Dickens draws upon contemporary news in the structure of *Our Mutual Friend*.

Dickens's last complete novel develops a tension between ordered miscellany and chaotic randomness in its structure and style, built on multiplications, repetitions, doubles and reversals that range from Mr Venus's 'warious' objects to replications embedded in the narrative itself. The novel is packed full of random lists and groupings including: the dust heaps that make Mr Harmon rich; the neighbourhood surrounding Headstone's school, which looks 'like a toy neighbourhood taken in blocks out of a box by a child of particularly incoherent mind';[25] as well as Mr Venus's shop, made up of 'human warious. Cats. Articulated English baby. Dogs. Ducks. Glass eyes, warious. Mummified bird. Dried cuticle, warious'.[26] On top of this jumble of disconnected places, objects and people, the novel unfolds countless acts of fraud, ranging from Silas Wegg's pretence of being educated to the Lammles's claim to wealth and security. *Our Mutual Friend* itself feels like a dust heap of fraudulent acts and miscellaneous objects, a contingent collection of characters and events.

But this appearance of randomness is set up against other repetitions that gesture towards a larger pattern, in the novel and beyond. A particularly notable example occurs at the beginning of the chapter in which Bradley Headstone, inflamed by his jealous desire for Lizzie, attacks Eugene Wrayburn near the Paper Mill. The narrator describes the happy scene of 'people going home from their day's labour' before the attack happens:

> Into the sheet of water reflecting the flushed sky in the foreground of the living picture, a knot of urchins were casting stones, and watching the expansion of rippling circles. So, in the rosy evening, one might watch the ever-widening beauty if the landscape – beyond the newly-released workers wending home – beyond the silver river – beyond the deep green fields of corn, so prospering, that the loiters in their narrow threads of pathway seemed to float immersed breast-high – beyond the hedgerows and the clumps of trees – beyond the windmills on the ridge – away to where the sky appeared to meet the earth, as if there were no immensity of space between mankind and Heaven.[27]

Here we once again encounter a doubling, this time of the sky reflected in the pool of water. The narrator calls it a 'living picture', as we see children tossing stones into the water and causing a series of circles to ripple across the reflection. These ripples reflect the enlarging circle that the narrator imagines, as it expands from the urchins, to the workers, to the cornfields, and finally to the horizon. It situates the minor disturbances created by the children within a larger sense of order, 'the ever-widening beauty of the landscape', while showing that their stones cause only a momentary ripple in the sky's reflection. It also gestures forward towards the attempted murder of Eugene Wrayburn. Just before the attack, Eugene hears a rippling in this same river, which he sees as a reflection of his own uneasy thoughts about Lizzie: 'He would have laid them asleep if he could, but they were in movement, like the stream, and all tending one way with a strong current.'[28] The river becomes a metaphor for the thinking and desiring mind, as Eugene's desires carry him beyond intentional action. But his thoughts are disrupted by Headstone's brutal attack: 'the reflected night turned crooked, flames shot jaggedly across the air, and the moon and stars came bursting from the sky'.[29] Eugene experiences this attack as a toppling of the natural world order. We see here not just a series of recurring metaphors, but also a series that resembles the 'the expansion of rippling circles' created by the 'knot of urchins'. These fire and water metaphors expand and constrict in meaning, inviting the reader to make connections forwards and backwards in the narrative, even within a single narrative moment. In a sense, this reformulates the serial structure of the novel in terms of cycles and circles rather than a chronological series of events.

Indeed, the novel as a whole features the forming and breaking of various kinds of communities, including Abbey Potterson's pub; the small community formed by Lizzie Hexam, Jenny Wren and Riah; and the partnership between Eugene Wrayburn and Mortimer Lightwood. These more generative communities are contrasted with those based in falsehood, self-interest and malice. The newly wealthy Veneerings derive their knowledge about society through their dinner parties, where they bring together acquaintances to mine them for information and social status. Silas Wegg claims to have incriminating information on Mr Boffin and threatens to share it if he is not financially rewarded. Eugene Wrayburn torments and teases the jealous Bradley Headstone into stalking him across London, leading him on endless circles around town. *Our Mutual Friend* is not just a novel about miscellaneous objects and trash; it also deals with the circulation of information and people as well as the role news plays in circumscribing social groups. These diverse instances of community encourage readers to read comparatively rather than linearly, considering the ways that communities are imagined and constructed across the novel.

Reading and storytelling are key to the moral value of these various communities in *Our Mutual Friend*. As Patrick Brantlinger argues, Dickens frequently associates illiteracy with innocence and morality, in characters such as Joe Gargery, Mr Boffin and of course Lizzie. By contrast, literacy is often coupled with deception and abuse, as in the case of Silas Wegg's manipulation of Mr Boffin. The practice of generative reading and fiction making is particularly highlighted in the character Lizzie Hexam.[30] One pivotal scene describes her 'reading' the fire, which prompts her younger brother Charley to comment, 'Your library of books is the hollow down by the flare, I think.'[31] Lizzie's fire-gazing is an act of make-believe that allows for alternative visions of the future and generative connections to those close to her, associating fire-gazing with 'childlike, unconventional, and unscripted modes of seeing'.[32] Her brother, however, can see only the fire's literal elements and the factual inaccuracies of Lizzie's stories: 'that's the gas, that is, coming out of a bit of a forest that's been under the mud that was under the water in the days of Noah's Ark'.[33] Later in the novel, he directs Lizzie to control her fancies and accommodate herself to reality: 'You are such a dreamer . . . It was all very well when we sat before the fire – when we looked into the hollow down by the flare – but we are looking into the real world, now.'[34] Lizzie, however, insists that she *is* speaking of the real world.

The novel features other acts of fiction-making and dreaming on the part of characters. Lizzie reveals her attachment to Eugene Wrayburn through an act of make-believe, by imagining she is a lady. Bella similarly imagines voyages for herself and her pa, particularly one that pretends John Harmon survived (as we later learn he did). When characters detach themselves from their immediate reality and imagine alternative realities, they push against the materially obsessed, chaotic world of the novel. As Lizzie, Bella and Harmon imagine alternative worlds, Rogue Riderhood falsely alleges that Gaffer Hexam committed murder, what Harmon/Rokesmith calls 'your trumped-up story'.[35] Even Mortimer Lightwood is guilty of spreading a story that is not entirely true. He becomes known in 'Society' for his storytelling capacity, particularly surrounding the Harmon Murder:

> like the tides on which it had been borne to the knowledge of men, the Harmon Murder – as it came to be popularly called – went up and down, and ebbed and flowed, now in the town, now in the country, now among palaces, now among hovels, . . . until at last, after a long interval of slack water it got out to sea and drifted away.[36]

Dickens's contrasting metaphors for storytelling – fire versus water – reveal the extent to which Lightwood loses responsibility for his story and allows it to gather force on its own. This pattern of oppositions, doubles and metaphors across the novel create a structure that goes beyond the newspaper and gossip, encouraging readers to look ahead, behind, or beyond the present moment of the narrative and to see interconnections across the serial instalments of the novel. Thus, *Our Mutual Friend* slowly and meticulously distinguishes between generative fictional patterns and 'trumped-up' frauds.

This distinction between the social effects of fictions and frauds becomes evident in the 'pious fraud' committed by John Harmon, who is nearly murdered by a shipman on his return voyage to London. When a dead body surfaces in the Thames, newspapers officially declare Harmon to be dead. He then takes on the name John Rokesmith, rents a room in the house of his intended wife, and becomes the secretary for the Boffins, who inherit the Harmon estate upon his supposed death. When the Boffins realise that Rokesmith is Harmon, they help him enact a fiction to school his intended wife Bella Wilfer on the consequences of overvaluing wealth and material comfort. The novel records the process of her moral and social development, from a fortune hunter who values money to a happy housewife who has absolute faith in her husband's integrity. The Boffins and John Rokesmith decide not to inform Bella that Rokesmith is actually her intended husband. They fabricate a story in which Mr Boffin becomes an unfeeling miser, mistreats his secretary, and announces his intentions to marry, or sell, Bella to a wealthy man. As Edwin Eigner suggests in *The Dickens Pantomime*, the telling of lies to measure and inculcate virtue is common in Dickens's novels and earlier short fiction.[37] Betsy Trotwood commits a similar 'pious fraud' in *David Copperfield* in order to complete David's education and to teach him to discipline his heart. Eigner adds that, while there may be nothing unrealistic about a character telling a lie, 'the implications of the aesthetics of such an action are contrary to the realist position'.[38] However, this assertion is not quite accurate; novelistic realism is built on fictions that are not true but suggest a larger truth. Dickens's pious frauds reveal a wider cultural sense that fictional narrative, through the readers' momentary removal from the real world into an imaginary reality, works productively on external reality in the form of 'the consciousness of listeners or readers whose way of being in the world has been altered by their reading'.[39]

In the first part of *Our Mutual Friend*, Bella is confident in her pragmatic and materialistic worldview, fixated on finding a husband who will set her up with a comfortable middle-class lifestyle. She acknowledges the moral vacuity of this outlook but also insists that it is necessary in a capitalist world like her own. It reflects the lessons of her parents' relationship, a marriage originally for love but now only a source of unhappiness and stress. However, Bella comes to question her worldview, first as she encounters the Boffins's affectionate marriage and then later as she watches Mr Boffin transform into a miser.[40] By the end of the novel, she abandons her old pragmatism and marries John Rokesmith (who is, unbeknownst to Bella, also John Harmon and Julius Handford), despite his apparent lack of position, fortune and name. Her experiences with the Boffinses enable her to imagine a world in which she can have something other than a marriage like that of her parents without becoming mercenary.

It turns out, of course, that Bella's transformation is partly the result of a 'pious fraud' concocted and enacted by her husband and Mr and Mrs Boffin. Mr Boffin has not truly transformed into a miser but has pretended to do so only in order to model for Bella the limitations of a materialistic life. Bella, believing herself a happily married mother satisfied with a modest social station in life, learns of the plots that were authored in her interests only after she has had her first baby. In this scene with Harmon and the Boffins, Bella insists that she does not understand what has happened. Mrs Boffin exclaims, 'How can you till you're told! So now I am going to tell you.'[41] Bella requires the storytelling skills of the Boffinses to recast the past into a new light.

John Harmon offers hints early in their marriage of this pious fraud; he warns Bella that she will undergo some trial in which she will need to put faith in him, and she reassures her husband that she has 'perfect faith in you'.[42] Indeed, Bella receives a number of hints of her husband's true identity: Rokesmith refuses to go to Lizzie and Eugene's wedding because he wishes to avoid Lightwood, Lightwood identifies him as Julius Handford when they run upon each other in the street, and finally the Inspector, upon learning her husband's true identity, gives Bella a 'knowing way of raising his eyebrows when their eyes by any chance met, as if he put the question "Don't you see?"'[43] Although Bella is willing to place her faith in the man she believes to be Rokesmith, she does not piece together the 'pious fraud' until it is told to her upon its conclusion. Bella's awareness of the full meaning of the plot does not emerge until its end, when what seemed to be disconnected, even baffling events fit together into an intelligible retrospective pattern.

While spinning this fiction, Harmon worries that Bella will fail to understand the intentions with which the fiction was conveyed:

> he had put a pious fraud upon her which had preyed upon his mind, as the time for its disclosure approached, lest she might not make full allowance for the object with which it had originated, and in which it had fully developed.[44]

Harmon's anxiety here reflects the postscript to *Our Mutual Friend* mentioned earlier in this chapter.[45] Dickens opens that postscript as follows:

> To keep for a long time unsuspected, yet always working itself out, another purpose originating in that leading incident, and turning it to a pleasant and useful account at last, was at once the most interesting and the most difficult part of my design.[46]

Dickens characterises deception as part of his design, gathering force and working itself out into a pattern that develops over the serial parts.

Dickens's postscript argues for an interpretation that regards the imaginary world as a privileged site for refiguring the readers' relationship to the lived, external world. This is a possibility available only to fictional narrative, since journalism is limited by the pressure to report events as they happen. Without the perspective of retrospection, journalists do not yet know how to talk about what has happened. As Clare Pettitt has argued, 'The newspaper mimes that aspect of presentness that resists known historical categories because the terms that will describe them are not yet fully formed or known, social relations remain inchoate and in the act of becoming in its pages.'[47] She quotes Richard Terdiman in calling the newspaper a 'form [that] *denies form*', and Kevis Goodman in arguing that the newspaper 'testified obliquely to the contradictions and complexities of ongoing events not by mapping them faithfully but by miming them with its own incoherences and dissociations'.[48]

For Pettitt, Dickens deals with this tension through the development of a new tense: the historical present tense. She suggests that Dickens imitates the form of the newspaper by miming the present through 'the production of spatial temporality'.[49] In her account, Dickens builds upon this paradoxical present in his Christmas stories and *Dombey and Son*, and, in doing so, 'strains toward a history that does not look backwards but rather forwards'.[50] But in many of his writings, Dickens also draws upon fiction's unique capacity to ask the reader to look forward and backward at the same time, what Dowling calls the 'double temporality of narrative structure'.[51] Even while aware of their limited knowledge, the reader is continually 'conscious of viewing events through the eyes of a narrator who, knowing the story as a whole, is already viewing them in terms of their outcome and who is viewing that outcome as an order of moral and ethical significance'.[52] Dickens's postscript to *Our Mutual Friend* encourages readers to look back on the novel's apparent hodgepodge of characters, objects and metaphors as a carefully planned pattern woven across the serial parts of the novel.[53] Dickens crafts this patterned appearance in the face of apparent chance happenings across his novel; as a result, the end invests earlier actions with inflated retrospective significance. John Harmon claims to better Bella through a 'pious fraud', but this pious fraud was made possible only because of a youthful prank gone wrong. *Our Mutual Friend* traces the movement of information and its influence on community through the narrative's formal operations. Serial form comes to mean not simply chronological publication in parts but also a system of repetition, retrospection and cumulative meaning that gives significance to its parts.

Reworking the News in *Our Mutual Friend*

At the time of *Our Mutual Friend*'s serialisation in 1864, London newspapers were clamouring over the trial, conviction and execution of a German immigrant named Franz Müller for the murder of bank clerk Thomas Briggs on July 9, 1864. Müller was accused of murdering 69-year-old Briggs for his gold watch and spectacles on the North London Railway and tossing his body out the carriage window. Müller fled to New York City and was apprehended there by British authorities, making him a transatlantic media sensation. Dickens's serialised novel about crime, imposture and murder intersected in fruitful ways with the news reports about Müller. Readers would have gossiped about Müller's trial while reading about the murders and attempted murders in *Our Mutual Friend*.[54] When examined against the backdrop of the Franz Müller case, Bradley Headstone's attempted murder of Eugene Wrayburn becomes a study of the self-reflexive quality of *Our Mutual Friend*, in which the journalistic murder story is reworked and theorised in fictional form. *Our Mutual Friend* began serialisation in May 1864, and its early instalments came out during the media hype surrounding Müller, who was apprehended in September 1864 and later executed in October 1864. Dickens introduced the character of Bradley Headstone in the sixth instalment, published in October 1864, during the Müller trial. Headstone finally attacks Wrayburn in the September 1865 instalment, a little less than a year after Müller's execution.

Although markedly different in terms of motive and context, the attempted murders in *Our Mutual Friend* invite an intertextual reading with the murder on the North London Railway. They all involve an attack on a middle class man in transit. Mr Briggs was sitting in a first-class compartment when he was murdered for his watch, and his body was later found lying between the railway tracks on the canal bridge between Bow and Hackneywick. Harmon watches his impersonator brutally beaten near the London docks, while Eugene Wrayburn suffers Headstone's jealous assault on the Thames. *Our Mutual Friend* intersects with the reportage of the murder on the North London Railway to interrogate the ways that murder stories are told and the kinds of publics they construct via sensation.

Müller became a sort of celebrity in his infamy, as readers clamoured for more information about the transatlantic story. *The Times* complained, 'Müller's name was on every tongue, and every family was discussing various theories of the murder.'[55] *Lloyd's Weekly Newspaper* bemoaned that 'Franz Müller, only a month or two since, was a poor German journeyman tailor ... and now his name is upon every lip; his portrait is in the shop windows; and he cannot speak without waking echoes throughout Europe.'[56] Upon his arrival and eventual arrest in New York, newspapers described crowds thronging the docks to glimpse the infamous murderer. *Lloyd's* criticised 'the wild greed of the public for the smallest crumb of news about a great murder', attributing the insatiable desire to 'the crowd' and the 'millions'.[57] Yet newspapers across the class spectrum continued to feed the public's desire, filling in factual gaps with speculative fictions. According to L. Perry Curtis, nineteenth-century murder news commonly rushed to speculation, devoting 'time and space to their own surmises and rumours gleaned from contacts or witnesses'.[58] It relied upon witnesses, conjectures and the frequently untruthful perpetrator to reconstruct the event; in doing so, the Victorian press shaped the narrative in their selection, composition and publication of these stories. For Curtis, then, murder news further silences the victim, and the gaps in knowledge serve only to promote further sensation and conjecture.[59] Murder news, thus, shapes a public based in sensational and speculative fictions that masquerade as a search for truth. This becomes evident in the conjectural account of the Müller attack in *Lloyds Weekly Newspaper*:

> The traveler falls into a light sleep in the corner of the carriage; the thief makes a dash at the watch-chain. . . . [T]he old man, roused by the attempt at robbery, wakes up and grapples boldly with his assailant. . . . It is probable, however, that the ruffian tried to escape with the watch and chain he had secured; that he had, in fact opened the door with such a purpose; and that his brave opponent sprang upon him, and endeavoured to hold him fast. Then came the death grapple.[60]

The fly-on-the-wall account requires linguistic acrobatics to provide a first-hand account of the event; it uses the present tense, omits the names of the perpetrator and victim, and includes qualifying phrases, such as 'it is probable'. It draws upon the language of melodrama and heroicises the 'old man' as he grapples with his attacker. By omitting the names, it encourages the reader to imagine himself in the scene, thereby cultivating a readership based in fear as well as sensation. In the aftermath of the Müller attack, newspapers stoked fears about the safety of the London railway and everyday middle-class life, warning that the attack could have happened to any 'elderly gentleman with a gold watch-chain'.[61] This is particularly true of *Lloyd's* and *Reynolds Weekly*, two Sunday penny papers that appealed to working-class readers through their mingling of crime news, politics and economics; but even staunchly middle-class newspapers, like the *The Times*, encouraged an interest in the murder.

Headstone attempts to murder Eugene Wrayburn in the September 1865 instalment of *Our Mutual Friend*, a little over a year after the North London Railway murder. Dickens manipulates the narrative tempo and perspective so as to foreground the experience of the victim. It lacks the clarity of an event that can be chronologically and factually reported; instead, Eugene experiences it as a series of disconnected and blurred impressions. The murder itself takes up only two paragraphs, although the imminence of such an act of violence has been a source of suspense for much of the novel:

> Was he struck by lightning? With some incoherent half-formed thought to that effect, he turned under the blows that were blinding him and mashing his life, and closed with a murderer, whom he caught by a red neckerchief – unless the raining down of his own blood gave it that hue. Eugene was light, active, and expert; but his arms were broken, or he was paralysed, and could do no more than hang on to the man.[62]

Unable to understand what is happening to him, Eugene attributes the violence to non-human forces. The description then shifts back to the third-person narrator, but one that draws upon figurative language to efface the literal events of the crime. We do not know the exact nature of the blows but only that they are taking away his sense of sight and 'mashing his life'; bereft of his senses, Eugene is unable to distinguish between his raining blood and the red handkerchief. Headstone becomes nothing more than a nameless 'murderer' and 'the man'. Whereas the news speculates about the details surrounding the North London Railway murder, *Our Mutual Friend* traces the tension and violence that leads up to the murder, but it narratively decentres the murder itself.

After the attack, and at Eugene's behest, Mortimer Lightwood seeks to control the circulation of gossip and conjecture surrounding the attempted murder. While still believing he will die from his injuries, Eugene urges Mortimer not to pursue Bradley Headstone: 'Don't think of avenging me; think only of hushing the story and protecting [Lizzie]. You can confuse the case, and turn aside the circumstances.'[63] Mortimer's discursive manipulation ensures that Headstone does not have authorial control over his crime. Hoping to learn of his rival's death, Headstone anxiously scours the city's newspapers for reports about his crime, and he lingers at the railway station, 'a place where any fresh news of his deed would be circulated'.[64] But instead of Eugene's death, he reads of Lizzie and Eugene's marriage: 'Bradley would far rather have been seized for his murder, than he would have read that passage, knowing himself spared, and knowing why.' Headstone becomes only a passive reader as Lightwood controls the public narrative surrounding Headstone's act and thereby 'put a fraud upon him'. Lightwood's control over the narrative of the crime protects Lizzie and Eugene from an amoral yet judgemental public sensation. The need to protect these characters from 'Society' and the unhampered circulation of news suggests the ways in which murder news threatens to derail small communities and interpersonal attachments. Unfamiliar consumers of murder news would leap to a faulty and speculative account harmful to Lizzie's reputation. In this sense, *Our Mutual Friend* problematises a 'Society' organised around gossip and dinner parties, valorising instead the small communities that are fostered apart from public circulation of information. By intersecting with the sensation surrounding the Müller case, *Our Mutual Friend* interrogates social groupings that emerge through pleasure in information independent of social and moral responsibility.

Although there is no record of Dickens writing explicitly about the North London Railway murder, Müller drew upon Dickens in defending his innocence to journalists. While he was in custody on a ship returning from New York, *Lloyd's Weekly* reported that Franz Müller 'ate, drank, and slept well, read the "Pickwick Papers", and laughed heartily over them. He says he never shall forget Sam Weller. He says he will be able to establish his perfect innocence.'[65] Müller invokes the emotional resonance and familiarity of Samuel Weller to construct a sympathetic imagination around his arrest, drawing upon Dickens's popularity to shape public perceptions of his detainment and trial. In the last section, I will argue that Dickens's aesthetic privileging of wholes and patterns emerged partly as a means to control unauthorised uses of his fiction in the public sphere. By envisioning his characters as part of a larger whole, he could make a clearer argument against adaptations, copies and borrowings of his fictions marshalled for competing political and social ends.

'A Striking Imitation of Boz'

In *Martin Chuzzlewit* (1840–41), Mr Pecksniff passes off an architectural blueprint designed by his former student, the young Martin, as his own. Martin, recently returned from America, learns that 'the great Mr Pecksniff, the celebrated architect' has designed and will 'help to lay the first stone of a new and splendid public building'.[66] Martin seethes as he realises that the new building is based on his own design of a grammar school: 'I invented it. I did it all. He has only put four windows in, the villain, and spoilt it!'[67] Even though Mr Pecksniff has made minor changes, Martin still insists on his claim to the design. Martin thus valorises the design as a whole, insisting that these small structural alterations do not substantially alter the larger vision. Just as Mr Pecksniff wrongly lays claim to Martin's work, he also pretends to act in the interest of the working classes in erecting the public building, when he is in fact only preoccupied with his own reputation. Mr Pecksniff's fraud is committed at the level of authorial creation as well as public feeling. This fraudulent act symbolically becomes a part of the public building itself, as Mr Pecksniff lays its first foundations. Thus, Mr Pecksniff's fraud poses a problem not only for Martin but also for the fabric of society, as its public architecture is reared on the basis of false claims.

At the time of *Martin Chuzzlewit*, Dickens had been fending off imitations and copies of his work for quite some time. Mr Pecksniff's theft of Martin's creative work parallels the borrowing of Dickens's writings in the literary marketplace. Dickens's anxieties surrounding these copies dealt with their implications for the growing and splintering reading public. As Patrick Brantlinger has noted, many Victorians worried about a volatile, unpredictable and even 'unknown public'. Dickens more specifically worried about the potential for his characters and plots to be repurposed for anti-social or self-interested motives. His vision of community was at odds with many of these imitations. Like Martin in this scene, Dickens increasingly valorised an aesthetic of pattern as a means to ward off the Pecksniffs of the literary marketplace. Many critics have offered convincing accounts of Dickens's pragmatic motivations in the fight for international copyright, but here I want to consider the formal and social ramifications of Dickens's defence of an author's rights to their own imaginative work. Pecksniff's plagiarism is not only a theft of Martin's invention but also erects a public building on false pretences. Dickens imagines the work of art and design as a social and moral practice with ramifications in how we envision the real world.

Critics have argued that the copyright debate encouraged Dickens and other writers to valorise aesthetic wholeness. Robert Patten recently contended that Dickens cultivated a coherent authorial persona over the course of his career, shifting from the scattered identity of the pseudonym Boz to the singular Charles Dickens. Central to this development, Patten believes that Dickens increasingly upheld narrative unity within and across his works, so as to display what Patten calls 'the hidden sense pervading their works'.[68] This emphasis on authorial and narrative coherence is commensurate with the rhetoric supporting the 1837–1842 copyright debate in Parliament, which eventually gave authors a longer monopoly over their work, although not the permanent rights that Dickens wanted. Beginning in 1837, Whig MP Thomas Noon Talfourd proposed a bill that would extend copyright protection to life plus sixty years; after several failed attempts, a revised and weakened version finally passed in 1842 by Lord Mahon (called the Copyright Amendment Act of 1842), extending copyright protection to seven years after death or 42 years from publication, whichever was longer. (Under the 1814 legislation, copyright in a literary work was to last 28 years from publication or for the remainder of the author's natural life.) Central to the debates was the question of which works deserved protection and which did not.

Proponents of the Talfourd bill determined literary value by distinguishing between 'imaginative literature' and 'useful knowledge', and in doing so, they valorised 'imaginative' literature as permanent, unique, original, coherent, complete and individual.[69] Chris R. Vanden Bossche writes:

> [S]uch works are permanent because the knowledge they contain is complete, and so cannot be added to meaningfully. This character of totality in turn results from the way the parts of the work are integrated to make an organic whole, because it emanates from the individuality of the author.[70]

Literary value, then, is determined by how effectively the parts of a work are integrated into the whole, a whole that could be created only by that particular author. In contrast, 'useful knowledge' can be detached from its original context and still retain its value, meaning that its arrangement does not justify protection on aesthetic and literary grounds. This argument – made by advocates of the copyright bill – also positioned artists to play an important role in imparting meaning to the real world. Indeed, they argued that imaginative literature should not mirror the demands of the marketplace but rather offer a 'cure for a fragmented culture'.

And yet copyists of Dickens drew upon similar rationales to justify poaching his characters. When encountered in the episodic narratives of Dickens's early career, characters could be disentangled from their imaginative origin and redirected to other purposes, because they were perceived as independent of the original creation. Detachable characters worked much like the heterogeneity of the newspaper form; they could be taken from their context and marshalled towards different social and political ends. Writers regularly borrowed Dickens's characters in ways not commensurate with Dickens's social beliefs. Dickens moved from episodic to planned narratives as a means to retain control over the ways his characters could be given meaning upon their entry into the real world. His understandings of authorship and literature emerged in tandem with his concerns over how literary form could be used to influence and shape readers' perceptions of their social reality. This anxiety developed particularly in relationship to the perceived threat posed by George W. M. Reynolds, an editor and writer who later took a leading role in the Chartist movement. Dickens famously despised George W. M. Reynolds, and in an 1849 letter, he wrote:

> If 'Mr G. W. Reynolds' be the Mr Reynolds who is the author of the *Mysteries of London*, and who took the chair for a mob in Trafalgar

Square before they set forth on a window-breaking expedition, I hold his to be a name with which no lady's and no gentleman's should be associated.[71]

In this respect, Dickens was not alone. Many of his contemporaries denounced Reynolds for his radicalism, his allegedly pornographic style, and his use of melodrama and sensation to titillate a new reading public. Reynolds authored nearly fifty novels, was the first editor of *The London Journal*, and founded the penny newspapers *Reynolds's Weekly* and *Reynolds's Miscellany*.

But Dickens was threatened by Reynolds not simply because he perceived him as an unprincipled hack who flooded the marketplace with writings of dubious quality; more importantly, his textual practices took Dickens's characters from their original imaginative context and repurposed them into new shapes. For instance, Reynolds's novel, *Pickwick Abroad; or, The Tour in France* (1837–38), ships Samuel Weller and Mr Pickwick off to France, where they come to question English political and social practices. In his opening to the novel, Reynolds playfully undermines Dickens's ownership of the *Pickwick* characters by suggesting that an author's rights do not extend past the original story: '[G]entle reader, allow me to remark that if the talented "Boz" have not chosen to enact the part of Mr Pickwick's biographer in his continental tour, it is not my fault. The field was open to him . . .'[72] In short, if Dickens failed to take Mr Pickwick to France, then the story is fair game. This suggests that characters enter the public domain as long as they are not fixed in the original narrative of *The Pickwick Papers*.

In the preface of the novel, Reynolds touted positive reviews of *Pickwick Abroad* that construe imitation as a skilful endeavour. The *Age* writes, 'Pickwick Abroad is so well done by G. W. M. Reynolds, that we must warn Boz to look to his laurels.' *The Dublin Pilot* represents Reynolds's skill as the submersion of his writerly identity into that of another:

> If the name of G. W. M. Reynolds did not stand upon the title-page, we should be induced to believe that the identical Cid Hamet Benengeli, who introduced us to the immortal club, had taken up his pen again to chronicle their sayings and doings.[73]

The Sunday Times calls *Pickwick Abroad* 'a striking imitation of Boz'.[74] Through collecting these snippets that celebrate imitation, Reynolds undermines the proprietary rights of authors over their literary creations. He blurs the distinction between what might be literary or unliterary, closed or open to imitation. Reynolds does not boast about his original voice but about his ability to sound exactly like Charles Dickens.

In doing so, Reynolds in one sense affirmed the arguments made by copyright supporters, because he treated Dickens's characters as parts of an episodic narrative that, when detached from their origin, are open to public adaptation. Yet Reynolds also challenged the rhetoric in favour of the bill by erasing the line between imaginary literature and useful knowledge. Reynolds's work shows the intermingling of fictional and political discourses, as he worked fluidly across non-fiction, advice columns and serial fiction in his novels and periodicals. As Ian Haywood has argued, Reynolds made his writing indistinguishable from his presence on the political platform: 'Reynolds's aim was to inscribe the people's perspective and agency onto his narrative by making his serials permeable to politics. He placed fictional representation on a continuum with social life.'[75] Haywood highlights the utility of serial fiction in enabling Reynolds to do so; it allowed for the reader to influence the plot and for the plot to intersect with and respond to current events, including the 1848 revolutions in Europe. (For instance, Reynolds interrupted *Mysteries of London* to include a long diatribe on the 1848 revolutions and then incorporated the events thematically into his story.) As Clare Pettitt has suggested, serial publications involved the reading public in the experience of assembling the story and thereby undermined traditional notions of art.[76] However, Reynolds takes this to another level. He stopped serial instalments mid-sentence, introduced characters in dramatic scenes and then never returned to them again, and gave the sense of an endlessly continuing bundle of disconnected narratives. *Mysteries of London* and its partner *Mysteries of the Court of London* continued on for more than a decade. According to Louis James, *Mysteries of London* 'has the kaleidoscope format of a journal rather than the unified focus of a novel'.[77]

Reynolds denies readers the sense that he is moving towards some final resolution, instead mimicking the contingencies of life. He plays in deferral and often structures his endings as a refusal of ending. At the end of the first volume of *the Mysteries of London*, he urges his readers not to deduce a moral because, though the end of the volume, he promises there is more to come. And when he does seem to offer a central narrative meaning, it is undermined through other sections of his hybrid storytelling methods. In so closely yoking his narratives to political reality, and allowing political discourse to disrupt his fictions, Reynolds does not ascribe any particular insight to fictional narrative in the way that Dickens does. Nor is there a clear distinction between his fiction and non-fiction, because of the ways that they discursively and structurally intersect.

Reynolds and Dickens demonstrate competing ideas about fraud, fiction and the periodical press. This becomes particularly evident in Reynolds's rip-off of Dickens's periodical *Master Humphrey's Clock*. Reynolds's serial, *Master Timothy's Book-case* (1840–1841), tells a story about a young engraver commissioned to copy a banker's check. The project is a difficult one, because the original banknote was designed to prevent forgery. But with hard work and natural skill, James Herbert produces an engraving that impresses his mysterious customer with its 'fidelity and delicacy of . . . execution'.[78] It turns out, unfortunately, that he has been duped into assisting an illegal counterfeiting operation. The criminals entrap James Herbert in an apartment near Notre Dame Cathedral and force him to produce more engravings. When they finally let him go, he is ruined and left with only a bundle of his own counterfeit currency. Herbert knows the penalty for using counterfeit bank notes is death, but he's unable to throw away the bills because he felt 'a species of attachment for them, because they were originated by his labour: he regarded them in the same light in which an artist surveys his picture—a sculptor his statue – a poet his ode – or a Pygmalion his Galatea'.[79] This story rejects an aesthetic privileging of original artwork; Herbert's counterfeits are situated in an imitative tradition of art reaching back to Pygmalion. It also makes labour central to the artist's relationship to his work. Herbert's story functions as a metaphor for another kind of artistic labour; the human labour involved in producing material printed texts. This story about artistic copies is situated within another copy: *Master Timothy's Book-case*. *Master Humphrey's Clock* features a frame story about the elderly Master Humphrey, who keeps old manuscripts in a longcase clock; he sets up a club for friends and acquaintances, including Mr Pickwick, to share these stories. *Master Timothy's Book-case* also features a frame story but takes serious liberties with the original: Sir Edmund Mortimer is the final descendent of a family visited by a spirit, Master Timothy, who grants each descendent one blessing. When Mortimer wishes for 'Universal Knowledge', Master Timothy reluctantly fulfils this wish by granting Mortimer a phantasmal bookcase visible only to him.[80] Mortimer mentions a person's name, and a parchment giving that person's history appears on the shelves. One of these parchments contains Herbert's story. Reynolds reworks Dickens's periodical featuring a domestic storyteller into a hopeless story of parchments and forgery.[81]

In his vulnerability to Reynolds's appropriation, and in watching his own creations repurposed to new ends, Dickens, I argue, became increasingly attentive to the social ramifications of form. Countless critics have argued that Dickens's writings have a fragmentary, newspaper-like quality to them. But rather than breaking down generic categories and allowing fiction and journalism to exist on the same plane, Dickens shows an increasingly discriminatory understanding of literary and extra-literary work over the course of his career.[82] Unlike Reynolds, there is a productive tension in Dickens's writings between fragmentation and wholeness, one that is constitutive of Dickens's form. Wholeness and fragmentation are not incommensurate; rather, Dickens's style shows an alternating pleasure in the distracting proliferation of details and in the crafting of a heterogeneous whole from these proliferating materials.[83]

Conclusion

Dickens plays on the differences between fiction and non-fiction, novelistic narrative and news reports. Readers approach fiction and non-fiction with different expectations as a result of the inherent form of these narrative orientations. While readers assume that non-fiction is true as long as they reasonably adhere to their external reference, readers require fiction to appear probable in light of perceived realities and characters' personalities. This means that fictions create the appearance that characters are acting on their own agency, therefore these narratives cannot rely too much on circumstance or chance. And yet Dickens, like many Victorian novelists, relies heavily on the appearance of chance in plotting his novels. I argue that, by emphasising the presence of contingency, he invites readers to imagine other possible outcomes.[84] Characters make sense of this contingency by telling stories that, at times, they know to be fictional. Expansive Victorian novels invite readers to imagine all other possible outcomes for a character, and thereby enter into the fiction-making process themselves. For instance, Andrew Miller has read Dickens's novels, particularly *Dombey and Son*, in terms of counterfactuals: that is, each 'character is the image of a viable alternate life', and thus suggests 'the peculiar contingency of modern experience'.[85] For Dickens, the 'pious fraud' is a means of fostering generative social connections and meanings out of contingent events. This is why Dickens's *Household Words* so earnestly emphasises the necessity of imagination. In turn, this allows for readers to make sense of the contingency of reality in ways that use the imagination to restore a sense of meaning and to compete with the apparent authority and influence of non-fictional narratives, like the newspaper.

I have argued in the past that Dickens draws upon fictional narrative to impose order on the dangerous miscellany of news, as a means of social control that parallels the functions of the novelist to those of the government. And indeed, Dickens's fictional storytellers – including John Harmon and the elder Martin Chuzzlewit – seem to exert something of a repressive network of power through their 'pious frauds'. John Harmon, after all, lies to Bella in order to remake her into the ideal Victorian wife. In his identity as Julius Handford, he lies to the police and stands in the way of an official investigation into his attempted murder. This reading draws upon Foucauldian approaches to the nineteenth-century novel, in line with D. A. Miller's famous account of the novel as a kind of 'diffuse social discipline'.[86] However, this sort of approach to Dickens's 'pious frauds' and Victorian novels more broadly is something of an interpretive injustice.[87]

In the specific instances of Harmon and the elder Chuzzlewit, we see two storytellers who do not have absolute regulatory power over their narratives. Harmon, in particular, originally plans his fraud to be a short-lived joke, imagining he could briefly test Bella's character and then abruptly reveal his true identity. However, his attempted murder prolongs this plan. Although Harmon takes credit at the end for more authorial power than he has, we see throughout the novel that the fiction itself disrupts his sense of self. Like the ebb and flow of the Thames, Harmon struggles to hold onto his identity and to make sense of a world in which he lives but in which official discourse has determined him dead. This experience of being a 'living-dead man' inhibits his ability to construct a linear narrative of his memory, particularly of that fateful night in which he was almost murdered. In an internal monologue, he tells himself:

> Again I ramble away from thinking it out to the end. It is not so far to the end that I need be tempted to break off. Now, on straight!
>
> I examined the newspapers every day for tidings that I was missing, but saw none. Going out that night to walk (for I kept retired while it was light), I found a crowd assembled round a placard posted at Whitehall. It described myself, John Harmon, as found dead and mutilated in

the river under circumstances of strong suspicion, described my dress, described the papers in my pockets, and stated where I was lying for recognition.[88]

By experiencing his own death, Harmon is forced to imagine a series of counterfactuals and also to find his own sense of reality falsified by discourses of the real, like placards and newspapers. The elder Martin Chuzzlewit similarly undergoes a self-reckoning as he pretends to lose his wits and to come under the influence of Mr Pecksniff. In the final scene, the elder Martin acknowledges that his fiction began not as a pious fraud but rather as a selfish plot to bring his grandson more firmly under his dominion. He acknowledges, 'I hoped to bring you back, Martin, penitent and humbled. I hoped to distress you into coming back to me.' But he comes to realise that his impulses are selfish and also that his grandson's 'old faults are, in some degree, of [his] creation'. In a sense then, all the characters become subject to this pious fraud: As Mr Tapley explains to the elder Martin, before his reveal of the pious fraud, 'I only mentioned my opinion that Mr Pecksniff would find himself deceived, sir, and that you would find yourself deceived, and that he [the young Martin] would find himself deceived, sir.'

Fiction-making can transform the teller as well as the recipient, partly because of its place within the larger fiction of the novel. The patterns involved in Dickens's fictions rework contingent repetitions, cycles and inversions evident also in news so that they develop over time into an imagined alternative reality, allowing the reader to re-enter the lived world with a new way of perceiving what is possible. As a result, in a novel full of parallels and metaphors for storytelling, Lizzie's unassuming and inadvertent practices of fictional creation may offer one of the best models for the transformative potential of fiction across Dickens's works. Lizzie discerns patterns and shapes in the random sparks of the fire, as she tells her brother stories about his future and hers. But she does not pretend to any sort of authority, and she does not pretend to prophesise; instead, she dreams up new possibilities for her family in a world that seems at risk of drowning in the Thames.

Notes

1. An earlier version of this chapter was published as 'Dickens's "Pious Fraud: The Popular Press and Narrative's Potential for Social Control"', Copyright © 2012 Johns Hopkins University Press. *Victorian Periodicals Review*, 44.4, pp. 377–400.

2. 'Valentine's Day at the Post Office', *Household Words*, 30 March 1850, p. 9.
3. While Dickens expresses concern about the miscellaneous character of British journalism, he articulates a greater anxiety about the American and French media. In an article called, 'A Paris Newspaper', printed Saturday, 1 May 1850, *Household Words* criticises the 'occult' power of French and American editors and their 'leaders': 'here is an instance amongst many that the French people are to be led in masses. Singly they generally have no ideas, either politically or commercially'. 'A Paris Newspaper', *Household Words*, 1 May 1850, p. 164.
4. Paul Ricoeur also suggests that the novel's fictional quality gives the reader greater access to the psychological processes of the human mind, both because it is focused on an actor around whom a series of events circulate and because the thought process is fictionalised and not restricted to the interpretation of exterior signs. Ricoeur, *Time and Narrative*.
5. Jesse Rosenthal has argued that the notion of what feels right in a narrative is tied up with Victorian ideas about morality. Rosenthal, *Good Form*.
6. [W. H. Wills], *Household Words* 10 (1 June 1850), p. 239.
7. Bagehot, *Literary Studies*, p. 197.
8. Drew, *Dickens the Journalist*, p. 194.
9. For related arguments on the construction of a national community in Romantic literature, see Trumpener, *Bardic Nationalism* and Garrett, *Wordsworth and the Writing of the Nation*.
10. In doing so, Dickens builds on and extends Coleridge's famous 'suspension of disbelief', which Margaret Russett argues is essential to the distinction of literary discourse from counterfeits and frauds.
11. Benjamin, 'The Storyteller', pp. 77–93.
12. By calling the journal 'household words', a reference to Shakespeare's *Henry V*, he also invokes its connection to a literary national past.
13. [Dickens], 'A Preliminary Word', *Household Words*, 30 March 1850, 1.
14. In 'A Preliminary Word' Dickens writes that *Household Words* will 'teach the hardest workers at this whirling wheel of toil, that their lot is not necessarily a moody, brutal fact, excluded from the sympathies and graces of imagination; to bring the greater and the lesser in degree, together, upon that wide field, and mutually dispose them to a better acquaintance and a kinder understanding – is one main object of our *Household Words*'. For more on fancy and *Household Words*, see Sumpter, *The Victorian Press and the Fairy Tale*.
15. Dickens as quoted by Clemm, *Dickens, Journalism, and Nationhood*, p. 7.
16. Jonathan V. Farina makes a related argument that Dickens's *Household Words* uses stylistic features of fictional characterisation to describe new abstractions and technologies as if they, like fictional characters,

were repositories of deep character. He suggests that this method is in contrast to alternative genres of representation, such as statistics, to validate abstract social phenomena that could not be seen. He writes, 'While others claimed to offer value-neutral, non-interpretative facts, Dickens aspired to offer characters, things with shadows and depths, inconsistencies and inscrutabilities.' One such example, for Farina, is the 'Shadow' behind *Household Words*, which Farina says appeals to an emergent epistemology of character, a way of knowing everything as divided and irreducible to systematization or simple description. This account is related to what I read to be Dickens's anxiety regarding newspaper coverage. Fictional narrative allows for the expression of inconsistencies and complexities that are reduced and lost within a newspaper account of an event. Farina, 'A Certain Shadow', p. 393.
17. Clemm, *Dickens, Journalism, and Nationhood*, p. 6.
18. This is parallel to Dickens's well-known critiques of educational systems that emphasised learning as accumulation rather than imagination and development. In line with utilitarian theories, nineteenth-century day schools instructed reading as a mechanical exercise that involved recitation and rote memorisation, and 'the institutions that fed teachers into the expanding elementary-school system were pedant-factories, whose machinery efficiently removed whatever traces of interest in humane culture the scholars had somehow picked up earlier in their careers'. Altick, *English Common Reader*, p. 162.
19. Dickens, *Martin Chuzzlewit*, p. 224.
20. Ibid. p. 235.
21. Ibid. p. 235.
22. Dickens as quoted in Hewitt, *The Dawn of the Cheap Press*, p. 828.
23. On the one hand, Dickens's pious frauds might look a lot like deceptive, perhaps even malicious, manipulation; after all, Dickens's characters and narrators who uphold 'pious frauds' orchestrate others' behaviour without their consent. In this sense, Dickens's novels might seem to facilitate a diffusive Foucauldian power that requires characters to adhere to social norms. An earlier version of this chapter published in *Victorian Periodicals Review* pursued this line of argument. Valdez, 'Dickens's "Pious Fraud"', pp. 377–400.
24. Dickens, *Our Mutual Friend*, p. 798.
25. Ibid. p. 219.
26. Ibid. p. 88.
27. Ibid. p. 672.
28. Ibid. p. 682.
29. Ibid. p. 682.
30. Brantlinger, *The Reading Lesson*, p. 5.
31. Ibid. p. 39. Both Headstone and Charley view learning as an accumulative endeavour, transforming education into a kind of consumerism. Headstone mechanically amasses his 'great store of teacher's knowledge'

and guards his collection: 'he always seemed to be uneasy lest anything should be missing from his mental warehouse, and taking stock to assure himself'. Headstone's education in no way affects him morally or socially. He does not draw on his imagination to create new patterns but rather simply accumulates and hoards information. p. 218.
32. Sullivan, 'Animating Flames', pp. 1–21.
33. Dickens, *Our Mutual Friend*, p. 37.
34. Ibid. p. 227.
35. Ibid. p. 355.
36. Ibid. p. 40.
37. He adds, 'The surprising fact is that very few legitimate writers besides Dickens have *ever* felt there was any virtue in these devices. . . . *pious frauds*, where the purpose of the deception is to benefit the person being deceived, are astoundingly hard to find.' Eigner, *The Dickens Pantomime*, p. 57.
38. Ibid. p. 53.
39. Dowling, *Ricoeur on Time and Narrative*, pp. 2–3.
40. Rosemary Mundhenk makes a related argument, suggesting that what Boffin does for Bella is what the novel does for the reader. She argues that Dickens limits the reader's knowledge of the Boffin deception, but informs the reader of the Harmon deception, in order to show the reader that perception is limited and knowledge is partial. Mundhenk, 'The Education of the Reader', p. 42.
41. Dickens, *Our Mutual Friend*, p. 751.
42. Ibid. p. 726.
43. Ibid. p. 743.
44. Ibid. p. 751.
45. Harmon becomes particularly aligned with Dickens's narrator when he has to decide whether to 'come alive' again and announce his identity, and thereby also decide the movement of the novel's plot. He is sensitive to the negative effects that his self-pronouncements could have upon his audience. His determination is in strict contrast to the newspapers that have rigidly proclaimed his death and that are impervious to considering the results that this claim may cause. Harmon's effectiveness as storyteller and story maker, specifically his motivation to transform Bella into a more moral subject, comes into relief against Eugene Lightwood's attempts at storytelling. Lightwood half-heartedly shuffles between genres in a way that sardonically parodies generic forms. This shift signifies his own lack of moral fixity and centrality as a narrator and prevents any real meaning from emerging cumulatively in the story. Lightwood seeks to please his superficial audience and increase his social standing, which causes him to take on an ironic tone of distance to his story. Lightwood's distance mimics that of the actual narrator, but it has no meaning-making impetus, unlike Benjamin's privileged oral storyteller. In contrast, the actual narrator's ironic

distance (based on Eugene) scathingly critiques the Veneerings and their 'bran-new' image.
46. Ibid. p. 798.
47. Pettitt, 'Dickens and the Form of the Historical Present', p. 131.
48. Goodman as quoted in Pettitt, p. 121.
49. Pettitt, p. 122.
50. Ibid. p. 120.
51. Dowling, *Ricoeur on Time and Narrative*, p. 88.
52. Ibid. p. 49.
53. Peter Brooks has called this quality of fiction 'the anticipation of retrospection'. Brooks, *Reading for the Plot*, p. 31.
54. Matthew Rubery argues that we can see journalism's influence on the novel by the way in which novels import journalistic narratives or directly represent newspapers in their pages. He writes that novels used newspapers as 'one of the primary tactics by which novelists sought to keep their work from becoming yesterday's news. Novelists used newspapers in a variety of ways: retelling events, reported by the press; reproducing journalistic voices, styles, and features; the pastiche of news items through headlines and quotations; recording the process of news production; and, most dramatically, portraying the individual reader's reaction to the news'. While I agree with Rubery, I contend that novelists represent news to reflect on discursive formations and aesthetic choices more broadly. Rubery, *Novelty of Newspapers*, p. 11.
55. 'Arrest of Francis Muller, the Suspected Murderer of Mr Briggs', *Reynolds's Newspaper*, 11 September 1864.
56. 'The Murderer Under the Microscope', *Lloyd's Weekly Newspaper*, 25 September 1864.
57. 'Murderer's Fame', *Lloyd's Weekly Newspaper*, 18 September 1864.
58. Curtis, *Jack the Ripper and the London Press*, p. 9.
59. Curtis argues, 'the silences in our newspaper texts problematise the narrative and create countless breaks or ruptures that invite more speculation', Ibid. p. 10.
60. 'The Railway Tragedy', *Lloyd's Weekly Newspaper*, 17 July 1864.
61. See, for instance, 'The Murder of Mr Briggs. – Police Incapacity', *Reynolds's Newspaper*, 24 July 1864. The article argued that the investigation had 'the effect of rousing the public to questions of police reform'. In turn, it contrasts their failure to protect the public with the police's capacity for 'political repression and working class degradation'. It concludes, 'To a certain extent, the police are a terror to evil doers; but they are intended to be a far greater terror to those workmen struggling for political amelioration.'
62. Dickens, *Our Mutual Friend*, 682.
63. Ibid. p. 710.
64. Ibid. p. 771.

65. 'Arrival of Müller: The Voyage to England', *Lloyd's Weekly Newspaper*, 18 September 1864.
66. Dickens, *Martin Chuzzlewit*, p. 473.
67. Ibid. p. 476.
68. Patten, *Charles Dickens and 'Boz'*, p. 20.
69. For more information about debates over the Talfourd bill and copyright more broadly, see the following: Vanden Bossche, 'The Value of Literature', 41–68, and Feltes, *Modes of Production*.
70. Vanden Bossche, p. 45.
71. Letter to W. C. Macready, 30 August 1849, *Letters of Charles Dickens*, p. 603.
72. Reynolds, *Pickwick Abroad*, p. 2.
73. Ibid. p. iv.
74. Ibid. p. iv.
75. Haywood, *The Revolution in Popular Literature*, p. 176.
76. Pettitt, *Patent Inventions: Intellectual Property and the Victorian Novel*.
77. James, 'From Egan to Reynolds', p. 105.
78. Reynolds, *Master Timothy's Book-case*, p. 74.
79. Ibid. p. 86.
80. In eliminating the central narrator, Reynolds opens up room for a different kind of moral lesson that emerges from unpredictability and inconsistency. *Master Timothy's Book-case* offers no clear moral code, for the actual reader or for Mortimer. When Mortimer learns the private histories of his acquaintances, it is unclear how he should react to these disclosures. Is he ethically obligated to take action, even when he cannot reveal how he obtained the information? Mortimer's request for 'universal knowledge' reminds us of the rhetoric surrounding the copyright debate described earlier in this chapter. The debate divided over 'imaginative literature' versus 'useful knowledge', and advocates for the bill characterised unfettered access to information as a danger to national coherence. That Reynolds's heroes are subject to this treatment parallels mainstream efforts to cultivate working-class morality by curating their access to the right kind of information. Indeed, in the 1830s, the Society for the Diffusion of Useful Knowledge published its own penny newspaper for the working class. It used fiction, but in such a way that dramatised working-class characters being rewarded for their good morals and adaptation to social constraints. Reynolds's stories do quite the opposite, challenging any sense of an overarching order.
81. Helen Hauser has argued that this book demonstrates Reynolds the 'tract writer' overwhelming 'Reynolds the novelist' in the sense that most of the tales are about man's inhumanity to man. She suggests that Mortimer is inadequate to Reynolds's purpose, because he is too naïve to grasp fully the injustices the book-case reveals. However, Reynolds

should not be separated into types: he is never *the* tract writer or *the* novelist but rather both and neither simultaneously. These distinctions disintegrate in his text. Hauser claims that Reynolds 'defies conventional categorization', and as such she terms his form the 'miscellany novel' – but to categorise Reynolds at all misses the point. His work demonstrates a conscious and radical refusal of categorisation, one that dismantles the growing divide between works defined as literature and other materials. Hauser, 'Form and Reform', pp. 21–40.
82. Another periodical run by Dickens, *All the Year Round*, subordinates other stories to its central novelistic text. In its monthly instalments, *Bleak House* was set off from the wrapper by a thick sheet of paper and two prints. The illustrations serve not only to render the story in visual form, but also signal the separation between the novel and its advertisements.
83. An attention to Dickens's heterogeneous whole, in Jonathan Loesberg's words, shows 'ways of arranging details so that we can see a new significance'. Loesberg, *A Return to Aesthetics*, p. 30.
84. Some apparently contingent events in Dickens's novel turn out not to be so contingent; we frequently find out that characters have some prior familial relationship or connection, which makes the chance-ridden occurrence seem less based on chance. In *Oliver Twist*, for instance, we find out that Oliver has been the offspring of a middle-class family all along.
85. Miller, 'Lives Unled in Realist Fiction', p. 119.
86. Miller, *The Novel and the Police*, p. 14.
87. My current approach is in line with Isobel Armstrong's argument in *Novel Politics* (2017), in which she argues that we need to seek out instances of the democratic imagination in our reading of the Victorian novel.
88. Dickens, *Our Mutual Friend*, p. 365.

Chapter 2

Arrested Development: Characterisation, the Newspaper and Anthony Trollope

Many of Anthony Trollope's novels return to the same plot line: characters read misleading depictions of themselves in the newspaper and feel overwhelmed by anxiety and isolation. This happens in *The Warden*, *Phineas Finn*, *Phineas Redux*, *Doctor Whortle's School*, *The Prime Minister* and others. The recurrence of this plot is no accident: it explores a tension between Trollope's serialised novels and the expanding Victorian newspaper press. By embedding the newspaper into fiction, Trollope interweaves its formal qualities into novelistic narrative; the newspaper disrupts the characters' processes of *Bildung* and inculcates a feeling of modern alienation. Georg Lukács famously argued that the limitlessness and formlessness of the novel – what he calls 'bad infinity' – is given shape through a biographical story that subordinates details to the development of a single individual. Yet Trollope's protagonists confront another kind of 'bad infinity' – the newspaper – that depicts them in ways deeply at odds with their developmental process of self-recognition. In experimenting with the formal qualities of novels and news, Trollope hypothesises that they enable divergent kinds of national publics to emerge.

Elaine Hadley has argued that Trollope's novels render into narrative the lived protocols of liberalism, as his characters seek to enact liberal values in practice.[1] In a sense, then, characters like Plantagenet Palliser and Phineas Finn are liberal heroes. *The Palliser* novels trace the gradual development of Finn from an Irishman into a member of British Parliament willing to subordinate his own personal and regional interests to the needs of the national community. These stories of liberal development, however, come into conflict with Trollope's fictionalised newspapers, as editors viciously slander characters in the public sphere, impeding and redirecting these characters' stories of personal and liberal growth.[2] Trollope's novels are not just about liberal development but also arrested development, as characters are paralysed by the disjunction between self and society.[3] The newspaper and the serial novel thus instantiate conflicting models of modernity for Trollope. The newspapers in his novels cultivate national feeling not through common feeling (as in Anderson's account) but through scapegoats.

While the first chapter of this monograph traced Dickens's varying metaphors for news and narrative, this chapter attends to practices of characterisation in Trollope's fictional construction of the newspaper press. Rather than depicting the world of newspaper production, as does George Gissing's much later *New Grub Street* (1891), Trollope's newspapers are generally represented by a solitary editor or writer who lacks the three-dimensional depth of his protagonists. Scholars of the newspaper emphasise its formal multiplicity, but Trollope renders the newspaper the output of a single individual who fraudulently claims to represent a multitude.[4] Trollope's reductive treatment of journalism stands in blatant opposition to the care with which he represents the world of British parliament and protagonists such as Phineas Finn and Plantagenet Palliser. Trollope thus seeks to make sense of a changing media ecosystem through novelistic form.

This chapter begins by examining the delayed immediacy of Trollope's *Palliser* novels. These novels mimic the structure and temporality of news but with adaptations in content and style so as to contrast newspaper and novelistic discursive operations, developing readerly interest not through plot-based suspense but through a character's arrested development. By mimicking real life events, the *Palliser* novels draw attention to the formal qualities of how events are told and the ethical consequences of these discursive strategies on individuals and the larger public. I then turn to Trollope's treatment of the newspaper's bad infinity, as it stymies characters' development with paralysis and alienation. Trollope not only represents the newspaper but also interweaves its formal processes into the novel, allowing it to disrupt these characters' processes of *Bildung*. I conclude by reflecting on what Trollope's critique of the newspaper suggests for his understanding of the public and general will. By flattening his journalistic characters into caricatures, Trollope problematises their claim to speak on behalf of a readership, suggesting divergences in journalistic and novelistic visions of a national public.

'Presence of the Present': Novelistic Adaptation of Journalistic Form

Many literary critics emphasise the serial structure of both the nineteenth-century novel and the newspaper. After all, many of these novels came out in instalments and would have been read alongside the prominent news of the day. According to literary critic Richard Altick, Victorian fiction shared with journalism a 'spirit' that 'sought to make the most of the present'.[5] Even novels that did not explicitly deal with contemporary issues still catered to readers who consumed fiction alongside newspapers and 'whose minds were filled with the happenings and issues of the day'.[6] Altick emphasises the role that serialisation played in prioritising the present: the public's saturation with newspapers, and the serial form of the novel, necessitated an association of current events and the content of the novel.

Trollope's novels not only dialogued with contemporaneous news, but they also closely paralleled recent events so as to reflect on the formal qualities of how events are told and the social consequences of these discursive practices. This is particularly true of the six *Palliser* novels that spanned a decade and a half, beginning with *Can You Forgive Her?* in 1864 and concluding with *The Duke's Children* in 1879. The *Palliser* series constructs a fictional version of mid-nineteenth-century British Parliament with characters and events that closely mirror the real world.[7] *Phineas Finn*, published serially from October 1867 to May 1868 in *Saint Pauls Magazine*, details the events leading up to the passage of the Reform Act of 1867. *Phineas Redux*, published serially in 1873 in *The Graphic*, dramatises fictional debates surrounding the disestablishment of the Church of England, echoing the 1871 disestablishment of the Irish Church.[8] Although the main characters of the novel are completely fictional, Trollope introduces versions of prominent politicians, such as William Gladstone (Gresham), Benjamin Disraeli (Daubeny) and John Russell (Mildmay) to encourage readers to see the contemporary parallel.[9]

By loosely basing his novels on historical events, Trollope mingles the expectations of fictional and referential narrative.[10] The Palliser novels mirror recent events but introduce minor alterations to render them fictional. They tease readers into making the external reference while simultaneously limiting the extent to which external knowledge can illuminate the reader's understanding of the novel. Fictionality thus becomes an analytical and evaluative tool for Trollope. Readers know what happened in real life, but they have to read the novel's version as if they do not know. This forces readers to reflect on the assumptions that they bring to news and other narratives of the real. In doing so, Trollope adapts journalism's 'median past tense', making his novels occupy a temporality in between journalism and history. Trollope selects events that are a few years old – no longer journalism, but not quite history either – and introduces small modifications to render them simultaneously strange and familiar. Readers thus have the uncanny experience of entering a fictional world that resembles their own and that is narrated 'from stage to stage' as if it were news.[11]

Rather than simply absorbing a cultural 'presence of the present', as Altick would suggest, Trollope's novels ask readers to recognise the divergences between novelistic and journalistic practices of serialisation. Newspapers report events as they happen and generate suspense over this uncertainty; as Lucy Brown argues,

> Old or irregular news, where the stages of an event are condensed in one report, has not the emotional force of news which proceeds from stage to stage, leaving the reader at any one time ignorant of the state of the situation.[12]

By contrast, Trollope situates events in terms of a longer continuing narrative revolving around key characters.[13] Trollope's novels draw upon the formal cues of journalism – its recentness, facticity and seriality – but he does so within the framework of novels that foreground character. For example, the 1869 novel, *Phineas Finn*, is not called 'Parliament' or the 'Reform Act of 1867'; it is named after a character who must undergo a process of liberalisation so that he, an Irishman, can assimilate into the British Parliament.[14] And the story is not fixed within the bounds of the novel; Trollope writes a series of Palliser novels and thereby examines the slow development of characters over time and the importance of tracing these gradual changes.[15]

In the posthumous *An Autobiography*, Trollope describes the Palliser novels as a continuing project rather than a series of separate, related novels. He writes,

> To carry out my scheme I have had to spread my picture over so wide a canvas that I cannot expect that any lover of such art should trouble himself to look at it as a whole. Who will read *Can You Forgive Her?*, *Phineas Finn*, *Phineas Redux*, and *The Prime Minister* in order that he may understand the characters of the Duke of Omnium, of Plantagenet Palliser, and Lady Glencora? Who will even know that they should be so read?[16]

He continues, 'I look upon this string of characters, – carried sometimes into other novels than just those named, – as the best work of my life.'[17] Charles Dickens famously professed that *David Copperfield* was his favourite 'child', but Trollope accords this privilege to characters – and specifically, later in *An Autobiography*, to *one* character: Plantagenet Palliser – that span a whole series of novels and even reappear in various other works outside the series proper. As Walter M. Kendrick has argued, the novel is never a static structure for Trollope: 'It is always dynamic, a process rather than an object.'[18] Trollope reshapes contemporary politics to trace the development of several key protagonists over the course of the series. In doing so, he relocates characters who were previously protagonists to peripheral roles, thereby allowing the centre of consciousness to shift. His novels refigure who is major and who is minor, constantly reorienting our perspective. Indeed, Palliser and Lady Glencora are minor characters throughout many of the *Palliser* novels, until they move into the limelight in *The Prime Minister*. This continuous, yet marginal involvement enables these characters greater entry into the lived experience of the reader.

Trollope's use of serial publication contrasts with his fictional depictions of the newspaper; his journalists are drawn to the latest outrage and expend little effort filling out context. Trollope's treatment of newspapers anticipates Pierre Bourdieu's account of twentieth-century journalism. Rather than providing context for each event, journalists 'show us the world only as a series of unrelated flash photos' in a practice that is 'dehistoricised and dehistoricising, fragmented and fragmenting'.[19] For Bourdieu, the media simply creates a sequence of events without any clear linkage or causation: 'events that, having appeared with no explanation, will disappear with no solution'. In contrast, Trollope's fictions remake seriality into a continuous form that explores the interconnections between geographically or temporally distinctive events. Trollope's emphasis on fictional narrativity becomes an important counterweight to the series of disconnected and decontextualised outrages published by his fictional journalists. In drawing this distinction, Trollope invites his readers to think analytically about the way that they relate to and absorb the news.

While Trollope's contrast between journalistic and novelistic discourses happens over the course of the Palliser novels, it becomes particularly evident in *Phineas Redux*, when Finn is accused of murdering his political opponent Mr Bonteen. The discovery of Mr Bonteen's murder and the subsequent general suspicion of Finn are narrated in a fashion that evacuates Finn's narrative centrality and parodies journalistic sensation. In doing so, it demonstrates the extent to which public opinion lacks coherence and rational self-control, titillated by the emotional force of a story whose end is unknown. The fragments of information cause characters to disregard their knowledge of Finn's character and instead to give way to conjectures based on public excitement.

Prior to the murder, Finn and Mr Bonteen are seen having a heated argument at a popular London club. The next chapter, called *What Came of the Quarrel*, reports the news that Mr Bonteen was murdered on his way home, implying in its very title that the murder resulted from the argument. This chapter's account of the murder and its resulting investigation differs dramatically from the previous chapters of *Phineas Redux*. The chapter is no longer narrated from the perspective of Finn; instead, it mimics newspaper form by reporting recent events from the perspective of a range of witnesses. Trollope's disinterested narrator gives way to a more sensational voice. The public comes to conclusions based on the limited time frame of the crime; they disregard previous experiences of Finn's character and recollect only the immediacy of the fight. Suspicion initially falls on Mr Emilius, who is an obvious subject of suspicion since he is a social outsider, but excitement grows as word spreads about the quarrel between Mr Bonteen and Finn:

> There had been so much talk about Mr Bonteen lately, his name had been so commonly in the newspapers, the ill-usage which he had been supposed by some to have suffered had been so freely discussed, and his quarrel not only with Phineas Finn, but subsequently with the Duke of Omnium, had been so widely known, – that his sudden death created more momentary excitement than might probably have followed that of a greater man. And now, too, the facts of the past night, as they became known, seemed to make the crime more wonderful, more exciting, more momentous than it would have been had it been brought clearly home to such a wretch as the Bohemian Jew, Yosef Mealyus.[20]

Trollope emphasises the fleeting nature of the public craze, the 'momentary excitement' that it generates, and Parliament's distraction from its duties. The public interest in the murder dwells in its exceptionality, in its throwing suspicion on a Member of Parliament rather than the expected outsider. It also derails the political focus of the novel, as Catherine O. Frank has suggested.[21] The first book of the novel highlights debate over disestablishment of the Church of

England, but this discussion disappears in the face of public excitement over the murder trial.

Finn himself is entirely absent from this account of the murder and does not yet know of the accusations gathering against him. The reader is walked through the accounts circulating around the crime. The majority opinion is against Finn, and the tone of these passages contrasts with the rest of the novel:

> And Finn, if he was the murderer, must, from the time he was standing at the club door, have contemplated a traitorous, dastardly attack. He must have counted his moments, – have returned slyly in the dark to the corner of the street which he had once passed; – have muffled his face in his coat; – and have then laid wait in a spot to which an honest man at night would hardly trust himself with honest purposes.[22]

These conjectures draw upon familiar melodramatic tropes and narratives common to nineteenth-century crime journalism, all the way down to the murderer's face hidden in his coat. The rationale here is logically flawed: it follows from the premise that Finn is the murderer, rather than reasoning from evidence that Finn committed the act. It also typifies Finn's categorical and narrative possibilities: he is either the murderer or the honest man. Finn's developed character, as it has been traced throughout the novel, is lost in the midst of these limited binary categories often associated with stories of crime and detection.

At this point, Trollope's disinterested narrator returns to his post and abruptly undercuts the building sensationalism, addressing the reader directly mid-chapter:

> The reader need hardly be told that, as regards the great offence, Phineas Finn was as white as snow. The maintenance of any doubt on that matter, – were it even desirable to maintain a doubt – would be altogether beyond the power of the present writer. The reader has probably perceived, from the first moment of the discovery of the body on the steps at the end of the passage, that Mr Bonteen had been killed by that ingenious gentleman, the Rev. Emilius.[23]

Trollope suddenly reveals the resolution of the mystery, long before the characters in the novel find out. In this intervention, the narrator explicitly gives readers a privileged understanding of Phineas and his innocence. In this way, the murder trial mimics the entire function of the *Palliser* novels. Just as the reader knows the real outcome of the reform bill and disestablishment of the church, the reader now knows Finn is innocent and must watch how the allegations affect his character. Indeed, Frank has argued that Trollope redirects suspense toward the outcome of the trial and its effect on Finn's character rather than the identity of the murderer.[24]

The novel explicitly develops a face-off between novelistic characterisation and journalism's claim to facts. Lord Cantrip, a friend of Finn, 'look[s] upon it [Finn's guilt] as quite out of the question' because of his familiarity with Phineas's character. But the Prime Minister, Mr Gresham, points out to Lord Cantrip that it is a conflict between two modes of knowledge, one based on character and another based on the 'facts': 'You are simply putting your own opinion of the man against the facts . . . but facts always convince, and another man's opinion rarely convinces.'[25] Mr Gresham unwittingly sets up the opposition of the epistemological framework of the realist novel and journalism. He disparages the reader's knowledge as mere prejudice rather than a cultivated understanding of character, although his 'facts' are largely based in circumstantial evidence and conjecture. In contrast, Madame Goesler suggests the utter impossibility of Finn's involvement in the murder: 'What judge of character would any one be who could believe that Phineas Finn could be guilty of a midnight murder?'[26] The resulting trial becomes not just a trial of Finn's guilt but also one of methods of characterisation more broadly, when Finn's lawyer, Mr Chaffanbrass, calls a novelist to the witness stand. Mr Chaffanbrass asks the novelist:

> The plot of a novel should, I imagine, be constructed in accordance with human nature? . . . Those great masters of human nature, those men who knew the human heart, did not venture to describe a secret murder as coming from a man's brain without premeditation?[27]

Mr Chaffanbrass valorises the fidelity to character of the novel and establishes it as an important framework of knowledge. In contrast, he points out the inadequacies of the *People's Banner*'s report on Finn's alleged crime, since it depends largely upon unreliable testimony against Phineas. Mr Chaffanbrass draws upon novelistic probability as a means to question whether Phineas is the likely murderer:

> If I understand you, then, Mr Bouncer, you would not dare so to violate probability in a novel, as to produce a murderer to the public who should contrive a secret hidden murder, – contrive it and execute it all within a quarter of an hour?[28]

The sensation surrounding Finn's potential guilt builds from a desire for the uncommon and the newsworthy. Suspicions are fuelled by conjecture, gossip and newspapers. The public succumbs to the 'momentary excitement' of a murder that seems 'wonderful, more exciting, more momentous' because of the identity of the suspected murderer. Trollope depicts public opinion as an uncontrollable force propelled by unreflective excitement and desire. As Trollope suggests the importance of knowing someone over time, he critiques the reliance of the press on its capacity to flesh out narratives solely on the basis of decontextualised and fragmented bits of information.

Yet even as Trollope warns of the tendency of the newspaper to scapegoat well-meaning characters like Plantagenet Palliser or Phineas Finn, it is key that Finn's innocence is built on Rev. Joseph Emilius/Yosef Mealyus's automatic guilt and Madame Goesler's eastern European connections. The novel itself reverts between the names of Emilius and Mealyus; we learn in *Phineas Redux* that the Rev. Emilius previously had been employed as Yosef Mealyus by a Jewish moneylender in the city, and before arriving in London, he lived under the name of Mealyus in Prague and married a 'Jewess' from Cracow.[29] Suspicious of Emilius/Mealyus and desirous of freeing Phineas from suspicion, Madame Goesler travels to Prague; there, she learns information that incriminates Emilius/Mealyus and undermines the case against Phineas. After Phineas is acquitted, the narrator explains that there is not enough evidence to arrest Mealyus/Emilius for the murder of Mr Bonteen, but that he is already in custody for bigamy:

> a charge which had subjected him to the peculiar ill-will of the British public. He, a foreigner and a Jew, by name Yosef Mealyus, – as every one was now careful to call him, – had come to England, had got himself to be ordained as a clergyman, had called himself Emilius, and had married a rich wife with a title, although he had a former wife still living in his own country.[30]

As the narrator explains after Mr Bonteen's murder, Mr Emilius's 'character was half sufficient to condemn him'.[31] The public is now careful to call him by his foreign name, a choice that seems condoned by the novel since the narrator makes the change as well. Thus, the major crimes in the novel originate in Prague and are committed by a foreigner who infiltrates British society through marriage and the Church of England. This sets up Mr Emilius as a contrast to

Mr Harding and other clergymen of the Barsetshire novels. Indeed, as Bryan Cheyette writes,

> It is Madame Goesler's intimate knowledge of the Prague 'ghetto' in *Phineas Redux* that finally vindicates Phineas Finn and exposes Emilius as a murderer and a bigamist. That the 'key' (in all senses) to Finn's innocence in this novel is to be found in the dark streets of the Jewish 'ghetto' indicates both the unfortunate necessity of accommodating the racial 'other' and the dangers of their unknowable powers of deception.[32]

In order to vindicate Phineas Finn, the novel makes Emilius/Mealyus the obvious outsider. Even as Trollope suggests the structural and formal tendency of the newspaper to create outsiders, his novels perform a similar move in the very act of resisting the category of the newsworthy. And yet, he simultaneously complicates this move in Finn's subsequent marriage to Madame Goesler. Although a foreigner and of dubious racial background, Madame Goesler is an appealing character throughout the *Palliser* novels: she is a good friend to Lady Glencora; she turns down the Duke of Omnium's offer of marriage but compassionately stays by his side in his final days; and her marriage to Finn makes him independently wealthy so he can continue his political career. In the novels following *Phineas Redux*, Finn is subsumed into Mrs Finn's more commanding presence. Through incorporating journalistic discourse into the narration of Mr Bonteen's murder, *Phineas Redux* sets up a conflict between the epistemological framework between the novel and the newspaper. In a sense, Trollope invites us to draw upon ideas of fictional probability in adjudicating the reality of news.

Novelistic *Bildung* and the Newspaper's 'Bad Infinity'

Finn's trial for murder derails his personal and professional development in *Phineas Redux*, even as his friends and the novel continue to testify to his good character. This section will argue that the newspaper poses a problem for the novel of self-development, as it reduces actors to types and reifies the judgement of a mass audience. *Phineas Finn* and *Phineas Redux* loosely adhere to the form of the classical *Bildungsroman* and its tension between ideals of self-determination and social conformity.[33] According to Lukács's

Theory of the Novel, this biographical form is the only way that the novel can overcome its 'bad infinity' and restore meaning via an individual's journey towards self-recognition. Twenty years later, however, Lukács argued that the historical novel provided a synthesis of individual and social life in representing character as a historical type.[34] As Ian Duncan explains, this means that the historical novel 'subsumes the *Bildungsroman* plot of individual sentimental and moral formation to the plot of national history', so that 'the nation supplies the horizon of totality'.[35] The novel thus curbs its 'bad infinity' and stabilises the character's internal formlessness by linking character to nation. The argument here is parallel to the one developed by Benedict Anderson in *Imagined Communities*: that the nation takes the role of the sacred in the modern age. In these admittedly divergent accounts, the nation provides meaning, or immanence, in a world that otherwise seems dissonant and alienating.

But Trollope's fictionalised newspapers destabilise this precarious balance, as they threaten novelistic *Bildung* with 'bad infinity', a quality also characteristic of the endlessly serialising newspaper. This formal conflict foregrounds the psychic toll enacted on Trollope's protagonists, who are made starkly aware of the irreconcilable gap between their self-determining ideals and the external pressures voiced by the newspaper. A *Bildungsroman* traditionally features characters that learn to accommodate and even internalise external social pressures; these characters, however, are incapacitated when they encounter versions of themselves in the newspaper. In this way, Trollope allows the newspaper, as a different textual medium, to destabilise his novelistic plots.

This sense of dissonance first appears in Trollope's earliest successful novel, *The Warden* (1855), when Mr Septimus Harding encounters unrecognisable and malicious depictions of himself in the *Jupiter*, a London-based newspaper satirically modelled on *The Times*. *The Warden*'s plot revolves around the *Jupiter*'s agitation for reforms to the Church of England, particularly its patronage system. The newspaper accuses Mr Harding, the private and meek warden of a Barchester almshouse, of corruption for occupying the well-paid but undemanding sinecure. Appointed by his old friend, the Bishop of Barchester, Mr Harding oversees twelve bedesmen at Hiram's Hospital, an almshouse supported by a medieval charitable bequest. The novel begins when local reformer John Bold insists the original bequest never envisioned such generous provisions for the warden; instead, it should have been divided among the bedesmen. Bold, despite his romantic interest in Mr Harding's daughter, approaches the *Jupiter* and encourages the editor, Tom Towers, to take on the issue in the newspaper's crusade against corruption. The *Jupiter*'s handling of the situation quickly outpaces what Bold thinks is just, as it makes the well-meaning Mr Harding into an object of public derision.

Mr Harding is paralysed by his depiction in the newspaper and a resulting sense of alienation from the newspaper's readers and the nation it claims to represent. While reading the *Jupiter*, Mr Harding envisions an anonymous multitude convinced that he is an 'avaricious, lazy priest':

> Four hundred thousand readers then would hear this accusation against him; four hundred thousand hearts would swell with indignation at the griping injustice, the barefaced robbery of the warden of Barchester Hospital![36]

The readers exist merely as an abstract mass public invoked by the newspaper, one that renders Mr Harding alienated not only from the newspaper's construction of a national public, but also from his immediate community.[37] The repetition echoes Lord Alfred Tennyson's 'The Charge of the Light Brigade', published only a year prior to *The Warden*, but it substitutes a faceless mass public for the imagined heroism of the Light Brigade, 'the noble six hundred'.

Yet the novel shows that Mr Harding is far from a villain, as he fulfils his responsibilities to the bedesmen with thoughtfulness and care. When he learns that his position may be ethically untenable, he remains dissatisfied with assurances from both his son-in-law and his lawyers that he is in the right. Towards the end of the novel, the barrister Sir Abraham Haphazard explains that the lawsuit against Mr Harding and the Church has been withdrawn, and the opposition has even agreed to pay their legal expenses. Nevertheless, the warden insists on resigning his position. When the barrister reminds him of his obligations to his daughter, Mr Harding responds, 'I would sooner that she and I should both beg, than that she should live in comfort on money which is truly the property of the poor.'[38] The careful rendering of Mr Harding in the novel and his ethical dilemma contrasts with the *Jupiter*'s characterisation:

> Another case, of smaller dimensions indeed, but of similar import, is now likely to come under public notice. We are informed that the warden or master of an old alms-house attached to Barchester Cathedral is in receipt

of twenty-five times the annual income appointed for him by the will of the founder. . . . Does he ever ask himself, when he stretches wide his clerical palm to receive the pay of some dozen of the working clergy, for what service he is so remunerated? . . . We must express an opinion that nowhere but in the Church of England, and only there among its priests, could such a state of moral indifference be found.³⁹

Whereas the novel develops the complex moral psychology of the humble Mr Harding as he seeks to accommodate the religious and social fractures of Barchester, the *Jupiter* uses the authoritative editorial 'we' in villainising Mr Harding as an unnamed but representative example of corruption endemic to the Church.⁴⁰ Its logic relies on conjectures as to Mr Harding's inward state, which readers know to be grossly unjust to Mr Harding's meek but insistent moral care.⁴¹

The article links up Mr Harding's case with that which precedes it in the newspaper, although the readers of the novel are not given access to that other case; in doing so, it suggests that Mr Harding's case is one among many such injustices committed by the Church of England. The serial structure of the newspaper, which connects Mr Harding's case with a prior story, encourages readers to perceive Mr Harding as part of a series of corrupt clerics. Luhmann argues that the media imagines morality by associating it with 'sufficiently spectacular cases – when scoundrels, victims, and heroes who have gone beyond the call of duty are presented to us'.⁴² These actors are rendered through familiar schema and an 'understanding which standardises'; readers (or 'receivers', in Luhmann's terms) typically do not align with these groups.⁴³ Readers thus develop a sense of shared morality based on the example of non-normative others with whom they rarely sympathise. We can see that, in *The Warden*, the *Jupiter*'s imagined national readership emerges through depicting Mr Harding as a typical corrupt cleric. *The Warden*, moreover, suggests that the typifying practices of the newspaper expand beyond its pages. When John Bold (who is now engaged to marry Mr Harding's daughter Eleanor) insists that the attack on Mr Harding has become too extreme, Tom Towers shows him that the story has been picked up by Mr Popular Sentiment (Charles Dickens) and Dr Pessimist Anticant (Thomas Carlyle). He proudly concludes, 'the fire had gone too far to be quenched'.⁴⁴ The satire suggests that Dickens and Carlyle participate in this unthinking and reactive public sphere, setting up *The Warden* as a space for discursive self-reflexivity.⁴⁵

The paucity of the *Jupiter*'s characterisation contrasts with the nuanced shifts in perspective developed by *The Warden*'s narrator. For instance, when the bishop and the archdeacon assure Mr Harding that their lawyer believes he is legally justified to his position, the narrator describes an unspoken emotional current between Mr Harding and his good friend the bishop:

> Mr Harding again sat silent for a while, during which the bishop once and again pressed his arm, and looked in his face to see if he could catch a gleam of a contented and eased mind; but there was no such gleam, and the poor warden continued playing sad dirges on invisible stringed instruments in all manner of positions; he was ruminating in his mind on this opinion of Sir Abraham, looking to it wearily and earnest for satisfaction, but finding none.[46]

The narrator reveals an unspoken emotional connection between the two older men. This feeling is expressed through touch and look, as the bishop tries to comfort and find comfort in Mr Harding. When Mr Harding doesn't return the bishop's gaze, the narrator shifts to describe Mr Harding's moral unease, which is expressed physically through his bodily contortions played out on an imaginary violin. Finally, we enter into Mr Harding's feelings of dissatisfaction. As the narrator moves fluidly from the bishop's perspective, to physical touch and expression, and finally to Mr Harding's perspective, the novel develops a complex network of emotional and physical connections between characters. This emotional current between the bishop and Mr Harding affirms their mutual respect and toleration; the bishop later acknowledges Mr Harding's feeling that he should step down from the wardenship, while the archdeacon focuses only on faction and struggles to force Mr Harding to adhere to his point of view. This multifaceted attachment as unveiled through the novel also reveals a moral sensitivity to others that picks up on subtle emotional cues.[47] *The Warden* allows for an intricate web of interconnections between Mr Harding, his friends and family, the Barsetshire community and the larger national public. The newspaper not only lacks access to Mr Harding's interiority; it also fails to register the unique affective attachments and local contexts of bonds that make up the public as a whole.

While the *Jupiter* vilifies Mr Harding, *The Warden* refocuses readerly attention on his feelings at finding himself the centre of a media furore. Initially, he responds with paralysis.[48] However, as the short novel progresses, Mr Harding begins to interrogate his right to the wardenship, progressing through stages of paralysis, self-pity, avoidance and finally confidence in the belief that he cannot in good conscience retain his sinecure. Although the archdeacon argues that Mr Harding owes it to his class to stay in possession of the position, Mr Harding tells his daughter, 'I have thought much of what the archdeacon has said, and of what this paper says; and I do believe I have no right to be here.'[49] Yet no one benefits from Mr Harding's resignation of the wardenship. The novel concludes with Hiram's Hospital in disrepair, the warden's house tenantless and the bedesmen receiving none of the money previously reserved for the warden. While the coverage of the newspaper contributes to Mr Harding's moral reckoning, it does not contribute to larger systemic change. As soon as Mr Harding relinquishes his position, the newspaper loses interest in this particular case. The *Jupiter* abruptly changes its characterisation of Mr Harding in between *The Warden* and the second novel of the Barsetshire series, *Barchester Towers*. It no longer vilifies Mr Harding but now 'waft[s] his name in eulogistic strains through every reading-room in the nation' and praises him as the author of 'the great musical work, Harding's Church music'.[50] Although Mr Harding is flattered, it is not long before 'Mr Towers of "The Jupiter" and his brethren occupied themselves with other names and the undying fame promised to our friend was clearly intended to be posthumous'.[51] The *Jupiter*'s searing critique of Mr Harding yields few positive outcomes for the bedesmen or the public on whose behalf it claimed to speak. However, Mr Harding becomes more self-aware of the ethical implications of his sinecure, allowing for some form of development to occur over the course of the novel. Unlike Matthew Rubery, who suggests the newspaper facilitates this development, I believe Mr Harding's development happens in spite of it.

The Warden is not just about a small sinecure in the fictional town of Barchester; it also critiques *The Times* at a time when it was seen as the ultimate representative of British public opinion, particularly in its coverage of the Crimean War (1853–6). This conflict pitted Russia against the Ottoman Empire; Britain entered the war in 1854 to prevent further Russian expansion. At first glance, the Crimean War, which saw for the first time the use of railroads and telegraphy in military manoeuvres and has thus been dubbed the first 'modern war', may seem worlds apart from the political intrigue of a rural parish. The origins of the war, though, lay in religious rivalries, namely a clash between the Catholics (backed by France) and the Greek Orthodox Church (backed by Russia) over who should control the Church of the Holy Sepulchre in Jerusalem and the Church of the Nativity in Bethlehem. As a historian of the conflict observes, this means that this major war of the nineteenth century emerged from a 'petty quarrel over some churchwarden's keys'.[52] *The Warden* is not so distant from the Crimean War after all.[53]

The Crimean struggle was the first modern war in another sense as well: it marked the first time that newspapers covered a conflict in real time.[54] The 1840s and 1850s saw the advent of the war correspondent; thanks to the development of the telegraph, reports from the front lines could be published within just a few days or, by the end of the war, within just a few hours. The immediate and firsthand accounts that appeared in *The Times* helped solidify that status of the paper as the mouthpiece of the British public and dramatically transformed the public's relationship to warfare. For the first time, newspapers allowed the public to be involved in debates about how the war should be fought; many wrote into *The Times* with opinions about how to fight the campaign.[55] These reports contributed to the public's growing disenchantment with the war, particularly after *The Times* revealed the horrendous conditions in which many of the wounded were kept.[56] The Crimean War catapulted newspapers, and *The Times* in particular, to an unprecedented level of influence.[57]

While writing *The Warden*, Trollope wrote a letter to John Lewis Merivale calling *The Times* a 'tyrant' because of its effect on public opinion:

> Ah! the Crimea. How impossible it is for anybody to be really happy, really at ease, while things are as they are. Not that I credit the *Times* throughout, not but that I think that waging a war with a corps of newspaper scribblers in one's camps is too great a lash for any one, but that I believe that had Caesar, Hannibal, Napoleon, Alexander or Wellington had been so attended the same sort of things would have been written . . .[58]

His letter playfully creates a sense of ambiguity as to whether Britain is 'waging war' with Russia or 'with a corps of newspapers scribblers'.[59] He suggests that the public malaise emerges not solely through wartime mismanagement but also through the close everyday involvement of the press and its public.[60]

The newspaper causes a similar paralysis in *The Prime Minister*. By moving from *The Warden* to *The Prime Minister*, we shift from a local cathedral town to the national and international stage, when the *People's Banner* castigates the prime minister, Plantagenet Palliser, for secretly supporting a candidate for Parliament. As a liberal advocate for parliamentary reform, Palliser announces publicly that he will not appoint a candidate for his family's borough. Landowning aristocrats traditionally had the right to appoint their borough's parliamentary candidate but nineteenth-century reforms sought to eliminate these 'rotten' boroughs and allow for more expansive representation of the British public in Parliament. As it turns out, Palliser's wife Lady Glencora clandestinely encourages Ferdinand Lopez to run for their seat. When the rascally Lopez realises he is likely to lose, he withdraws from the race and demands reimbursement for his election expenses. Palliser feels compelled out of a sense of honour to reimburse Lopez. When Quintus Slide, the editor of the London populist paper *The People's Banner*, learns of the reimbursement, he accuses Palliser of using his wealth and influence to buy a seat in Parliament.

The novel provides a detailed account of Palliser's reflective process in deciding that he is ethically bound to reimburse Lopez as a result of his wife's misguided support. Slide, however, nurses a grudge against Palliser for not inviting him to a party earlier in the novel, and he portrays Palliser's financial assistance to Lopez in a nefarious light in the *People's Banner*:

> Were those expenses paid out of the private pocket of the present Prime Minister? If so, we maintain that we have discovered a blot in that nobleman's character which it is our duty to the public to expose. . . . We happen to know also the almost more than public manner, – are we not justified in saying the ostentation? – with which at the last election the Duke repudiated all that influence with the borough which his predecessors, and we believe he himself, had so long exercised. . . . What are we to think of the Duke of Omnium as a Minister of this country, if, after such assurances, he has out of his own pocket paid the electioneering expenses of a candidate at Silverbridge?[61]

Slide takes issue with Palliser for an action seemingly incongruent with his public pronouncements of political disinterestedness, and he does so in the guise of speaking on behalf of 'the public'. Many of the allegations are framed in the form of questions, drawing on conjecture and implication to fill out the details in a story that has only a basic skeleton of information. The novel contrasts Slide's account with what we as readers know about Palliser: 'That he had done so from the purest motives he knew and the readers know; – but he could not even explain those motives without exposing his wife.'[62] Palliser's situation echoes that of Mr Harding in *The Warden*, but the problem is amplified because of Palliser's national role. Although Slide causes Palliser to reconsider beliefs he felt to be right, it is not the kind of 'ethical confrontation' that John Stuart Mill would advocate.[63] Whereas Mill argues for constant dialogue and disputation to 'form the truest opinions', Palliser feels unable to explain his motives to the press – in fact, his private motives no longer seem justifiable when explained publicly.[64] Palliser cannot defend himself, because he would expose his wife to the critical eye of the public. Slide has shifted what should have been a private exchange between two individuals into the public arena.

The allegations of the newspaper cause a crisis of conscience in Palliser, who grapples with the way that public scrutiny blurs his private sense of what is right and wrong. Although aware that Quintus Slide has a personal vendetta against him, Palliser takes the allegations to heart and suffers from the disjunction between his own self-image and his portrayal in the newspaper. The narrator writes:

> In his old happy days two papers a day, one in the morning, and the other before dinner, sufficed to tell him all that he wanted to know. Now he felt it necessary to see almost every rag that was published. And he would skim through them all till he found the lines on which he himself was maligned, and then, with a sore heart and irritated nerves, would pause over every contumelious word. He would have bitten his tongue out rather than have spoken of the tortures he endured, but he was tortured and did endure.[65]

This passage draws a contrast between Palliser's regular newspaper reading habit – twice per day, with breakfast and dinner – and his sudden, solipsistic compulsion to read every newspaper with any reference to himself. Palliser is consumed by the 'bad infinity' of the newspapers, constantly looking from newspaper to newspaper for references to himself. Rather than connecting him to a larger community, the news causes him to collapse into self-absorbed paralysis and impotence. Palliser loses the capacity to make his own judgements and obsesses over what others think of him, even unconsciously adopting the newspaper's language. He inadvertently adopts Slide's phraseology, 'lethargy on the country', when speaking to his friend, the Duke of St. Bungay: 'Then the Duke of St. Bungay knew that his friend had read that pernicious article in the "People's Banner", for the Duke had also read it and remember that phrase . . . and understood at once how the poison had rankled.' Whereas free indirect discourse mingles the language of character and narrator, here Palliser unthinkingly incorporates Slide's language and perspective into his dialogue. Palliser's ability to respond and adapt to external pressures is suspended by the allegations of the newspaper.

Although Matthew Rubery argues that the newspaper, particularly in *The Warden*, allows for private expression and self-reflection, Palliser is paralysed by this disjunction between public representation and his own knowledge of the process by which he reached his controversial decision. Instead of taking on a position of leadership, he is coddled by his staff: 'The old Duke's work at this time consisted almost altogether in nursing the younger Duke.'[66] So 'goaded' by the newspaper, '[h]e was beginning to have the worn look of an old man. His scanty hair was turning grey, and his long thin cheeks longer and thinner.'[67] The newspaper sends Palliser into a simultaneous infanthood and old age, locking him into isolated inaction. Palliser knows his innocence but struggles against a consciousness that the newspapers have made him look, and feel, guilty. His private life is opened out for the public eye and misconstrued by the press to fit a particular pattern of legibility. As Palliser says to the Duke of St. Bungay, 'It cannot be explained. I cannot explain it even to you; and how then can I do it to all the gaping fools of the country who are ready to trample upon a man simply because he is in some way conspicuous among them?'[68] Palliser feels he has been judged by a whole nation, when in fact he is the victim of a single man pretending to be more than one. *The Prime Minister* shows the larger political effects of Palliser's sense of alienation, as his coalition falls apart over the rest of the novel.

Similarly, in *Phineas Redux*, Phineas Finn finds himself unmanned by the allegations that he is a murderer. Marginal characters question his manliness as he emotionally breaks under the pressure of the murder trial. Lord Chiltern urges Phineas, 'the time has come in which you must show yourself to be a man' and valorises an enacted show of manhood.[69] When Phineas is 'prostrate' as a result of the emotional stress, Mr Low reflects regretfully to his wife, 'I thought he would have been more manly.'[70] Phineas is prostrated because he is trying to understand how to position himself in a world where he has been tried for, and believed by many to be guilty of, murder. In both cases, Palliser and Phineas grapple with a two-dimensional depiction of themselves in the newspaper and public opinion; they are unable to reconcile this portrayal, and a public that would believe it, with their self-perception. In one sense, they are unable to fulfil the development of *Bildung*: Palliser fades out of the political limelight, and Phineas becomes a shadow to his more assertive wife. Made painfully conscious of the gap between their ideals and the pressures imposed by the newspaper, both Palliser and Finn grapple with the newspaper's 'bad infinity' and the lack of shape to their place within a larger world. Yet it is notable that, in vindicating Finn and castigating the newspaper's rendering of his character, Trollope suggests that there are subjects worthy of communal suspicion and exclusion, including Mr Emilius, who is characterised in terms of a Jewish stereotype.

A 'People's Friend': Representing Public Opinion

The protagonist's disillusionment with society and their subsequent removal from the public sphere are recurrent plot points across Trollope's novels. These characters show a moral sensitivity ill-equipped to handle a world of newspapers, gossip and judgement. And yet, even as characters like Mr Harding, Palliser and Finn grapple with their malicious and reductionist treatment in the newspaper, Trollope's novels similarly flatten out journalists and the newspaper press more broadly. After all, *The Warden* satirises the *Jupiter* with an over-the-top style similar to the journalistic practices it critiques. This section argues that Trollope's use of caricature reflects the limits he perceives in journalistic discourse. Not only does caricature mimic the strategies of the newspaper editors, it also conveys the distortion Trollope perceives in their representative methods and their construction of the reading public. He substitutes the novel for the newspaper as the ultimate form of political representation, particularly in its capacity to represent other forms and to work through their imagined effects on the reading public.

While the *Jupiter* claims to be a disembodied representative of public interest, everyone knows that its editor, Tom Towers, is working behind the scenes. This means that the newspaper constructs the fiction that it represents the public, while it also depicts that public as the product of a single individual. When we first meet Quintus Slide in *Phineas Finn*, the narrator describes his simplistic understanding of 'the people':

> To be a 'people's friend' suited the turn of his ambition, and he was a 'people's friend'. It was his business to abuse Government, and to express on all occasions an opinion that as a matter of course the ruling powers were the 'people's enemies'.[71]

Although ostensibly acting on behalf of the people, Quintus Slide is motivated by personal, commercial and professional interests; yet he erases those interests when assessing his motivations. When Slide accuses Phineas of having an affair with the married Lady Laura Kennedy, the narrator gives us a brief moment of insight into Slide's self-rationalisation: 'the anonymous accusation of sinners in high rank was, on behalf of the public, the special duty of writers and editors attached to the public press. Mr Slide's blood was running high with virtuous indignation.'[72] Slide's mingling of private and public interests suggests a contradiction inherent to the commercial press more broadly.[73]

Slide's unreflective claim to mirror the public reflects changing definitions of the word 'public' over the course of the nineteenth century. Sally Ledger has argued that the period saw a larger shift from an eighteenth-century conception of the people as a political entity towards an understanding of the people, or populace, as a commercial entity, partly because of the rise of the mass-market commercial newspaper press in the 1840s. The idea of the public no longer signified 'an ideal of civic life, but simply "the country as an aggregate" and thus "the members of a community"'.[74] These accounts are in line with Jürgen Habermas's argument that the liberal public sphere of the eighteenth century gave way in the nineteenth century to a degraded commercial environment.[75] Slide's orientation towards the public shifts across the Palliser novels, beginning with Slide's claim to represent 'the People', a term which seems to mingle both the political and commercial iterations of the word. By *Phineas Redux*, when he has inverted his political identity from Radical to Conservative, Slide claims, 'We go in for morals and purity of life, and we mean to do our duty by the public without fear or favour.'[76] But towards the end of this very chapter, he reminds Phineas Finn, 'I needn't tell you that such a letter as that would sell a great many copies.'[77] Here we see Slide unreflectively mingling commercial and political conceptions of the public.

For Trollope, Slide's claim to speak on behalf of public opinion is not only self-deceiving but also an unreflective act that has real consequences for how public opinion is represented. It has been argued that free indirect discourse is a novelistic technique for representing general opinion, whether this is perceived as a coercive mechanism of social control, as in the case of D. A. Miller, or a communal contribution to individual development, as in the case of Frances Ferguson. If we take this association to be even partly true, the claim of the newspaper to speak on behalf of a public competes with the claim of the novel to represent communal language through free indirect discourse. Trollope's narrator, however, demonstrates the extent to which public feeling is not as consistent or coherent as Slide believes it to be. Frances Ferguson has argued that public opinion does not operate according to the same psychology as an individual, and thus it does not register a problem when it is inconsistent: 'the public is never able to see itself as a whole, it never recognises its changeability as significant'.[78] She concludes, 'A person may feel the need to explain a point of view and the changes in it; public opinion never does.'[79] When Quintus Slide claims to speak on behalf of a whole public, he substitutes his own personal interest for public opinion, giving himself the ability to change positions without seeming inconsistent. Indeed, this happens in between *The Warden* and *Barchester Towers*, when Tom Towers transforms Mr Harding from a villain into a hero, and then in between *Phineas Finn* and *Phineas Redux*, when Quintus Slide sees the political benefit in swapping the political leaning of the *People's Banner* from radical to conservative. In claiming to speak on behalf of general will, Trollope's journalists partly project their own psychology onto a whole public. This means that Trollope's editors are not thinking about the mechanics of representing general will in a self-conscious or critical way. But if Trollope's novels problematise claims of the newspapers to speak on behalf of a public, then it would seem that his own novels, which represent an expansive swath of society, might fall into the same trap. After all, Trollope is a single author claiming to represent a whole society.

Trollope's narrator, however, imbricates general will and individual perspective in a far more complicated and generative way than his fictional newspapers do. To demonstrate this point, I want to look at a passage that brings Phineas and Palliser together towards the end of *The Prime Minister*: it follows Phineas Finn's speech to Parliament on Palliser's behalf, which helps to explain away the *People's Banner*'s allegations. Thankful for Phineas's support, but also freed from the pressure of the *People's Banner*, Palliser gives a spontaneous defence of liberalism and the ethical obligation to 'march on to some nearer approach to equality':

> The Duke in his enthusiasm had thrown off his hat, and was sitting on a wooden seat which they had reached, looking up among the clouds. His left hand was clenched, and from time to time with his right he rubbed the thin hairs on his brow. He had begun in a low voice, with a somewhat slipshod enunciation of his words, but had gradually become clear, resonant, and even eloquent. Phineas knew that there were stories told of certain bursts of words which had come from him in former days

in the House of Commons. These had occasionally surprised men and induced them to declare that Planty Pall, – as he was then often called, – was a dark horse. But they had been few and far between, and Phineas had never heard them. Now he gazed at his companion in silence, wondering whether the speaker would go on with his speech. But the face changed on a sudden, and the Duke with an awkward motion snatched up his hat. 'I hope you ain't cold,' he said.[80]

At the beginning of this passage, it is not clear whether we watch Palliser through Phineas's perspective or that of the narrator. Phineas makes sense of Palliser's speech by reflecting on the gossip he has heard in the past. In this case, Phineas draws upon public opinion to help him construct a better sense of Palliser's character over time, and to situate this moment, which might seem out of character, in a pattern of behaviour. It also conveys a sense of lost opportunity, since Palliser has not lived up to the dark horse potential. The Duke's abrupt and awkward shift to commonplace pleasantries reveals his liberal beliefs to be deeply felt, not put on for an audience like Slide. This scene may appear unimportant, but it offers a striking contrast to Palliser's earlier incorporation of Slide's jargon into his dialogue. Novelistic poetics allows for the nuanced interaction between public opinion and the character whose psychology is depicted. It allows for a productive accommodation between the character and a more communal language; at the very least, it invites analysis of the shaping influence of public opinion on the individual character in ways that go beyond that individual's consciousness.

The problem of representing general will is formally embedded in Trollope's methods of characterisation, particularly in his rendering of journalists through caricature. Trollope is known for his detailed, psychologised characterisations, with mainstream characters like Mr Harding and Plantagenet Palliser, as well as those guilty of theft and fraud, such as Lizzie Eustace of *The Eustace Diamonds* and Lady Mason of *Orley Farm*. This situates his journalistic caricatures at odds with his practices of characterisation more broadly. I contend that Trollope's use of caricature in these limited circumstances distinguishes between novelistic approaches to public opinion and those of journalism. Political caricature was synonymous with nineteenth-century journalism, and Mike Goode argues that the formal logic of caricature informed how readers imagined themselves as a national public. Whereas many scholars of caricature argue that it reflects and illuminates public opinion, Goode suggests that the logic of caricature limits the ways that individuals can imagine a national public.

Caricatures reduce newsworthy actors and events to familiar tropes, a taxonomy that encourages viewers and readers to imagine the public as a series of static types.[81] Complicating Benedict Anderson's argument, Goode writes,

> [C]aricatures functioned to install a sense of the public as itself a kind of caricature collection moving through calendrical time ... they further implied that the main formal – and indeed, logical – possibilities for change lay in adding and subtracting more character types and kinds of situations in which they might perform.[82]

This reduces the idea of the public to something that changes through addition or subtraction but is not substantially altered by any particular individual's participation in it. Thus, it makes sense that Trollope depicts journalists through the framework of caricature, because it enables his critique of their political and formal logic. Trollope suggests the out-sized effect the journalist can have on his surrounding environment. In contrast, his other characters are not exchangeable types but inhabit their communities in highly singular ways. Trollope's novels create a world that develops across his novels that shapes and is shaped by unique individuals.

Trollope further develops this contrast through formal analogy. In *Phineas Finn*, radical politician Mr Monk Parliament's representative logic is analogised to a portrait rather than a mirror. He writes to Phineas:

> Another great authority has told us that our House of Commons should be the mirror of the people. I say, not its mirror, but its miniature. And let the artist be careful to put in every line of the expression of that ever-moving face ... In America the work has been done with so coarse a hand that nothing is shown in the picture but the broad, plain, unspeaking outline of the face. As you look from the represented to the representation you cannot but acknowledge the likeness; – but there is in that portrait more of the body than of the mind. The true portrait should represent more than the body.[83]

Mr Monk argues that the aim of political representation is to be attentive to the lines and nuances of an expressive and changing face. This renders general will as an individual's likeness, one that registers the actions of individuals and their communities as changes in facial expression. This imagines the public as a single entity, but one that accounts for the importance of individual actions and situates them within a larger whole, in contrast to the kind of public envisioned by caricature. Slide, however, believes that he offers a direct kind of representation, more akin to the mirror. The irony is, of course, that he does not realise he is simply reproducing his own reflection.

Rather than offering a critique of the medium of photography in this scene, as Hadley has suggested, I argue that Trollope criticises the rhetoric surrounding newspapers and 'the fourth estate'.[84] Mid-century newspapers based their claims to social and political importance in their mirror-like reflection of popular opinion. Fergus O'Connor, for instance, claimed that the paper was a 'mirror' of the people's mind.[85] Mr Monk defines realist political representation in terms of detail that captures movement and development over time and that is attentive to qualities not immediately or physically visible. Yet Mr Monk's use of the miniature portrait does not exactly free itself of the problems of journalistic representation. The analogy of the portrait requires an artist, or artists, who will decide how best to create the portrait. Mr Monk is deeply conscious of the place of the working class in a national consciousness, and his rendering of the public would take their interests into account; but his portrait analogy still relies upon the judgement and responsibility of a single person or group of people. While the novel represents Mr Monk's portrait theory sympathetically, it does not straightforwardly adopt it as a motto for the novel. Trollope's novels force readers to think through representative techniques; he shows that issues of novelistic and journalistic style are not simply aesthetic questions but also of social and political import.

Conclusion

This chapter has argued that Trollope develops a novelistic aesthetic in relationship and sometimes in opposition to the newspaper. Although a political writer himself, Trollope's novels rarely represent novelists but instead fixate on journalists rendered as absurd caricatures. This is where Trollope's 1869 novel, *He Knew He Was Right*, departs from other novels examined in this chapter. The novel's hero, Hugh Stanbury, is a journalist; he gives up a legal career to become first a war correspondent and later a regular writer for *The Daily Record*. Stanbury superficially resembles his counterpart in *The Warden*, since he is said to write 'two or three rather stinging articles in the *Daily Record*, as "to the assumed merits and actual demerits of the clergy of the Church of England"'.[86] However, that is where the resemblance ends. Instead, Stanbury is far more modest in his representative claims. He is motivated to pursue journalism partly out of self-interest and partly due to a fondness for the work. His work ethic and self-reflectiveness is contrasted with his fiancée's father, Sir Marmaduke, the incompetent colonial governor of a fictional island in the West Indies who disapproves of his daughter's engagement to a journalist.

On one level, *He Knew He Was Right* reflects the changing social situation of journalists, who became more respectable as their field increasingly professionalised. But I also think that Stanbury instantiates a different relationship to journalism than Trollope's other fictional journalists. Rather than speaking in grandiose terms about his lofty place on Mt. Olympus, as does Tom Towers, Stanbury articulates his position to Sir Marmaduke via sharp pragmatism:

> Talk of permanence, Sir Marmaduke, are not the newspapers permanent? Do not they come out regularly every day – and more of them, and still more of them, are always coming out? . . . You have complained that my work is not permanent. I have shown that it is so permanent that there is no possibility of its coming to an end. There must be newspapers, and the people trained to write them must be employed.[87]

Stanbury does not claim to be the people's mirror or banner, but rather situates himself within a larger field of journalism. In *He Knew He Was Right*, newspapers provide a backdrop of stability and permanence.

Yet even though Stanbury does not disrupt communities in the way that Tom Towers and Quintus Slide do, he generates a low-level anxiety wherever he appears in the novel. As a writer for a penny paper, Stanbury's presence forces others to rethink their assumptions and values. Characters ranging from Sir Marmaduke to his aunt Jemima Stanbury have to re-orient their ideas about what confers social value in order to accommodate Stanbury's profession. Trollope thus doesn't reject journalism per se, but a historically contingent set of journalistic practices and pretentions that made instantaneous telegraphic reporting and scandalous exposés equivalent to truth. Stanbury's example offers a closer parallel to Trollope's vision for his realist novelistic project. Through the continual presence of his serial parts in readers' everyday lives, Trollope makes readers think about how they build communities and respond to narratives about other people's lives. Stanbury does not claim to represent anyone or anything absolutely, but instead necessitates a rethinking of what some characters might accept as fact.

Trollope characterises the claim of the newspaper to represent all of public opinion as fraudulent, but he positions the novel form as an expansive canvas for the imbrication of individual and social feeling at the levels of small groups and national publics. The novel traces complex movements of feeling through gestures, speech and other less explicit modes. Although Trollope instils many liberal values, he also suggests the importance of often unspoken connections in the construction of a larger public. Indeed, Amanda Anderson rightly points out, 'For Trollope, there appears to be a persistently felt concern that disembodied communication will fail to capture the elusive elements of manner that constitute ethos and character.'[88] But whereas his journalists construct a sense of belonging based in disembodied imaginings, and at the cost of a scapegoat, the novel depicts the public as an expanding and contracting series of intimate relationships. The idea of the common good is often acted out first by means of a felt connection to another character or group of characters, one that sometimes entails setting aside critique in favour of generous belief in others. And yet this vision simultaneously relies upon the identification and exclusion of characters like Mr Emilius from the community. The next two chapters concern characters like Mr Emilius and the social and formal ramifications of their exclusion.

Notes

1. Elaine Hadley argues that 'liberalism's abstracted individual' had to adhere to principles that were individual but 'were not expressly partisan or contingent on any vested interest'. In her account, Trollope's main characters demonstrate these liberal values in lived practice and, in doing so, link novelistic character to liberal ideals of character. Hadley, *Living Liberalism*, p. 19.
2. Deborah Denenholz Morse also complicates the relationship between Trollope and nineteenth-century liberalism. For Morse, Trollope's *The Way We Live Now* (1875) presents a retreat from his customary liberal reformist stance and instead interrogates the 'liberal subject's ability to effect moral change'. Morse, 'The Way He Thought Then'.
3. Elaine Hadley perceives these journalistic interruptions in terms of a media environment out of sync with Trollope's visions for a liberal public sphere.

4. Marshall McLuhan has argued that the forms of the book and the newspaper are 'as incompatible as any two media could be' (p. 216), since the book form is a 'private voice' (p. 204) that 'yields the inside story of the author's mental adventures', while the newspaper 'yields the inside story of the community in action and interaction' (p. 205) and 'provides communal participation' (p. 204). McLuhan, *Understanding Media*. For examples of scholars who highlight the ephemeral and multivalent quality of the newspaper, see the following: Sinnema, *Dynamics of the Printed Page*; Brake, *Investigating Victorian Journalism*; Shattock and Wolff, *The Victorian Periodical Press*.
5. Altick, *The Presence of the Present*, p. 1.
6. Ibid. p. 59.
7. Indeed, some critics, including John Halperin, have traced the resemblance between the Palliser novels and real-life parliamentary events and personalities. Halperin, *Trollope and Politics*. More recently, Lauren Goodlad and Frederik Van Dam argue that Trollope's political dialecticism can be appreciated by placing his novels in their specific political context. See Goodlad and Van Dam, 'Trollope and Politics', pp. 15–34.
8. It is significant that Trollope published *Phineas Redux* in *The Graphic*, a weekly, illustrated newspaper designed to compete with the *Illustrated London News* for a middle-class audience. However, *The Graphic* was more expensive than its competitor and covered more serious topics. Artist William Luson Thomas founded the newspaper in response to what he felt was the poor treatment of artists in the *ILN*.
9. When Trollope was criticised for 'ungentlemanly conduct' in representing real politicians, Trollope insisted that he did not mean these characters to correspond to actual people. He wrote in a letter dated 31 March 1869, 'It was also my object so to draw the character that no likeness should be found in our political circles.' However, later on, he acknowledged that these characters resembled their originals, but only in terms of their political views. Halperin, 'Trollope's Phineas Finn and History', p. 121.
10. Narrative theorists have argued that readers approach fiction and non-fiction with different assumptions. For James Phelan, the most significant assumption underlying the reading of fiction is the audience's double perspective: 'Readers of fiction simultaneously participate in the illusion that the characters are independent agents pursuing their own ends and remain aware that the characters and their trajectories toward their fates are part of an authorial design and purpose' (p. 3). This theory of audience requires the fiction writer to preserve the illusion that characters are operating autonomously and therefore cannot rely too heavily on circumstance, chance, or events outside the characters' probable actions. The non-fiction writer, however, is free to shape characters and events as they like, independent of this appearance of probability, as

long as they remain faithful to external events. Phelan, 'Rhetoric, Ethics, Aesthetics, and Probability', p. 3.
11. Goodlad and Van Dam have argued that Trollope's novels offer a complex historicism, a form of realism that depicts the 'present as history'. Serialisation makes each instalment a recurrent event in time, presenting new material from week to week or month to month; this renders serial fiction a current event in itself, in contrast with the book, which is a single event. Goodlad and Van Dam, 'Trollope and Politics', p. 17.
12. Brown, *Victorian News and Newspapers*, p. 96.
13. Linda K. Hughes and Michael Lund also emphasise the importance of serial form to the experience of reading. They ask what it means to read a work that we customarily read in two weeks over the course of two years or longer. Unlike the Romantics who highlighted brief moments and personal epiphanies, the Victorians 'responded to the sequence of time, to its motion and unfolding perspectives'. They add that serialization fostered an approach to narrative as a gradually developing story that asks the reader to pause between parts for reflection and speculation. Hughes and Lund, *The Victorian Serial*, p. 5.
14. For more on Phineas Finn and the Irish question, see Frank, 'Trial Separations', pp. 30–56, and Patrick Lonergan, 'The Representation of Phineas Finn', pp. 147–58.
15. I argue that Trollope is interested in the effects of different kinds of serial reading on the reflective subject. Other critics have been attuned to the psychological and physiological effects of serial reading. For instance, Mary Hamer claims that the subliminal effect of serial form helped Trollope to write with greater psychological penetration. In an argument that goes beyond Trollope, Nicholas Dames identifies a substantial body of criticism in this period that highlighted reader's physical reception of serial texts. He writes, 'Physiological novel theory imagined novelistic form as produced by reading in time, particularly in the rhythms of attention and inattention, slow comprehension and rapid skipping ahead, buildups and discharges of affect.' Dames, *The Physiology of the Novel*, p. 11.
16. Trollope, *An Autobiography*, p. 183.
17. Ibid. p. 183.
18. Kendrick, *The Novel-Machine*, p. 4.
19. Bourdieu, *On Television*, p. 7.
20. Trollope, *Phineas Redux*, II.60.
21. Frank mentions that the second volume of *Phineas Redux* is largely focused on the trial and is 'in many respects . . . disconnected from the political questions that framed the novel's first half'. She adds that 'The trial thus supplants the novel's explicit political questions, refocuses attention onto Phineas's moral character, and raises the question of just what role law plays in transforming politics into personal character.' Frank, 'Trial Separations', p. 35.

22. Trollope, *Phineas Redux*, II.65.
23. Ibid. pp. II.77–8.
24. Frank writes, 'This knowledge changes the object of suspenseful narrative for them: less about discovering whether Finn is in fact innocent, the plot assumes a sociological interest in whether the court will find him so.' Frank, 'Trial Separations', p. 39.
25. Trollope, *Phineas Redux*, II.65.
26. Ibid. p. II.68.
27. Ibid. pp. II.193–4.
28. Ibid. pp. II.194–5.
29. Mr Bonteen travels to Prague to find out if Mr Emilius is married, which would invalidate his marriage to Lizzie Eustace and free her from demands on her fortune: 'There had been written communications with Cracow, and information was received that a man of the name of Yosef Mealyus had been married to a Jewess in that town. But this had been twenty years ago, and Mr Emilius professed himself to be only thirty-five years old, and had in his possession a document from his synagogue professing to give a record of his birth, proving such to be his age. It was also ascertained that Mealyus was a name common at Cracow, and that there were very many of the family in Galicia.' Ibid. pp. II.45–6.
30. Ibid. p. II.287.
31. Ibid. p. II.64.
32. Cheyette, *Constructions of 'the Jew'*, p. 36.
33. Over the course of the *Bildungsroman*, the protagonist comes to accept and internalise social demands and 'fuse the external compulsion and internal impulses into a new unity until the former is no longer distinguishable from the latter'. Moretti, *The Way of the World*, p. 15.
34. Lukács, *The Historical Novel*.
35. Duncan, 'History and the Novel After Lukács', p. 391.
36. Trollope, *The Warden*, p. 68.
37. Trollope's liberalism emphasises the 'role of individual character in the unfolding of narrative', but journalism's mass public is absolutely abstract, disembodied and unindividuated. Hadley, *Living Liberalism*, p. 35.
38. Trollope, *The Warden*, p. 176.
39. Ibid. pp. 67–8.
40. This, of course, contrasts with Trollope's exhaustive treatment of Barchester across a series of six novels, beginning in 1855 and ending in 1867 with *The Last Chronicle of Barset*. Helena Michie has noted Trollope's formal representation of the process of thinking and the ways that people 'change their minds'. She writes, 'If we look at the verbal and syntactical differences between sentences in Trollope as accretive – that is, slowly adding up over time – we can also see them as the perfect vehicle for representing the process of thinking.' This

formal quality of Trollope's novels is exactly what the *Jupiter* fails to accomplish. Michie, 'Rethinking Marriage', p. 154.
41. Amanda Anderson reads characters like Mr Harding as examples of Trollope's liberal ethos. She writes, 'Trollope is deeply engaged by questions having to do with argument, sincerity, and the relation between psychology and principle; this is less an active promotion of liberal ideology or the importance of the liberal state than a dynamic engagement with core ideas of liberalism.' Anderson, *The Powers of Distance*, p. 259.
42. Luhmann, *Reality of Mass Media*, p. 31.
43. Ibid. p. 32.
44. Ibid. p. 150.
45. The satire also mischaracterises Hiram's original will, which did not identify a specific annual income for the warden but rather allowed the warden to keep whatever remained after the bedesmen took their portion. In contrast to *The Jupiter*, *The Warden* details the circumstances of Mr Harding's sinecure with almost tedious care. Towers is right that the warden receives more than the will originally intended, but he does not account for the substantial increase in property value over time. Because of the nature of daily journalism, the *Jupiter* is unequipped to provide such a detailed history of Barchester but instead omits local specificities to appeal to a national readership.
46. Trollope, *Barchester Towers*, pp. 86–7.
47. Similarly, John Bold's well-intentioned reformist actions are later tempered by his affection for the warden and his love for Eleanor.
48. The *Jupiter* fosters a national public based in the suffering of Mr Harding, a meek warden rendered into a social outcast. Trollope illustrates the experience of representative methods that categorise and reduce the individuals they depict. Matthew Rubery has argued that Trollope's fictional newspapers often foster a 'whispering conscience' in his characters, but the *Jupiter* disrupts Mr Harding's sense of self and his relationship to a larger community.
49. The sensitivity and care of Mr Harding's moral reflection contrasts dramatically with the inflated language in the following chapter that describes Tom Towers' self-interested motivations and his newspaper office as 'Mount Olympus'. Towers enjoys the 'hidden but still conscious glory' of a newspaper editor, and 'he walked on from day to day, studiously striving to look a man, but knowing within his breast that he was a god'. Trollope, *The Warden*, p. 141.
50. Trollope, *Barchester Towers*, p. 11.
51. Ibid. p. 11.
52. Figes, *The Crimean War*, XXIII.
53. Figes, *The Crimean War*, XIX.
54. I argue that Trollope distinguishes between the potentialities of novelistic and journalistic realisms, countering recent critics who identify

shared practices of realism across the Victorian literary marketplace. Rachel Teukolsky has argued that novelistic realism developed in tandem with journalistic coverage of the Crimean War. She identifies in the writing of war correspondents – particularly William Howard Russell – a 'self-conscious language of "hard truths"' positioned as counternarratives to the claims of British leaders and war stories back home, one that contributed to the development of novelistic realism in the 1850s, with George Eliot's *Adam Bede*. Teukolsky suggests that both journalistic and novelistic realism emerge in tandem with the 'hard facts' of Russell's wartime reporting. She concludes that newspaper journalism and realist fiction of the 1850s drew upon discursive operations to create 'similar imagined communities in pursuit of newly real representation'. This chapter, by contrast, argues that Trollope pits his novelistic practices in opposition to journalistic operations. Teukolsky, 'Novels, Newspapers, and Global War', p. 51.
55. Figes, *Crimean War*, p. 305.
56. Newspaper accounts of the war were often inaccurate. Military communication received priority when it came to the telegraph, so war correspondents often could not finish their reports before the newspaper went to print. This meant that newspapers were known to publish false or partial reports, including an account in *The Times* on 2 October 1854 that wrongly reported the fall of Sevastopol.
57. Jon P. Klancher has argued that nineteenth-century periodical texts shaped their readers' ideologies. Trollope worries about the kind of national identity that *The Times*'s war coverage cultivates in its readership. Klancher, *The Making of English Reading Audiences*.
58. Anthony Trollope, Letter to John Lewis Merivale, 2 January 1855, Robert H. Taylor Collection, Box 20 Folder 16, Princeton University Library, Princeton, NJ.
59. In a letter dated 1 May 1854, he wrote, '[I]s the genius of the country to be wasted, is able talent to lie hid under a bushel, because the opinions of the *Times* may not be controverted?'
60. Other critics have observed the influence of the Crimean War on *The Warden*. For instance, Goodlad and Van Dam argue that the war manifests itself in the novel through the war imagery used to describe clerical conflicts; they argue that the 'geopolitical crisis is domesticated through a comic contest between the established clerical elite and a cadre of Evangelical pretenders'. Goodlad and Van Dam, 'Trollope and Politics', p. 18.
61. Trollope, *The Prime Minister*, p. 429.
62. Ibid. p. 430.
63. Waldron, 'Mill and the Value of Moral Distress', p. 416.
64. Mill, *On Liberty*, p. 23.
65. Trollope, *Prime Minister*, p. 327.
66. Ibid. p. 480.

67. Ibid. p. 540.
68. Ibid. pp. 434–5.
69. Trollope, *Phineas Redux*, II.135.
70. Ibid. p. 251.
71. Trollope, *Phineas Finn*, I.242. The only explicit reader of *The People's Banner* is Phineas's landlord, Mr Bunce, yet its stories pervade the halls of Parliament. For analyses of public opinion and changing conceptions of 'the people' in the nineteenth century, see J Parry, *The Rise and Fall*.
72. Trollope, *Phineas Redux*, p. 250.
73. Indeed, his claims to be the 'people's friend', and Towers' belief that he represents the public, echo the language circulating around *The Times* and other newspapers of the period. As a result, Slide's flatness and internal contradictions partly stand in for the flaws of commercial journalism more broadly. It is important to note that *The People's Banner* is a dramatically different publication than the *Jupiter*. Whereas Trollope's early fiction satirised *The Times*, the Palliser novels redirect their satire towards the penny newspaper. This shift suggests changing conceptions of the public over the course of the Victorian period. When writers spoke of a public in the early to mid-nineteenth century, they tended to mean only middle-class men. However, the Reform Act of 1832 increased the electorate by almost 250,000 men, broadening the conception of the public; indeed, in 1858, Wilkie Collins called readers of the penny press the 'unknown public'.
74. Barrell as quoted in Kreilkamp, *Voice and the Victorian Storyteller*, p. 37.
75. Similarly, Elaine Hadley imagines the mass media as a threat to mid-century liberalism, which advocated for a kind of politics in which individuals joined together through shared, deliberated opinions independent of self-interest, not a politics of mass or group interest.
76. Trollope, *Phineas Redux*, I.200.
77. Ibid. p. I.203.
78. Ferguson, 'Jane Austen, *Emma*, and the Impact of Form', p. 164.
79. Ibid. p. 164.
80. Trollope, *Prime Minister*, p. 585.
81. Goode, 'The Public and the Limits of Persuasion', p. 120.
82. Ibid. p. 122.
83. Trollope, *Phineas Finn*, p. 335.
84. In her analysis of this scene, Hadley argues that Trollope sees the antiquated medium of the painted portrait as a more effective means of political representation than the photograph, since the latter is too close to mechanical reproduction. Aesthetic and political representation requires the interpretive skills of an artist. Hadley, 'No Representation Without Mediation', 29 September 2012, North American Victorian Studies Association.

85. Barker, *Newspapers, Politics and English Society*, p. 25.
86. This could also be seen as a reference to Trollope himself, since he recently had written a similar series of articles Trollope, *He Knew He Was Right*, p. 361.
87. Ibid. p. 595.
88. Anderson, 'Trollope's Modernity', p. 529.

Chapter 3

'The End is No Longer Hidden': News, Fate and the Sensation Novel

Early in the 1866 sensation novel, *Armadale*, middle-aged clergyman Mr Brock reads *The Times* to his friend and neighbour Mrs Armadale. The narrator emphasises the repetitive habit of their reading:

> Mr Brock and his newspaper, appearing with monotonous regularity at her tea-table three times a week, told her all she knew, or cared to know, of the great outer world which circled round the narrow and changeless limits of her daily life.[1]

This introductory scene at first seems to illustrate Benedict Anderson's famous theorisation of the newspaper and its construction of national community. The newspaper reading sessions organise the monotony of Mrs Armadale's mundane life and give her a sense of the outer world that encircles her own changeless reality. The narrator continues,

> On the evening in question, Mr Brock took the arm-chair in which he always sat, accepted the one cup of tea which he always drank, and opened the newspaper which he always read aloud to Mrs Armadale, who invariably listened to him reclining on the same sofa, with the same sort of needlework everlastingly in her hand.[2]

The structure of this long and meandering sentence underscores the repetitive regularity of their habitual reading and thus crafts a sense of an eternal present.

Yet this time the reading ceremony is suddenly disrupted; Mr Brock sees an advertisement on the front page requesting communication from 'Allan Armadale', a boy of the same name as Mrs Armadale's son. The newspaper ceases to invoke an imagined community but calls specifically for someone Mr Brock knows in his 'little group of characters'.[3] An agitated Mrs Armadale insists that the advertisement's Allan Armadale must be another person: 'Another family, and other friends. . . . The person whose name appears in that advertisement is not my son.'[4] In asserting her son's singularity, Mrs Armadale resists the serial imagining that associates her with the world of the newspaper and its readers. In the meantime, Mr Brock has the uncanny sense that their lives are affected by influences outside his knowledge and control. This is affirmed six years later, after Mrs Armadale's death, when Mr Brock sees another newspaper advertisement for this Allan Armadale, causing him to intuit that events 'were tending steadily to some unimaginable end'.[5] Mr Brock feels a sense of superstitious fatality, as the scene's temporality shifts from a cause and effect view of a presentist history to a sense of history beyond nation. In this early scene, readers of *Armadale* see their own practices of reading doubled in Mr Brock and Mrs Armadale, but this doubleness is a not a source of community but of dread. The Allan Armadale invoked in the newspaper is not a representative body but a double of Mrs Armadale's son, even though she denies their association. In turn, Mr Brock is discomfited by Mrs Armadale's extreme dread of the newspaper and comes to realise how little he knows her.

In *Armadale*, the newspaper generates nervous anxiety and jolts the novel from the mundane everyday into the realm of melodrama. It is a source of the uncanny and the mysterious, a sign of a larger providential plot rather than a national temporal orientation. Peter Brooks shows that the melodramatic imagination in fiction often entails investing ordinary objects and gestures with symbolic, even sacred meaning.[6] I argue that not just *Armadale* but the sensation novel more broadly invests this meaning particularly in the newspaper, the most everyday of objects. These fictional newspapers do not foster an Andersonian national community or a disinterested and rational Habermasian public sphere. Rather, they reveal the intersections in novelistic and journalistic uses of the melodramatic mode in constructing understandings of reality.

This chapter pushes against received views, at the time and since, that the sensation novel and the newspaper (particularly crime news) functioned in tandem as symptoms of modernity.[7] In 1863, reviewer H. L. Mansel conflated the sensation novel – which he called 'the Newspaper Novel' – with crime news and argued that it was representative of a general decline in the public sphere.[8] Mansel was not alone in his linkage of crime news and sensation novels; many Victorian commentators considered them both debased versions of older forms, seeing the newspaper as an inferior mode of history and the sensation novel as a degenerative mode of Gothic sensibility. Critics today continue to see the forms as deeply interrelated.[9] Richard Altick and Deborah Wynne, for example, argue that the sensation novel drew upon crime news in order to authorise their byzantine plots with the newspaper's ostensible facticity, laying claim to reality through their resemblance to true crime.[10] This chapter argues, however, that the novels of Wilkie Collins and Mary Elizabeth Braddon deconstructed journalistic and novelistic discourses in their fictionalisation of news and newspapers. These sensation novels incorporate melodrama in self-reflexive ways to show the narrative heterogeneity of constructions of the real and to demonstrate that devices commonly seen as particular to sensation and melodrama are also an integral part of the newspaper and its practice of community building.[11] Thus, the sensation novel defines itself and its hybrid novelistic realism through the capacity to analyse the workings of news discourse.

This chapter focuses on two sensation novels – Mary Elizabeth Braddon's *Aurora Floyd* (1863) and Collins's *Armadale* – that feature marginalised characters who use the newspapers in unorthodox ways. In *Aurora Floyd*, the newspaper becomes essential to the mystery, sensation and 'atmospheric menace' for which the sensation novel is so famous.[12] Rather than enabling a shared community, the newspaper isolates Aurora Floyd as someone who does not live according to normative practices. I then turn to Wilkie Collins's *Armadale*, a novel that amplifies and exaggerates the truth claims of the newspaper, as the protagonist of the novel Lydia Gwilt invests the newspaper with mythic meaning. Collins's novel dialogues with contemporaneous news about Madeleine Smith, a real-life Glasgow socialite accused of poisoning her ex-lover in 1857, as well as Elizabeth Gaskell's realist domestic novel, *Wives and Daughters*, published concurrently in the pages of *Cornhill Magazine*. The newspaper figures as an embodiment of the uncanny in these novels because of the ways in which marginalised characters understand their position in society and the limited agency they have available to them. Sensation novels thus reflect critically on the violence at the heart of community, and they underscore the ways in which such figures – excluded from mainstream society – might approach news media in non-normative ways.

Melodrama, the Body and News

Sensation novels obsessively play out scenarios in which newspapers act on their readers in determinative ways, deploying melodrama to unpack the effects of the newspaper on readers. Although melodrama is traditionally associated with the nineteenth-century stage, critics identify a more diffusive melodramatic mode in other forms and media; this mode is characterised by rigid personifications of good and evil, visual depictions of physical pain, intense emotion, and 'atmospheric menace and providential plotting'.[13] Most famously, Peter Brooks argues that melodrama is a mode for the 'post-sacred era', as readers find meaning in signs and thereby make 'the world morally legible'.[14] News in the sensation novel often instigates these traces of melodrama: newspapers cause their readers bodily suffering and generate highly charged emotion, as characters see 'false significations' in the news. This tendency to find inflated meaning in the news parallels the newspaper's creation of a fictional national imaginary through a random assortment of regional and global events, letters, leaders and advertisements.

Characters encountering the newspaper in sensation novels often find themselves at odds with their communities, suggesting that the ability of the newspaper to construct an imagined community relies upon practices of exclusion and categorisation. This feeling of exclusion partly emerges from the effects of the newspaper on the character's body, a sense that they are antagonistic to normative society and a heightened attention to sensations incongruous with the surrounding environment. Critics have long argued that sensation novels act on the reader's body in ways that either register, or prepare readers for, the shocks of modernity.[15] However, newspapers in the novels of Mary Elizabeth Braddon and Wilkie Collins participate in an atmosphere of fatality at odds with the association with modernity and the everyday of the newspaper. An attention to the sensation novel's formal and thematic treatment of the newspaper reveals a self-reflexive theorisation of media and the public sphere, one that ties the bodily sensations of these novels to the bodily marginality of the figures at the centre of them. In doing so, the sensation novel reveals the frequently exclusionary practices of newspapers, as a community of readers relies upon the constructed abnormality of the people represented in its pages.[16]

In Braddon's novel, *Aurora Floyd*, the newspaper is a source of nervous anxiety on several levels. First, Aurora's unconventional reading of a sporting journal causes her suitor to experience excruciating discomfort, as her reading of such a paper raises questions about her moral worth. Second, the newspaper spreads a lie upon which the sensation plot of the novel is built: it reports that Aurora's first husband has died, which she later learns to be a falsehood authored by her husband. And finally, the newspapers spread rumours that Aurora is guilty of murder. In all cases, Aurora is positioned outside the normative society crafted by the newspaper.

Aurora Floyd scandalously enjoys reading *Bell's Life*, a newspaper that does not imagine her as part of its reading public, revealing the practices of exclusion on which the newspaper is structured. *Bell's Life* was a sporting journal associated with an audience of working class and middle class men interested in sports and gambling. Aurora's unorthodox choice of reading material is one of the main sources of nervous anxiety in the novel. Talbot Bulstrode, who briefly becomes her fiancé, is deeply unnerved by her reading: 'how restless he was when Aurora read *Bell's Life*, and how the very crackle of the newspaper made him wince with nervous pain'.[17] He is 'shocked at [her] purposeless manner' and how he sees 'her poring over *Bell's Life*'.[18] Aurora's reading practices exceed the norms of newspaper consumption; she reads the newspaper in ways that are physically strong ('crackle') and voracious ('poring'), associating her with the newspaper's imagined masculine reader.[19] Indeed, for Bulstrode, Aurora's reading seems to suggest a degenerative quality potentially inherent to her heredity. Although her father is a wealthy banker, Aurora's late mother was a young, dark-complexioned actress rumoured to have been a 'daring, disreputable creature'; Bulstrode desires Aurora, but he is not certain that she is respectable enough to be his wife.

Yet it is not one of Aurora's habitual readings of *Bell's Life* that instigates the main plot of the novel. Instead, the plot begins when Aurora faints after she receives a clipping from *Bell's Life* in the mail. As soon as she recovers consciousness, she calls Bulstrode by his first name and abruptly accepts his proposal of marriage, even though she had rejected it just the day before. Once she leaves the room, Bulstrode picks up the paper from the floor:

> He shuddered in spite of himself as he looked at the title of the journal; it was *Bell's Life* – a dirty copy, crumpled, and beer-stained, and emitting rank doors of inferior tobacco. It was directed to Miss Floyd, in such sprawling penmanship as might have disgraced the pot-boy of a sporting public house.[20]

The materiality of the newspaper – its dirtiness, its smell of beer and tobacco and the barely comprehensible English of the note – associates Aurora with the original reader of this copy and also by extension the masculine intended audience of the newspaper. Bulstrode reacts with physical repulsion to the journal and the readership it implies. Yet Bulstrode cannot comprehend why the sender directed Aurora to this particular bit of news:

> Bulstrode ran his eye eagerly over the front page; it was almost entirely filled with advertisements (and such advertisements!), but in one column there was an account headed 'FRIGHTFUL ACCIDENT IN GERMANY: AN ENGLISH JOCKEY KILLED.'
>
> Captain Bulstrode never knew why he read of this accident. It was in no way interesting to him, being an account of a steeple-chase in Prussia, in which a heavy English rider and a crack French horse had been killed.[21]

The story's newsworthiness derives from the jockey's Englishness and his death abroad; the jockey is important primarily for his representativeness. But this is not the way that Aurora responds to the story. Instead, Aurora faints because, as we later learn, the jockey is James Conyers, her secret abusive and estranged husband. It has a meaning fully comprehensible only to Aurora, one that is distinguished from the intended readership of the newspaper. However, it also suggests to the reader and to Bulstrode the underlying plot of Aurora's mysterious past. In doing so, the newspaper clipping sets off the sensational plot of the novel beginning with Bulstrode's rejection of Aurora, as he comes to distrust her moral worth. Thinking she is free, Aurora marries John Mellish of Yorkshire, but it later turns out that the story in the newspaper was wrong, and Aurora finds herself with two husbands: John Mellish and James Conyers. Thanks to the newspaper, Aurora becomes a bigamist and is later accused of killing her first husband. When Conyers is actually murdered while working as a servant in Aurora and John Mellish's household, she immediately becomes an object of suspicion in the newspapers and in local gossip. The real murderer, Steven Hargraves, fans the rumours at the local pub and encourages others to believe suppositions in the news. He insists, 'The papers are cleverer nor me. . . . [I]t wouldn't do for a poor fond chap like me to go agen such as them. I think what they think.'[22] Conjectures about her part in the murder spread as far as Manchester as Aurora's past becomes a regional sensation.

Aurora Floyd demonstrates the ways in which newspapers fracture the larger reading public and render individuals like Aurora Floyd suspect. Bulstrode absorbs the worldview of the newspaper in imagining that Aurora's reading of *Bell's Life* makes her morally questionable. That same sporting journal enables her husband to fake his own death and instigate her inadvertent steps towards bigamy and sensation. Indeed, Aurora is a victim of these newspapers and the male gaze that they enable, as characters like Bulstrode and later those at the local pub believe in Aurora's inevitable fall. Yet *Aurora Floyd* proves its sense of fatality wrong by the end of the novel. Bulstrode's worries that Aurora is fated to live a cursed life are unfounded, and the novel concludes with Aurora living a happy and nondescript life with her husband John Mellish. *Aurora Floyd* makes evident the acts of violence and exclusion necessitated by the newspaper's vision of a nation as well as the segmented readerships that make up that nation.

Published in 1863, Braddon's novel, like many sensation novels, came out in a decade of economic depression, electoral reform and global conflict resulting from Britain's imperial influence.[23] News about electoral reform was printed alongside accounts of the American Civil War (1861–5), the Taiping Rebellion in China (1850–64) and the Morant Bay Rebellion in Jamaica (1865). Although Great Britain officially outlawed the slave trade in 1807, these global conflicts revealed its continued involvement in slavery and global violence as an imperial power. Even as newspapers constructed a sense of community through accounts of distant conflicts, they are also evidence of the violence on which nation and empire was built.

The Newspaper and Lydia Gwilt's Providential Plot

It is key that Aurora Floyd never doubts the news of her first husband's death. This is partly due to the assumptions that readers bring to news. As Ralph Rader has argued about true stories, the news 'invites us to believe it is an account of fact' because of its formal claim to be 'reality referring'.[24] Yet the whole concept of regularly produced news is based in falsehood. Rather than waiting for events to happen, 'the serial production of news' requires what Luhmann calls 'deception' in making it appear that news happens on a regular basis.[25] Thus, while news discourse lays claim to accuracy, it also transforms readerly perceptions of the probable and the real. Many nineteenth-century newspapers – particularly the weeklies with which the sensation novel was compared – featured stories that went beyond the everyday, uncommon events that, by virtue of their prominent place in the daily paper, paradoxically came to seem part of everyday reality.

Wilkie Collins's sensation novel, *Armadale*, published serially in *Cornhill* from 1864–6, self-reflexively amplifies the truth claims of the newspaper and makes it a major contributor to the melodramatic plot line of the novel. Like many sensation novels, *Armadale* features an adventuress guilty of poisoning her husband and committing a series of frauds; what is notable about this adventuress, named Lydia Gwilt, is that she regards the newspaper as a sign of a larger providential plot in which she is fixed as the villain.[26] She repeatedly looks to newspaper stories, often read out of context from their actual publication date, to get a sense of what she is fated to do.

Armadale is infamously difficult to summarise because it is rife with characters that share the same name. The Prologue opens in 1832, one year before the Slavery Abolition Act of 1833, with a deathbed confession: the dying man admits to murdering his cousin. As a youth, this man became heir to his distant cousin's West Indian estate under the stipulation that he and his heirs take the cousin's name: Allan Armadale. The estate was originally supposed to go to the owner's son, also named Allan Armadale, but he was disinherited because of his youthful wild behaviour. Shortly after learning of his good fortune, the new heir befriends a young man named Fergus Ingleby. Worried about the friend's bad influence, the heir's mother seeks to arrange a marriage between him and her friend's daughter. However, before the young heir can arrive at his mother's friend's estate and meet the daughter, Ingleby (actually the disinherited Armadale in disguise) impersonates the heir and woos the daughter under his name. He and the daughter (the woman that Mr Brock later knows as Mrs Armadale) convince her 12-year-old maid, Lydia Gwilt, to forge a letter enabling their marriage. Once the heir learns of this marriage, he jealously pursues the couple and murders Ingleby/Armadale by locking him inside the cabin of a sinking ship (although not before the couple conceives a child, also named Allan Armadale). The heir later marries a West Indian woman and fathers a son whose name is Allan Armadale but decides as an adult to go under the name of Ozias Midwinter.

The main action of the novel begins once young Armadale and Midwinter have matured into adulthood. The first half of the novel features third-person narration focused on the male protagonists.

The suspense of this first half circulates around whether Midwinter is fated to harm his friend Armadale and also whether the mysterious but beautiful governess Lydia Gwilt is part of this fate. Lydia first appears in the story as the girl who facilitated the fraud; she then drops out of the narrative and only appears sporadically in newspaper reports, rumours and dreams, until her letters and diary take over the second half of the novel. This second half consists of Lydia's plot to marry Midwinter (knowing, secretly, that his name really is Allan Armadale) so that she can impersonate Allan Armadale's wife and secure a fortune upon his death.

Both Lydia and Midwinter believe themselves to be agents of an already determined destiny.[27] Midwinter feels he is destined by what Taylor calls his 'social and psychic inheritance',[28] understanding both his father's criminality and his mother's racial otherness as hereditary: as he explains to Mr Brock, 'I, an ill-conditioned brat, with my mother's negro blood in my face, and my murdering father's passions in my heart, inheritor of their secret in spite of them!'[29] He believes that he and young Allan Armadale are their fathers' doubles and fated to re-enact the murder. After first meeting the young Allan Armadale, Midwinter explains, 'I thought I was looking him in the face as *my* father looked *his* father in the face when the cabin door closed between them.'[30] Midwinter imagines their commonplace daily encounters through the lens of his father's act of murder, thereby collapsing the distinction between time periods and seeing his relationship with Allan as an exact doubling of their fathers.[31] Lauren Goodlad calls Midwinter's superstitious nature 'the Atlantic uncanny', since it 'is figured, on the one hand, as a racialised attribute of African descent and, on the other, as the expression of a complicated transatlantic past'.[32] The novel conveys the entwinement of capitalism and slavery through Midwinter's sense of historical guilt and the uncanny doublings across the novel. The newspaper is an important technology of the uncanny in *Armadale*, as it helps to structure the series of repetitions and doubles of the novel; it introduces the doublings of Allan Armadales, the unsettling power of Lydia Gwilt and Midwinter's premonition that he is fated to harm his friend. Collins's conflation of dreams and the newspaper muddies the distinction between the rationalised tools of modernity and the irrational and inexplicable phenomena of the mind.

Lydia's sense of self is influenced by Ozias Midwinter's belief that they are fated to murder young Armadale. Midwinter's father warns his son that he has inherited his father's guilt and is fated to re-enact the crime: 'I see My Crime, ripening again for the future in the self-same circumstance which first sowed the seeds of it in the past.'[33] Although he imagines time as circular and repetitive like a blossoming fruit tree, he warns Midwinter to avoid anyone connected to the murder, including the young maid we later learn to be Lydia Gwilt. The novel initially seems to bolster his sense of inherited guilt as Lydia haunts Midwinter and Armadale's lives. We first learn of Lydia's uncanny influence from a mysterious event reported in the newspapers. A woman 'neatly dressed in black silk, with a red Paisley shawl over her shoulder' tries to commit suicide by jumping off a London steamship but is saved by Arthur Blanchard, the heir to the property that Allan Armadale later inherits. He subsequently dies of exposure, paving the way for Armadale's inheritance.[34] Although readers later learn that this woman is Lydia Gwilt, she flees the scene before she can be identified and remains a mystery for reporters and authorities: 'Who was the woman? The man who saved her life never knew. The magistrate who remanded her, the chaplain who exhorted her, the reporter who exhibited her in print – never knew.'[35]

After Armadale inherits Thorpe-Ambrose, his friend Ozias Midwinter hears that a woman in 'black silk, with a red Paisley shawl' has been seen in the village; he immediately recognises in this description the woman from the police report in the newspaper. He worries that there is some mysterious connection between this woman, himself and Armadale. He whispers to himself, 'Can it be the same? . . . *is* there a fatality that follows men in the dark? And is it following *us* in that woman's footsteps?'[36] Moreover, Lydia's shadow reappears in Allan Armadale's dreams, in which his murdered father takes him by the hand and shows him 'the Shadow of the Woman and the Shadow of the Man', dream-world doubles of Lydia and Midwinter. This dream convinces Midwinter that he is fated to follow in the footsteps of his murderous father. However, a doctor reassures Midwinter that Allan's dream simply derived from impressions taken from the newspaper he read prior to falling asleep. Despite the doctor's assurances, 'the terrible conviction of the supernatural origin of the dream, from which he had tried to escape, had possessed itself of him again'.[37] The newspaper and the police report link up with Armadale's prophetic dreams and Midwinter's superstitious dread, so that the tools of modernity become part of a broader supernatural order beyond Midwinter's ken. Indeed, after her marriage to Midwinter, Lydia comes to believe that she *is* the shadowy woman in Armadale's dreams, fated to ensure

Armadale's death and thereby replicate the murder of Armadale's father in a new generation.

Lydia comes to believe in Midwinter's premonitions and his attachment of overdetermined symbolic truth to everyday objects and occurrences, influenced by a life of marginalisation. As a child, Lydia is reduced to an object of exchange, as she is traded for her labour and beauty. Lydia never knew her parents; her earliest years were spent with a woman who took in children to nurse, and there she was beaten and starved. At eight years old, she was sold to the Oldershaws, 'a traveling quack doctor, who dealt in perfumery as well as medicines' and his wife, who procured her through an advertisement to sell their wares. While helping to sell Oldershaw's goods in the marketplace at Thorpe-Ambrose, she strikes the fancy of Mr Blanchard's daughter, who convinces her father to take Lydia in as a maid, or 'plaything'. Shortly thereafter, Lydia travels to the West Indies with Mr and Miss Blanchard, where she commits fraud in assisting Miss Blanchard to become Mrs Armadale. She is then sent to a school on the Continent under the condition that she promises never to return to England. The exile renders literal Lydia's exclusion from a normative English world represented by the young Allan Armadale. It is no wonder, then, that she is convinced that she is fated to wreak havoc on Armadale and Midwinter. As the novel progresses, Lydia sees her life as part of some metanarrative: 'I begin to think that events are forcing me nearer and nearer to some end which I don't see yet, but which I am firmly persuaded is now not far off.'[38] Drawing upon well-known melodramatic plots that 'reinforced the sense of destiny out of control', Lydia imagines herself as a flat character and an archetypal villain.[39]

Seeking to learn of her inevitable fate, Lydia consults the newspaper as if it holds predictive power. She reads old newspaper stories in her diary, recent newspapers collected at a local archive and the daily newspaper over breakfast. At one point, she stumbles upon a newspaper story in an old letter from her ex-lover, in which he urged her to murder her husband; he explains that he found it in 'yesterday's newspaper . . . among the law reports'. Her former lover tells her the story of a 'married woman charged with fraudulently representing herself to be the missing widow of an officer in the merchant service, who was supposed to have drowned'. She interprets it as a blueprint for her next action:

> The end is no longer hidden. The cloud is off my mind, the blindness has gone from my eyes. I see it! I see it! . . . When I had got on, line by line, to those words, it burst on me like a flash of lightning. In an instant I saw

it as plainly as I see it now.... The whole thing has been in my Diary, for days past, without my knowing it! ... And I never saw, never suspected it, till the reading of the letter put my own thoughts before me in a new light. ... The whole series of events under which I have been blindly chafing and fretting for more than a week past, have been one and all – although I was too stupid to see it – events in my favour; events paving the way smoothly and more smoothly straight to the end.[40]

Lydia reads the old news story out of its original publication as a premonition of what is to come. There is no sense of cause and effect but rather an understanding of time as already determined. For Lydia, the newspaper illuminates a plot that has been implicit in her diary for days, suggesting that even her diary, a space of internal expression, is merely a reflection of a larger external and timeless unity.

The article is extracted from its temporal context and newspaper layout. Lydia learns of the story from her ex-lover, Captain Manuel, and thus her understanding of the article is refracted through his interpretation. He writes,

> Do you think such a woman as that would have written to tell me I was pressing her farther than she had courage to go? A handsome woman, too, like yourself! You would drive some men in my position to wish they had her now in your place.[41]

He empties out Lydia's individuality and instead highlights Lydia's potential to substitute for the handsome woman in the newspaper. At the time the letter was written, this lover sought to convince Lydia to murder her husband; but now, the similarity between the woman in the newspaper and Lydia persuades her that she needs to marry Midwinter under his real name (Allan Armadale) so she can impersonate the widow of Allan Armadale of Thorpe-Ambrose 'if [she] can count on Allan Armadale's death in a given time'.[42] She disregards the temporal fixity of both texts – the letter and the news story – and instead attributes to them a truth that continues across time.

Later in the novel, Lydia consults newspapers once again to investigate whether Armadale has died at sea, which will determine if she can follow through on the plot to impersonate his widow. Like a good archival researcher, she asks the hotel landlord to find her back numbers of *The Times*: '[The landlord] has politely offered to accompany me himself to-morrow morning to some place in the

City where all the papers are kept, as he calls it, in file.'[43] The news comes, however, from the daily newspaper rather than the archive: 'Saturday's newspaper *has* lifted the veil! Words are vain to express the panic of astonishment in which I write.'[44] Lydia does not see herself as an individual agent but rather locked into larger structures of meaning instigated and signified by the news. She reacts to the newspaper with emotion and anxiety, very much like the imagined reader of the sensation novel. Her perspective more closely resembles Anderson's understanding of premodern time, 'what Walter Benjamin calls Messianic time, a simultaneity of past and future in an instantaneous present'.[45] This form of consciousness imagines that all events are part of a plan originating from Divine Providence, '*simultaneously* something which has always been, and will be fulfilled in the future'.[46]

This Messianic worldview is reflected in how she reads the newspaper; she draws on practices of bibliomancy, when a reader flips randomly to a passage in a book as a form of divination. Daniel Defoe's *Robinson Crusoe* includes one of the more famous literary examples of bibliomancy, as Crusoe finds spiritual consolation in a random passage from the Psalms and thereby links up early novelistic realism with suggestions of the divine. Collins's 1868 novel, *The Moonstone*, ironically echoes Defoe's novel: the servant Gabriel Betteredge regularly turns to random pages of *Robinson Crusoe* for divine guidance. Lydia's treatment of the newspaper as an agent of fate, and her reading of it outside the daily framework in which it was intended, converts the most everyday of forms – news – into a divine key to understanding. This reflects Peter Brooks' account of the melodramatic imagination, in which everyday objects and gestures become invested with spiritual and moral meaning: it 'represents both the urge toward re-sacralisation and the impossibility of conceiving sacralisation other than in personal terms'.[47] Lydia's superstitious faith takes readers' customary belief in the news to the extreme, so that the news becomes more like an oracle than a product of the modern print marketplace.

Simply a Domestic Romance: Melodrama and Character

Lydia Gwilt was the subject of intense controversy among reviewers and readers when Collins's novel first came out. The *Athenaeum* called Lydia 'one of the most hardened female villains whose devices and desires have ever blackened literature'.[48] The *Spectator* insisted that Collins 'revolted every human sentiment' in giving

> us for its heroine a woman fouler than the refuse of the streets, who has lived to the ripe age of thirty five, and through the horrors of forgery, murder, theft, bigamy, gaol and attempted suicide, without any trace being left on her beauty.[49]

Reviewers criticised Lydia based on probabilistic and moral objections, finding her an unlikely character in light of Victorian beliefs about feminine morality. Yet this character reviled by reviewers was partially based on a real woman that readers would have recognised and remembered: Madeleine Smith, an elite Glasgow socialite who was tried in 1857 for poisoning her ex-lover. In drawing upon this newspaper craze and transforming a real life newspaper sensation into novelistic narrative, Collins reveals the interplay between news and melodrama in Victorian narratives of the real and their construction of a reading public.[50] It is also key that he bases this plot line in *Armadale* on a media sensation ten years old, allowing him to tap into a sensation that has grown somewhat stale in readers' memories. Rather than drawing upon the immediacy of recent news, Collins reworks old news to give the reader some critical distance. Adaptations of the Smith story recur across several of Collins's novels, inviting readers to attend to the workings of news discourse in different contexts. In the case of *Armadale*, Collins transforms the wealthy socialite into a marginalised 35-year-old adventuress of misleadingly youthful appearance.[51]

The media frenzy surrounding Smith's trial for murder spanned all kinds of newspapers and readerships. Writers sought to discern the extent of Smith's guilt through examining her countenance, perceiving it as a window to her character (both in the sense of personality and morality). Newspapers described the efforts of people in the courtroom to catch a glimpse of Smith's face and in turn parsed her expressions for their readers. Rather than emphasising the evidence and testimony at trial, newspapers looked for signs that might make Smith's inward morality legible to an outsider. The *Caledonian Mercury* reported, 'Many anxious glances were cast towards her as she came up the stair, the most of the people present rising in order to get a better glimpse of her countenance.'[52] The *John Bull and Britannia* concluded that 'her demeanour is certainly not that of a guilty person'.[53] Newspapers made sense of 'Scotland's trial of the century' by placing it within the framework of familiar stage melodramas, largely attributing Smith's crime to the villainy of her lover. The *Glasgow Herald* called the whole situation a 'horribly romantic case', in which the innocent and trusting Smith was seduced by her lover. Similarly, *The Derby Mercury* blamed the 'black villainy . . . of her heartless seducer' for Smith's crime.[54] When the jury returned the verdict 'not proven', a leader in the *Glasgow Herald* attributed moral certainty to the case by repackaging it as a morality tale for newspaper readers:

> The awful tale of immorality and unrestrained appetite is concluded. . . . The tale which has been nine days telling in Edinburgh has left its impress upon the minds of thousands of persons . . . [S]he fell into the snare planted for her by a vain and boastful braggart, and we know not what arts may have been employed to lead her away from the paths of innocence. . . . Though his arts may never be known, it would be of vast importance to ascertain, if it were possible, how much he had acquired of the vile knowledge to effect seduction which is so extensively diffused and put in practice in France.[55]

The leader frames Smith as an innocent victim to a villain's foreign arts of seduction, signalling a moral threat from outside of Great Britain. Thus, even though the trial returns the verdict unproven, the leader re-affirms moral certainty for its Edinburgh readers, situating them within a larger national community under threat by the invasion of French sexuality. These newspaper accounts are unable to imagine Smith outside of the rigid melodramatic role of the victim.[56]

Lydia undergoes a similar trial for murder before the novel's plot begins, inviting readers to reflect on the way that Madeleine Smith's story and other news sensations circulate in the public sphere. *Armadale* does not provide direct access to the newspaper reports surrounding Lydia's trial; instead, it is relayed from the perspective of the detective, 'Bashwood the younger', after he is hired by his father to investigate Lydia's past. We learn that, under the influence of her lover, Lydia poisoned her landowning husband and later was brought to trial for her crime. Bashwood's description of the media furore surrounding Lydia's trial and her presumed innocence echoes the account of Smith's case in the real-life newspaper press:

> [T]wo or three of the young Buccaniers [sic] of Literature went down to two or three newspaper offices, and wrote two or three heart-rending leading articles on the subject of the proceedings in court. The next morning the public caught light like tinder; and the prisoner was tried

over again, before an amateur court of justice, in the columns of the newspapers. All the people who had no personal experience whatever on the subject, seized their pens, and rushed (by kind permission of the editor) into print. Doctors who had *not* attended the sick man, and who had *not* been present at the examination of the body, declared by dozens that he had died a natural death. Barristers without business, who had *not* heard the evidence, attacked the jury who *had* heard it, and judged the Judge, who had sat on the bench before some of them were born. The general public followed the lead of the barristers and the doctors, and the young Buccaniers who had set the thing going. . . . The British Public rose to protest as one man against the working of its own machinery . . .[57]

This passage highlights the arbitrariness behind the apparent serial structure and facticity of newspaper form. News coverage relies not upon perceived external reality but the whim of a few articles that then galvanise a series of people with 'no personal experience whatever' to write. The outcry on Lydia's behalf emerges from the original 'heart-rending' articles and also a rendering of Lydia's character into melodramatic victim.[58] The newspaper coverage surrounding Lydia's trial is based in circulating fictions that lay claim to veracity, largely on the basis of mass public outrage. It percolates down from the leaders to professionals and then finally to the general public, who write to the newspaper to add their own voices to the uproar. Thus, the newspapers create a 'British Public' positioned against its own legal operations, united in emotional outrage at Lydia's perceived victimisation.

When Bashwood describes this trial by newspaper, he is not entirely clear about the sections of the newspaper, or the kinds of newspapers, he has read. His account blurs the newspaper press together into an indistinguishable clamour kindled by the emotional appeal of a few leading articles. This outrage spreads across the columns of the newspaper; it is unclear whether the outburst happens solely among readers' letters to the editor, or if it also spreads to other sections of the paper as professionals write in with their supposed expertise. Bashwood's imprecision is symptomatic of a larger tendency in Collins's *Armadale*, and in sensation novels more broadly, to blur the distinctions between the parts of the newspaper. Whether it is an advertisement, a law report, a leader, or sports news, all parts of the newspaper contribute to the novel's fatality.

Yet it is also worth noting that this quotation comes from Bashwood's perspective, not from an omniscient narrator. Bashwood offers a pointed critique of the newspaper press and its creation of public opinion, but he also treats Lydia as an object to be reduced to black and white.[59] In this sense, he joins the newspaper's clamour and holds Lydia up for judgement, and he becomes part of the network of masculine discourses circulating around Lydia throughout the novel. *Armadale* thus demonstrates that the construction of a British public occurs through the public adjudication of what Luhmann calls a 'norm violator', on the basis of melodramatic and sensational plots. The public comes together through a trial by newspaper that holds Lydia up to different expectations and narratives than the court of law.

Lydia Gwilt in the Pages of *Cornhill*

Armadale not only absorbs and reworks real-life media sensations; it also interacts with the predominantly realist framework of its publication context. Indeed, the attention of the novel to constructions of reality is foregrounded in its serial publication in *Cornhill Magazine*, a shilling monthly founded in 1859 to rival Charles Dickens's *All the Year Round*.[60] Some critics have read *Armadale* as a subversion of the conservative journal *Cornhill*, but I believe its inclusion speaks to a complex network of Victorian realism, sensation and melodrama. *Cornhill* famously enforced a rigid definition of reality. In a letter to potential contributors in November 1859, *Cornhill*-cofounder William Makepeace Thackeray announced the journal's valorisation of the factual and the everyday: '[F]iction of course must form a part, but only a part, of our entertainment. We want, on the other hand, as much reality as possible.'[61] Thackeray regulated the periodical's treatment of the 'real world' through censoring its contributions, thereby making reality 'a construct within the periodical's pages'.[62] It is striking that a novel like *Armadale* was published in a periodical known for its commitment to a highly limited conception of reality.

Armadale's overlapping serial publication with Elizabeth Gaskell's *Wives and Daughters* brings out the multifaceted dimensions of novelistic realisms. At first glance, *Wives and Daughters* might seem the ultimate example of Thackeray's rigid notion of reality. Published from August 1864 to January 1866, *Wives and Daughters* was subtitled 'An Every-Day Story' and focused on the daily life of a small-town doctor's daughter. Yet its structure resembles the mingling of melodrama and everyday reality that *Armadale* also identifies in the newspaper. Gaskell's novel lays claim to its domestic realism in its very first sentence:

> In a country there was a shire, and in that shire there was a town, and in that town there was a house, and in that house there was a room, and in that room there was a bed, and in that bed there lay a little girl.[63]

Suggestive of Eliot's *Middlemarch* (published five years later), or of Dickens's concentric circles of duty in *Bleak House*, the first sentence situates Molly Gibson within a larger national community of simultaneous everyday activity. And yet this opening begins with the one uncommon event in Molly's young life: her trip to Cumnor Towers, the country seat of an aristocratic family. After this singular event, the narrator skips over most of her quiet, but uneventful childhood: 'Molly grew up among these quiet people in calm monotony of life, without any greater event than that which has been recorded – the being left behind at the Towers – until she was nearly seventeen.'[64] The novel stakes its claim to everyday realism, but the forward movement of the plot relies upon events that are uncommon in Molly Gibson's everyday life. In this sense, *Wives and Daughters* reflects the same tension characteristic of serial news. Just as the news media must make uncommon events appear common in order to sustain the regularity of serial news, so does Gaskell's novel rely upon the uncommon to build the foundations of a plot, even if it *is* an 'every-day story'.

The novel is also rife with melodramatic traces, from the unknown background of Molly's father Dr Gibson (whose mother is conjectured to be French because of his dark complexion), to Osborne Hamley's secret marriage to a French bonne. Hyacinth Kirkpatrick responds in hysterical tears when Dr Gibson proposes to her, and her beautiful stepdaughter (and Molly's stepsister) Cynthia Kirkpatrick has a mysterious relationship with the villainous Mr Preston. The 'every-day story' seems every moment to be veering into melodrama. The intertwining of melodrama and realism in *Wives and Daughters* becomes particularly evident in Molly's bemusement at learning of Osborne's secret wife: 'She would never have guessed the concealed romance which lay *perdu* under that every-day behaviour.'[65] Readers of *Cornhill* eager for tales of secret liaisons and clandestine marriage could turn to *Wives and Daughters* as surely as *Armadale*.

Molly Gibson continually consigns herself to the background in the interest of her friends and family. Yet *Wives and Daughters* is partially a history of Molly Gibson's emotional upheavals, ranging from her traumatic visit to the Towers to Roger Hamley's engagement to Cynthia. After the latter event, Molly becomes so emotionally overwrought that she makes herself ill, showing the kind of emotions more commonly associated with sensation novels. In an early chapter, called 'A Crisis', Molly's father informs her of his engagement to Hyacinth Kirkpatrick, the former governess of the Towers family, but she is too overwhelmed to respond:

> She did not answer. She could not tell what words to use. She was afraid of saying anything, lest the passion of anger, dislike, indignation – whatever it was that was boiling up in her breast – should find vent in cries and screams, or worse, in raging words that could not be forgotten. It was as if the piece of solid ground on which she stood had broken from the shore, and she was drifting out to the infinite sea alone.[66]

As Molly restrains herself for fear of a hysterical outburst, Mr Gibson finds her silence to be 'unnatural'. Yet Molly knows that her father would condemn her emotions as unnatural as well. She worries that an outburst would result in incomprehensible hysterics or, worse, 'raging words that could not be forgotten'. Indeed, once she collapses into tears after her father's departure, Roger Hamley considers her grief 'unreasonable and possibly exaggerated'.[67] Molly's restrained outburst came out in the November 1864 instalment of *Cornhill*, the first issue in which *Armadale* began serialisation. In this sense, *Wives and Daughters* seems to register the introduction of a sensation novel to *Cornhill*'s highly constructed reality. Molly finds herself pushed to the side to make way for her father's new wife, at the same time that *Wives and Daughters* is pushed further back into the instalment to allow *Armadale* the first page. Molly's inward storm presages the outbursts that Lydia details in her letters and diary entries.

Armadale's dialogical relationship with *Wives and Daughters* suggests the melodramatic latency of this novel of domestic realism. As a character of little power and status, Molly must refrain from speech because she fears to transgress the proper boundaries of her story. Her stepsister Cynthia might seem more like a sensation novel heroine, but Molly reveals the intense feeling that is an undercurrent to her calm and retiring exterior. The community of the novel regains stability at its end only through Molly's pain and unnoticed victimisation. By intersecting with the plot of *Wives and Daughters*, *Armadale* suggests the artificiality of a construction of reality that represses the 'raging words' that result from disempowerment.

An Upside-Down Pamela

This dialogue between novels that were serialised contemporaneously in *Cornhill* parallels another formal interaction in *Armadale* itself: news discourse versus epistolary writing. The first half of *Armadale* is written in third-person narration from the perspectives of Ozias Midwinter and Allan Armadale, but much of the second half gives way to Lydia's letters and her private diary. But whereas Molly resists putting her feelings in words, Lydia obsessively documents every minute emotional fluctuation in epistolary form. In some ways, Lydia's diary entries mimic the structure of the daily newspaper, characterised by the specific date lines and the daily ceremony involved in their writing. However, they substitute Lydia's inner emotional life for the kinds of events customarily deemed newsworthy.

The novel deepens the connection between the diary and the newspaper when Lydia consults the news to see if Armadale has died at sea. On 20 November, she writes,

> Not a word of news yet, either in the obituary column, or in any other part of the paper. . . . The newspaper is to meet me at the breakfast-table every morning till further notice – and any day now may show me what I most want to see.[68]

The next day she writes, 'No news again.' Her diary entries are increasingly structured by her breakfast newspaper reading, a reminder of the contemporary passage of time that would be further reinforced by *Armadale*'s serial publication in *Cornhill Magazine*. They also invoke the early epistolary tradition of the novel, in which the modern individual subject emerges with a character like Samuel Richardson's Pamela, whose worth derives not from her social status but from her rich interiority.[69] It is Pamela's capacity for written self-expression that eventually wins over Mr B and persuades him to marry her, and Richardson called his epistolary style 'writing to the moment' because the letters traced Pamela's emotions as they happened in real-time.[70] For Michael McKeon, the epistolary format also serves as a claim to historicity, the alignment of *Pamela* with documentary history rather than romance because of its temporal specificity and appearance of reality.[71] But rather than offering a claim to veracity, Lydia's writing to-the-moment brings out her exaggerated and hysterical emotional outbursts, as she feels that each entry brings her closer to an inevitable end. The dates do not mark a sense of an eternal present but rather the unfolding of time as she approaches her ultimate climax as part of a larger providential plot. Her diary entries trace the intense fluctuations of her emotions, far more extreme than anything we see in *Pamela*. Lydia's story is perhaps an upside down version of Pamela's, in which Lydia's guilt, rather than her interior worth, has already been determined.[72] Indeed, as Mariaconcetta Costantini highlights, Lydia's emotions go beyond what Victorians perceived as appropriate, 'since she alternates romantic feelings with violent, unladylike passions springing from the dark recesses of her psyche'.[73] Whereas Mr B discovers Pamela's singular worth through reading her letters, Lydia's diary (unread by anyone in the novel) documents her unavoidable march towards an already determined fate.

And essential to this fate, once again, is the newspaper. After her wedding to Midwinter, Lydia initially disavows her plans to impersonate Armadale's wife to secure his inheritance, intending to be a good wife to Midwinter. But she is driven back to her plots and her diary by Midwinter's developing career as a journalist:

Naples, October 10th. – It is two months to-day, since I declared that I had closed my Diary, never to open it again.

Why have I broken my resolution? Why have I gone back to this secret friend of my wretchedest and wickedest hours? Because I am more friendless than ever; because I am more lonely than ever, though my husband is sitting writing in the next room to me. My misery is a woman's misery, and it *will* speak – here, rather than nowhere; to my second self, in this book, if I have no one else to hear me. . . .

Day after day, the hours that he gives to his hateful writing grow longer and longer; day after day, he becomes more and more silent, in the hours he gives to Me. . . . All he remembers is the newspaper.[74]

The dateline echoes the situated temporality of the newspaper, and Lydia opens her entry by measuring the passage of time since she last wrote in the diary – 'it is two months to-day'. She imagines this diary as a second self and as a 'secret' competitor to Midwinter. She traces the growing intensity of her feelings by the day, as Midwinter continues to devote time to the newspaper. Lydia believes that Midwinter's journalistic success drives her providential plot forward in a manner beyond her control and as part of her fate as a woman with a 'woman's misery'. Shortly after her marriage to Midwinter, Lydia vows to give up her diary:

> The eve of my wedding-day! I close and lock this book, never to write in it, never to open it again. . . . My love! my angel! when to-morrow gives me to you, I will not have a thought in my heart which is not *your* thought, as well as mine![75]

However, she later feels compelled to return to her diary when Midwinter prioritises his journalistic writing. The newspaper represents the exclusive world that absorbs her husband and leaves her out.[76] While the diary might structurally resemble the newspaper in its relationship to daily time, Lydia feels her writing to be at odds with the newspaper and the supposedly rational world that the newspaper represents.

Lydia's superstition and hysteria would seem to locate *Armadale* firmly outside of the realist tradition. Nevertheless, *Armadale* suggests the significant power that melodramatic narratives have over individuals' orientations to their worlds, as well as the importance of melodrama and sensation to narratives of the real.[77] Lydia's hysterical dread of her predetermined fate reflects her marginal condition in society. Her self-perception has also been structured by conditions that force her to look upon herself from external perspectives, whether it be in the newspaper accounts of her trial or the mysterious story of the lady with the Paisley shawl. Contrary to the philosophy of self-help so popular in the early and mid-nineteenth century, Lydia rightly perceives that she is not a free agent settling her own fate.[78]

In rendering Lydia an upside-down Pamela, Collins suggests the felt social reality of the melodramatic mode. He recasts a melodramatic villainess as the protagonist of the novel.[79] Alex Woloch has argued that the realist novel is an 'inequitable distribution', in which minor characters are flattened out to make way for the bulging psychology of the protagonist. In *Armadale*, however, Lydia retains her minorness – that is, her lack of depth and her failure to develop over the course of the novel – even as she is brought to the forefront. It reflects Lydia's feeling that her fate is beyond her control. As a marginalised person, Lydia truly feels flat, because roundness is limited to the select few (like Allan Armadale, whose social advantages as a white British man she resents). Rather than a character that imagines himself to be a hero in a romance, like Don Quixote, Lydia quite accurately sees herself excluded from a society constructed of Armadales and relegated to the role of the villain. This reflects the ways in which Victorians have been said to draw upon melodrama to understand and make sense of their experience.[80] Melodrama is truly real in this sense, both inherent to the newspaper, novelistic realism and the making sense of everyday experience. *Armadale* reveals the intermingling of apparently competing genres and modalities in conveying the experience of an unequal world; moreover, it highlights these tensions within less reflexive media like the newspaper.

Conclusion

Some critics have argued that sensation novels interrogate the ideological and moral certainty of the realist novel through injecting the everyday with melodramatic qualities.[81] I have argued in this chapter, however, that the sensation novel brings out more explicit tensions that are already present within narratives of the real. The novel – whether realist or sensational – incorporates melodrama in more self-reflexive ways, such that it reveals the narrative heterogeneity of the 'every day'. In contrast, the claim of the newspaper to reality and facticity distorts its relationship to melodrama, as it fails to interrogate its practices of representing some of its actors as villains. The newspaper generates anxiety, pain and suspense throughout sensation novels, and thus it is structurally linked up with these melodramatic plots in the novel. Just as Peter Brooks, Elaine Hadley and Fredric Jameson recognise a melodramatic mode in otherwise realist novels, the sensation novel recognises this strand in narratives of the real; by re-centring a melodramatic villainess, Lydia, *Armadale* suggests the power exerted by melodramatic narratives on perceptions of probability and reality.[82]

In his dedication to the novel *Basil*, published in 1852, Collins began what would be a long-term effort to think through what constitutes literary 'realities'. He explains, 'I have not thought it either politic or necessary, while adhering to realities, to adhere to everyday realities only.'[83] Rather than restricting himself to the constrained experience of the imagined reader, Collins claims that he appealed 'to other sources (as genuine in their way) beyond [the reader's] own experience' so 'that [Collins] could hope to fix his interest and excite his suspense, to occupy his deeper feelings, or to stir his nobler thoughts'.[84] Collins distinguishes between the 'realities' of his novel and 'every-day realities': he suggests the representative quality of his fiction goes beyond its probabilistic resemblance to the perceived immediate real world. Collins's 'realities' seem rooted in the very fact of the novel's distance from what the reader thinks could happen in his or her own sphere: 'by appealing to other sources (as genuine in their own way)'. Much later, in his preface to *The Law and the Lady*, published in 1875, Collins challenges facile uses of the words 'natural' and 'unnatural' that make assumptions about established truths that appear to be essential and unchanging. In this preface, he reminds the reader of 'certain established truths' that the reader of fiction sometimes forgets: 'That Characters which may not have appeared, and Events which may not have taken place, within the limits of our own individual experience, may nevertheless be perfectly natural Characters and perfectly probable Events, for all that.'[85] Collins here refers to the cliché that haunts fictional narrative: that truth is stranger than fiction. Because fiction does not have the referential authorisation of non-fiction, Ralph Rader argues that fiction must create an appearance of internal probability, whereby characters appear to act autonomously in ways consistent with their personality, rather than relying upon the artifice of chance and circumstance.[86] In contrast, the non-fiction writer is free to shape characters and events to their own vision within the limits imposed by external reference.

And yet the newspaper is somewhat at odds with Rader's account of non-fiction, since its attention to the newsworthy requires reporting the aberrant as simultaneously remarkable and commonplace. The news generates and sustains social norms by encouraging readers to judge examples of those who violate them. While readers might perceive themselves to be aligned with other imagined readers, and thereby construct their relationship to the nation serially, this sense of national identity is constructed on the basis of the improbable. Thus, newspapers offer a peculiar relationship to the real, relying upon the authority of their factual basis, while covering events and actors that are unusual, improbable, or excluded from the national imaginary constructed by the newspaper.

While deeply involved in shaping the representation and production of our perceptions of a spatial and temporal reality, newspapers – particularly the crime news seen as the origin of the sensation novel – measure newsworthiness according to how unusual or improbable an event is. The sensation novel brings out this structural tension in the newspaper by making it a source of melodramatic imagination. The sense that the newspaper must be true, and yet the realisation that it is not true or that it is at odds with a character's experience, helps to generate the atmosphere of superstition and menace in the sensation novel. Mr Brock reads of an Allan Armadale in *The Times* but is assured that it is not the Allan Armadale that he knows. Aurora Floyd reads of a jockey's death in *Bell's Life* only to learn that this jockey, also her husband, did not actually die. These characters are made to feel helpless, anxious and abnormal, as they find uncanny resemblances of their own life in the news. The newspaper, in a sense, *is* uncanny – it feels both familiar and unfamiliar, like and unlike.

Collins ends the novel with an appendix telling a story that he heard from reporters and later saw in a variety of newspapers, including *The Times* and the *Daily News*. He writes, 'In November, 1865, that is to say, when thirteen monthly parts of "Armadale" had been published, and, I may add, when more than a year and a half had elapsed since the end of the story, as it now appears, was first sketched in my notebook', three ship-keepers died in a vessel docked at Liverpool. Collins then emphasises, '*The name of that ship was "The Armadale"*. And the proceedings at the Inquest proved that the three men had been all suffocated *by sleeping in poisoned air!*' Collins's appendix thus moves beyond the framework of his novel, as he emphasises the doubling of his plot in real life. In doing so, he mysteriously mimics Lydia's practice of attributing symbolic significance to the most everyday of objects, the newspaper.

Notes

1. Collins, *Armadale*, p. 56.
2. Ibid. p. 56.
3. Ibid. p. 53.
4. Ibid. p. 56.
5. Ibid. p. 76.
6. Brooks, *The Melodramatic Imagination*.
7. This chapter builds upon Dallas Liddle's claim that Victorian journalists imagined sensation and crime news in very different terms than sensation fiction.
8. [Mansel], 'Sensation Novels', pp. 482–514.
9. Nicholas Daly argues that the sensation novel trained readers' bodies to absorb the shocks of modernity, tapping into anxiety fostered by the expansion of urban life, the newspaper and the railroad. Daly, 'Railway Novels', pp. 461–87. Daly's argument is in line with prior work on the sensation novel; Jenny Bourne Taylor, for instance, argues that the sensation novel was perceived as a symptom of modern cultural degeneration. Taylor, *In the Secret Theatre*.

10. For an example of a critic who sees the sensation novel as a challenge to realism, see Gilbert, *Disease, Desire and the Body*.
11. Alexander Welsh argues that the expansion in information technology in the 1860s led to pathological side effects that show up symptomatically in Victorian novels, including *Lady Audley's Secret*.
12. Kathleen Tillotson calls sensation novels 'novels with a secret', but I want to emphasise that it is the newspaper that often divulges or withholds this secret. See Tillotson, 'Introduction', *The Woman in White*, XV.
13. Elaine Hadley identifies a mid-nineteenth-century 'melodramatic mode' as a response to social, economic and epistemological changes 'that characterised the consolidation of market society' (p. 2). She identifies the melodramatic mode in texts not traditionally understood as melodramatic. Hadley, *Melodramatic Tactics*, p. 3.
14. Brooks, *Melodramatic Imagination*, p. 42.
15. Many Victorians saw sensation novels as symptoms of social degeneration, or 'a collective cultural nervous disorder . . . that worked directly on the body of the reader and as an infection from the outside'. Taylor, *In the Secret Theatre*, p. 4.
16. Many critics have associated the sensation novel with the nineteenth-century stage, melodrama and Gothic fiction. Indeed, Winifred Hughes argues that the sensation novel diverged from realism by adopting Gothic practices.
17. Braddon, *Aurora Floyd*, p. 50.
18. Ibid.
19. Jon Klancher argued that the Romantic British periodical was a 'paradigm of audience-making', as writers developed new ways of influencing "readers" interpretive frameworks and shaping their ideological awareness'. Aurora, however, does not function according to the readership imagined by the periodical. Klancher, *The Making of English Reading Audiences*, p. 4.
20. Braddon, *Aurora Floyd*, p. 68.
21. Ibid.
22. Ibid. p. 381.
23. Indeed, Nicholas Rance associates the sensation novel with a 'particular "structure of feeling" . . . in a decade labouring under economic depression and, fairly strictly connected, campaigns for extension of the franchise'. Rance, *Wilkie Collins*, p. 4.
24. Rader, 'Defoe, Richardson, Joyce', p. 179.
25. Luhmann, *Reality of the Mass Media*, p. 25.
26. As Jenny Bourne Taylor has argued, 'Modernity in Dickens is externalised and melodramatised as a visible force. . . . In Collins, on the other hand, what is visible on the surface is an eerily incomplete and sometimes apparently motionless landscape, where signs of change are omnipresent but the processes of change are subterranean and mysterious. . . . The

evacuation of meaning from character to plot in the sensation novel implies that characters are rarely able to act openly or freely.' Taylor, 'Introduction', *Cambridge Companion*, p. 17.
27. Indeed, as Lyn Pyket points out, sensation novel heroines and heroes are often structured around some secret from the past that makes their current life a sham. Pykett, *The Nineteenth-Century Sensation Novel*.
28. Taylor, *In the Secret Theatre*, p. 163.
29. Collins, *Armadale*, p. 89.
30. Ibid. p. 101.
31. Several critics have highlighted the novel's implicit critique of the slave trade, including Lauren Goodlad and Nathan Hensley. Hensley argues that the doubling in *Armadale* highlights the 'tension between singularity and universality crucial to the smooth functioning of a modern democracy'. It ironises the move from particularity to exchangeability and its links up with 'the most basic form of human interchangeability: slavery'. Hensley, '*Armadale* and the Logic of Liberalism', p. 608.
32. Goodlad, *The Victorian Geopolitical Aesthetic*, p. 116.
33. Collins, *Armadale*, p. 47.
34. Madeleine C. Seys points out that this shawl 'functions as an evocative colonial symbol'. Seys, *Fashion and Narrative*.
35. Collins, *Armadale*, p. 80.
36. Ibid. p. 105.
37. Ibid. p. 150.
38. Ibid. p. 442.
39. Walkowitz, *City of Dreadful Delight*, p. 86.
40. Collins, *Armadale*, pp. 444–6.
41. Ibid. p. 445.
42. Ibid.
43. Ibid. p. 578.
44. Ibid. p. 579.
45. Anderson, *Imagined Communities*, p. 22.
46. Auerbach, *Mimesis*, p. 74.
47. Brooks, *Melodramatic Imagination*, p. 16. For Brooks, Balzac's novels are examples of 'real' melodramas, when 'he is using the things and gestures of the real world, of social life, as kinds of metaphors that refer us to the realm of spiritual reality and latent moral meanings. Things cease to be merely themselves'. Brooks, p. 9.
48. [H. F. Chorley], *Athenaeum*, 2 June 1866, 732–3. Indeed, Sue Lonoff argues that Lydia Gwilt and Collins's other female characters 'tend to upset the reader's expectations' and 'offended against propriety and assaulted Victorian standards'. Lonoff, *Wilkie Collins and His Victorian Readers*, 28.
49. '*Armadale*', *The Spectator*, 9 June 1866, 18. According to Lisa Niles, reviewers were disturbed by Lydia's use of cosmetics in achieving a fraudulent appearance of youth. As Niles writes, 'to be thirty-five and

not look it is analogous to perpetrating fraud'. Niles 'Owning "the dreadful truth"', p. 67. Similarly, Piya Pal-Lapinski writes, 'What most disturbs the Victorian reviewer of Wilkie Collins's *Armadale* about Lydia Gwilt's body is its capacity to absorb and transform *traces*.' Pal-Lapinski, *The Exotic Woman*, p. 35.

50. As Lonoff points out, Collins did not always take his stories from the contemporary press; he also used older sources, including Maurice Méjan's *Recueil des Causes Célèbre* (Paris, 1808).
51. When the murder is first revealed, *The John Bull and Britannia* emphasises the elite status of Smith's family in their 'report that a gentleman had been poisoned by the daughter of a family which moves in the better classes of society, . . . the granddaughter of the late Mr David Hamilton, the celebrated architect of Glasgow Exchange and Hamilton Palace'. 'Extraordinary Case', *John Bull and Britannia*, 4 April 1857, 222.
52. 'High Court Judiciary: Trial of Miss Smith', *Caledonian Mercury*, 1 July 1857. The *Mercury* was one of Edinburgh's oldest newspapers and was owned by a locally based family until it was sold to its editor James Robie and then to a London journalist in 1866. By the 1860s, it was associated with the Edinburgh Radical group and known for its support of social reform and the early Scottish nationalist movement in the mid-1850s.
53. 'Extraordinary Case', p. 254.
54. 'Madeleine Smith and Emile Langelier', *The Derby Mercury*, 15 July 1857.
55. 'Friday Morning, July 10', p. 9. This aligns with Rohan McWilliam's argument that 'the world of mustache twirling aristocrats and seduced milliners is a key to the construction and presentation of the Victorian self'. McWilliam, 'Melodrama and the Historians', p. 58.
56. My reading differs from John Hariman's argument that the media's treatment of Smith showed a shift from objectifying spectacle to an interest in accessing her subjectivity. For a summary of John Hariman's argument, see Fiske, *Heretical Hellenism*, p. 46.
57. Collins, *Armadale*, p. 530.
58. The younger Bashwood explains that documentation on Lydia is widely available because she is a 'public character': 'If we had a less notorious woman to deal with, she might have cost us weeks of inquiry . . . A day did it in Miss Gwilt's case; and another day put the whole story of her life, in black and white, into my hands.' Collins, *Armadale*, p. 519.
59. Characters like Allan Armadale seek to understand Lydia in terms of the stereotypical Victorian woman, supported by melodramatic and newspaper narratives. Early in the novel, when Lydia is still a local governess, Allan learns of her checkered past and strives to reconcile this information with his idea of a victimised heroine: 'One conclusion, and one only – the conclusion which any man must have drawn, hearing

what he had just heard, and knowing no more than he knew – forced itself into his mind. A miserable, fallen woman, who had abandoned herself in her extremity to the help of wretches skilled in criminal concealment . . .' (p. 345). Equipped with only a skeletal sense of Lydia's history, Armadale constructs a melodrama around Lydia in which he represents her as a passive victim worthy of his feeling, one that resembles the language circulating in newspapers about Smith.

60. For more on *Cornhill*, see Colby, 'Into the Blue Water', pp. 209–22.
61. Thackeray as quoted in Turner, *Trollope and the Magazines*, p. 10.
62. Turner, *Trollope and the Magazines*, p. 11.
63. Gaskell, *Wives and Daughters*, p. 35.
64. Ibid. p. 67.
65. Ibid. p. 249.
66. Ibid. p. 145.
67. Ibid. p. 154.
68. Collins, *Armadale*, p. 579.
69. McKeon, *Origins of the English Novel*, p. 46. Also, see Armstrong, *Desire and Domestic Fiction*.
70. Yet Ralph Rader emphasises that *Pamela*'s epistolary form only imitates reality; it does not ask readers to believe that Pamela is a real person and that they are reading real letters. The fictional quality of *Pamela* is ever present to the reader, whereas Daniel Defoe's *Moll Flanders* is written to be read as non-fiction: 'though the difference is not easily perceived by those who think of realism as involving a single kind of imaginative relationship to the natural world'. Richardson's letters only *seem* to be real letters because they must continually remind us that they are a fiction: 'In fact, the dramatic vividness of the letters (and the events they relate) is not the result of their likeness to real letters (and real events) but of their unlikeness to them.' Rader, 'Defoe, Richardson, Joyce', pp. 177–8.
71. McKeon, *Origins of the English Novel*, p. 46. McKeon argues that *Pamela* reveals the 'radically subjective bases of all cognition' in its obsessive effort to record historical truth and experience (p. 363). Rebecca Tierney-Hynes adds that Pamela's record does not show her 'radical individuality, but rather its dependence on a readership'. Tierney-Hynes, *Novel Minds*, p. 162.
72. One of these unladylike passions is an intense hatred of Midwinter's journalistic writing and 'the whole tribe of authors'. She feels that her fate is reaffirmed when Ozias Midwinter, now her husband, decides not to accompany her back to England, since his editor prefers him to stay in Europe: '[If] he had persisted in his first resolution to accompany me himself to England . . . I firmly believe I should have turned my back on temptation for the second time. . . . No man who really loved me would have put what he owed to a pack of newspaper people before what he owed to his wife.' Collins, *Armadale*, p. 547, p. 578.

73. Costantini also argues that the epistolary correspondence between Lydia and Maria Oldershaw is a parody of the relationship between conduct books and their audience. Lydia's transition from letter writing to journal writing signifies, for Costantini, her rejection of this conduct-book format and of Oldershaw's authority. Costantini, 'Wo/Men of Letters', p. 44.
74. Collins, *Armadale*, pp. 545–7.
75. Ibid. p. 515.
76. Piya Pal-Lipinski argues that 'Lydia's desperate attempts to poison Allan signify an attack on everything that he stands for – the hierarchies of class and imperial identity that refuse to acknowledge their own ideological fissures.' Pal-Lipinski, 'Chemical Seductions', p. 14.
77. Fredric Jameson contends that melodrama finds a 'self-conscious working through' in George Eliot's novels, particularly in *Daniel Deronda* (p. 156). In his account, *Daniel Deronda* features a return to melodrama in the aristocratic villain Henleigh Mallinger Grandcourt and the protagonist's mother, Leonora Halm-Eberstein, who abandoned Deronda so as 'to live the life that was in me, and not to be hampered with other lives' (Eliot p. 626). Even the realist novel *Middlemarch* contains traces of melodrama in Tertius Lydgate's past romance with a Parisian actress. Of the Princess and Lydgate's first love, Jameson writes, '[W]e find the beating heart of George Eliot's work and the place in which the conventional sub-generic narratives both of melodrama and of the drama of adultery are revealed to be the merest of disguises and fronts for an unequal drama of liberation. . . . [T]he work of realism lies in dissolving these archetypes . . . and in appropriating their archetypal plots for new acts of freedom' (p. 160). For Jameson, the realist novel contains a clash of aesthetic ideologies, between the older conception of fate and modern contingency. Jameson, *The Antinomies of Realism*.
78. Nicholas Rance argues that the sensation novel challenged 'the doctrine of free will and the moralism which the doctrine underpins', and that it did so in formal ways, particularly in character. This is why reviewers were so outraged by many of Collins's heroines.
79. Lonoff has argued that Collins took his 'out-and-out villains and Jezebels' from a 'long tradition of melodrama'. While this is true, I think Collins is self-consciously experimenting with melodrama's expression of social limits. Lonof, *Wilkie Collins*, p. 86.
80. Joyce, *Democratic Subjects*. Indeed, Rohan McWilliam argues, 'Communication in the nineteenth-century public sphere was governed by ways of seeing derived from melodrama.' McWilliam, 'Melodrama and the Historians', p. 58.
81. Although the sensation novel draws upon a melodramatic tradition, Linda Hughes argues that it also reworks the meaning of melodrama by relocating this tension into the heroine herself and making her represent moral ambivalence rather than moral certainty. She suggests that the

sensation novel strains romance and realism to their limits. Other critics, like Christopher GoGwilt, see sensation novels as precursors of modernism, arguing that *The Moonstone*, for instance, captures the modernist alienation of modern life. GoGwilt, *The Fiction of Geopolitics*. Many critics have agreed that the sub-genre of the sensation novel was generated not by novelists but by reviewers. Jonathan Loesberg argues that the sensation novel 'was as much a creation of the literary journals who grouped the novels together as it was of the novels themselves'. Loesberg, 'The Ideology of Narrative Form', p. 116. Similarly, Richard Nemesvari insists that reviewers used the sensation novel as a means to solidify and define the realist novel: 'the sensation fiction controversy served not to oppose a new genre to a preexisting one, but rather that the formulation of "the sensational" was an essential, constitutive strategy which reified "the realistic" in ways which had been unachievable before'. Nemesvari, 'Judged by a Purely Literary Standard', p. 17.
82. Moreover, it suggests the extent to which narratives of the real rely upon melodrama. Although melodrama, romance and modernism are often posed as foils to realism, Fredric Jameson argues that they are actually inherent to the realist novel. He identifies the work of realism as the gradual dissolving and attenuation of the archetypes of melodrama and other older genres in favour of more modernist tendencies. Realism, thus, is not a codified genre but rather a form made up of generic and modal oppositions.
83. Collins, *Basil*, XXXVII.
84. Ibid.
85. Collins, *The Law and the Lady*.
86. The sensation novel sits on the border between these kinds of narratives described by Rader. On the one hand, many sensation novels are blatantly referential, as they draw upon true crime stories that readers would recognise. On the other hand, they are not limited by journalists' claim to facticity; they adapt and at times exaggerate true crime stories.

Chapter 4

Israel Zangwill, or 'The Jewish Dickens': Representing Minority Communities in Novel and Newspaper

In 1888, the Orthodox English-language newspaper, *The Jewish Standard*, published a series of articles called 'Jews in Fiction' that looked critically at Jewish characters across British literature.[1] The series began with Sir Walter Scott's *Isaac of York*, then featured Benjamin Disraeli's *Sidonia* and George Eliot's *Daniel Deronda*. After finding fault with Dickens's Fagin and Riah, the April 20th column conjectured what it might look like for Charles Dickens to use his 'magician's wand' to write a more nuanced treatment of everyday Jewish life:

> How he would have reveled in the description of the ostentation, the generosity, the kindliness, the harshness, the thousand and one contradictions to be found in our fellow-Jews and Jewesses. [How he would have treated] . . . Mr and Mrs Z –, with all their children – how they went to synagogue Saturday morning gorgeously attired . . . Then Dickens would describe how the family go home to luncheon, a better luncheon most likely than on weekdays, because paterfamilias is at home. How our author would revel over the fried fish and various orthodox dainties.[2]

This column envisions Jewish life through the lens of an outside observer; it focuses more on Dickens's imagined pleasure in the spectacle, how he would 'revel' in the scene, than on the characters themselves. And importantly, the column chooses Saturday for this everyday rendering, which situates religious practice at the centre of Jewish life. The writer then exclaims, 'Shade of Dickens! would that your mantle might descend on my shoulders, that I might worthily describe all this.' He elevates Dickens's writing into a 'magician's wand' and calls upon the novelist to give him the same powers, treating Dickens as an otherworldly power rather than a writer of social fiction. The irony is, of course, that the writer has already described this scene, but as the imagined Dickens.[3]

This article from *The Jewish Standard* dramatises the pressure of external Jewish stereotypes on the self-conception of the nineteenth-century Anglo-Jewish community. In the very act of portraying this community, the columnist negates the act by calling upon Dickens to make the anonymous columnist a worthy narrator for depicting Jewish life. On one level, this negation seems to present an ambivalence about the potential for Jewish authorship and literature. Yet the writer also imagines Dickens relishing the material culture of Anglo-Jewish life and finds charm in its difference from the English everyday: the synagogue, the fried fish and the 'orthodox dainties'. The writer in effect calls for a Jewish Dickens, a persona that is both English and Jewish, one that also seems magical in nature and made possible by a non-Jewish power.

The 'Jews in Fiction' series imagines Jewish newspapers as gate-keepers for the portrayal of the Jewish community, a gaze that is persistently directed outwards toward mainstream English readers. This vision of an alternate Dickens raises questions about representation, aesthetics and nineteenth-century conceptions about national community. The article is invested not only in a construction of a Jewish community but also in the portrayal of that Jewish community to an English public. This construes the Anglo-Jewish community as both particular and universal, requiring particularised representation in a 'Jewish novel' while also situating them within the larger English public. The imaginary Dickens is both outside and inside; he must have access to the Jewish community but still remain the novelist synonymous with Britishness.[4] This article is an instance of the representative problems encountered by Anglo-Jewish communities and their writers, as they negotiated national, racial and ethnic stereotypes that irrevocably located them outside of the liberal nation. As Amanda Anderson has argued, the Jewish question unveiled the limitations of nineteenth-century liberal thought, since it 'typically asks whether and how the particularity of the Jew might be assimilated to, or alternately accommodated by, a project conceived as modern in its pretensions to universality'.[5]

At the time of this column, Israel Zangwill – the man who would later be called the 'Jewish Dickens'[6] – was subeditor of *The Jewish Standard* and writing a satirical column about Anglo-Jewish life called 'Morour and Charouseth'. Born to Jewish immigrants from tsarist Russia in 1864 and raised in London's East End, Zangwill became famous for his realistic depiction of Jewish East End life in his 1892 novel, *Children of the Ghetto: A Study of a Peculiar People*, which was long considered the foremost representation of Jewish life in both Great Britain and the United States.[7] Rather than dealing with specific news stories reworked by novelists, as did the previous chapters, this chapter argues that Zangwill's *Children of the Ghetto* adapts English generic practices to cultivate a hybrid representation of Jewish experience. He depicts discursive practices of meaning making surrounding what was often considered a racial identity; in doing so, he juxtaposes a range of storytelling practices, including novelistic realism, the newspaper, Yiddish-language oral storytelling, communal newspaper reading and fin de siècle aestheticism.

In particular, Zangwill reworks George Eliot's novelistic approaches to community in *Children of the Ghetto* and problematises the role of the newspaper in developing nineteenth-century Anglo-Jewish identity. Whereas *Daniel Deronda* concludes with Daniel's yearning towards Palestine and an independent nation for his people, *Children of the Ghetto* valorises the Jewish ghetto as a place of nostalgic attachment, a setting that fosters affective attachment based not in anonymous nationalist imaginings but in lived and material communal proximity. Acknowledging the centrality of newspapers to the Jewish community, Zangwill dramatises the limitations of newspaper form and function to the cultivation of a broader affective attachment. Franco Moretti has argued that *Daniel Deronda*'s failure signified the decline of the *Bildungsroman* as the symbolic form of modernity, and Mikhal Dekel similarly argues that Eliot grapples with the impossibility of creating a male Jewish *Bildungsroman* hero. Zangwill, however, reinvigorates the *Bildungsroman* and novelistic realism by hybridising it with practices of Yiddish storytelling. This hybrid realist form enables Zangwill to convey the complex feelings that the Jewish ghetto elicits in his main character, Esther Ansell, both when she resides there and later returns. Its value is set up in opposition to the newspaper and its production, which necessitates routinised labour and desensitisation to the passage of time. The newspaper looks like a form conducive to affective connections only when it is repurposed by readers and made to work more like a novel.

In analysing *Children of the Ghetto*, Joseph Childers insists that individuals tend to identify more or less with a particular discourse and identity; they cannot be both English and Jewish since these identities and discourses are in tension. He concludes,

> At the very least, this novel makes it apparent that participating in both Englishness and Jewishness may increase the number of possible subject positions available to the characters of this book, but there is no place of compromise that allows a subject to be completely English *and* completely Jewish.[8]

I argue, however, that Zangwill's novel problematises compartmentalised Jewish and English identities in order to foster a tenuous intermingling. Even as Zangwill feels a wistful nostalgia for the ineffable idea of an authentic Jewishness, his novel advocates for what approximates a hybrid of the two identities in the figure of Esther, who grows up in the East End, becomes socialised in the West End and later emigrates to America. She is a figure of the melting pot, a metaphor Zangwill later coins, rather than one-dimensionally Jewish or English. By fostering this hybrid, acculturated identity, Zangwill challenges approaches to Jewishness that understand them solely through late-nineteenth century racial pseudosciences.[9] While he calls the newspaper the 'ever-whirling wheel' of Sisyphus, the *Children of the Ghetto* offers a generic melting pot that captures the experience of being part of a fractured community within a larger liberal nation.

While the prior chapters centred largely on the newspaper, this chapter expands its focus to argue that *Children of the Ghetto* draws upon a range of generic and cultural traditions, including the newspaper, the Bible, Yiddish literature, oral storytelling practices, fairy tales and other British novels. In the first section of this chapter, I will consider the treatment of realism in the novel as a representative modality for the Anglo-Jewish community, as writers felt compelled to speak to but also on behalf of their community to a wider readership. I argue that *Children of the Ghetto* both explicitly and formally dialogues with George Eliot's works; it engages not only with *Daniel Deronda* but also with *Middlemarch* by paralleling Raphael Leon with Eliot's Will Ladislaw. While *Daniel Deronda* evacuates the importance of the newspaper to the Anglo-Jewish community and instead valorises ethnic nationalism, *Children of the Ghetto* draws more upon *Middlemarch* in exploring the use of *Bildung* in constructing nationalism. In the end, rather than valorising Raphael and Ladislaw, *Children of the Ghetto* recentres its attention on Esther Ansell, who taps into not just the *Bildungsroman* but also into biblical and Jewish traditions. She is both of the ghetto and outside it, thereby offering another kind of cosmopolitanism. When Zangwill's contemporaries admired the realism of *Children of the Ghetto*, they meant its sociological observations of the Jewish East End. This chapter argues, however, that the realism of the novel actually consists of an intermingling of various discursive, cultural and literary modes in capturing the hybrid Anglo-Jewish experience.

Representing the Jewish Community

Children of the Ghetto (1892) features a heroine who grows up in the Jewish East End and later becomes the author of a realist novel, *Mordecai Josephs*.[10] Esther Ansell's novel, written under the name of Edward Armitage, presents a searing portrayal of the materialist, status-oriented Jewish West End, where she lives after being adopted by a wealthy Jewish family. Esther's novel is widely criticised by characters for realistically and caustically portraying West End Anglo-Jews rather than providing an idealised assimilated portrait.[11] By situating a realist writer at the core of his novel, Zangwill interrogates the representative and aesthetic dilemma at the centre of the Anglo-Jewish condition: how to represent a necessarily hybrid identity and write for both a Jewish audience and a less sympathetic general English audience.

Characters in *Children of the Ghetto* reject realism because it presents a self-critical portrayal of the middle-class Jewish community. They highlight the importance of tailoring such representations for the benefit of the non-Jewish reader. When discussing *Mordecai Josephs* over dinner at the Goldsmiths' house (where the adopted Esther now lives), characters point out that 'Yes, the book's true enough,' but add, '[I]t's plain treachery and disloyalty, this putting of weapons into the hands of our enemies.'[12] Although alive to the realism of the portrayal of the novel, these characters perceive the novel as disloyal because of its refusal to advocate for the Jewish community against broader social stereotypes. What they want is an idealised anglicised portrayal of the Anglo-Jewish community, one that glosses over the cultural differences that distinguish them (particularly more recent immigrants) from their English counterparts. These characters approach Esther's novel through the perspective of an English reader, and they filter their reactions through the mainstream reader's imagined responses. As a result, they consider the use of Yiddish – 'jargon' – in the novel to be an attack on the community's efforts to intermingle with English society. Although the characters are willing to joke about their community within closed doors, even in terms of stereotypes, it becomes reprehensible when a member of the community sounds as though he or she is confirming the stereotype for outsiders. Indeed, when it emerges that Esther is the author of the despised novel, she is accused of treachery.

Painter and aesthete Sidney Graham (whose real name is Abrahams) responds to this pressure by abandoning his identification with a Jewish community. Sidney explains to Esther why he refuses to call himself a Jew:

> [I]t would be a lie to say I was. It would be to produce a false impression. The conception of a Jew in the mind of the average Christian is a mixture of Fagin, Shylock, Rothschild and the caricatures of the American comic papers. I am certainly not like that, and I'm not going to tell a lie and say I am. In conversation always think of your audience. It takes two to make a truth. If an honest man told an old lady he was an atheist, that would be a lie, for to her it would mean he was a dissolute reprobate.[13]

Sidney articulates himself within the framework of English literature and American journalism, abandoning his Jewish identity in order to conform to mainstream assumptions. At the core of Sidney's argument is an aesthetic denial of reality outside art. He rejects the external truth of a Jewish community and suggests that identity is only socially constructed. He also questions the capacity of realism to represent mimetically in the midst of social and literary tropes. As I will explain later in this chapter, Zangwill's project of novelistic realism rejects this ambivalent aestheticism and asserts the tangible reality of Anglo-Jewish life.

In depicting these different responses to realism, Zangwill dramatises the representational question central to the Anglo-Jewish situation, both politically and aesthetically. The situation of Anglo-Jews differed dramatically from their European counterparts, regarded with 'anti-Semitism of tolerance'.[14] By the late nineteenth century, Anglo-Jews had won new political rights and could serve in Parliament. However, they often felt pressured to represent themselves as a unified religious community consistent with the lifestyle of the English middle class.[15] The literary trope of Shylock, the unyielding usurer, persisted in popular depictions of the Jewish community. Jewish artists could not represent their community without taking into account the competing representations produced by non-Jewish writers. Anglo-Jews were generally interpreted and understood via the discursive construct of 'the Jew'. More strikingly than ever, 'the Jew' was overdetermined: infinitely wealthy and yet abjectly poor; refusing to assimilate and yet assuming a false English identity; cosmopolitan and trivial; alien and yet almost overly familiar.[16]

Anglo-Jewish writers persistently articulated the difficulties posed by these stereotypes, which by the end of the century were bolstered by the purported evidence of pseudosciences.[17] Jewish difference was reformulated through the lens of race. This meant that signs of difference were legible on the body as 'a kind of visible proof text'.[18] As Susan David Bernstein points out, Jewish identity took on the contradictory meanings of race, nationality, culture and religion.

At the core of this representational question is George Eliot's novel *Daniel Deronda*, an influence that *Children of the Ghetto* directly acknowledges. Over Christmas dinner, the Goldsmiths and their guests argue over Eliot's representation of 'the Jewish character'. Raphael Leon criticises Eliot's simplistic treatment: 'We are made either angels or devils. On the one hand, Lessing and George Eliot, on the other, the stock dramatist and novelist with their low-comedy villain.'[19] Mrs Goldsmith, however, is not fully convinced by Raphael, and Cissy Levine responds, 'They are the only writers who have ever understood it.' Sidney has the final word, when he claims that *Mordecai Josephs* has more 'actuality' in it than *Daniel Deronda*, even though he faults *Mordecai Josephs* for its propensity to moralise. Raphael and Sidney are not alone in their criticism of Eliot's Jewish characters; countless readers have faulted Eliot for the simplicity and shallowness of Daniel Deronda, Mordecai and Mirah.[20] Most famously, F. R. Leavis understood *Daniel Deronda* as two novels – the English plot and the Jewish plot – and advocated rescuing Gwendolen Harleth by excising the entire Deronda plot from Eliot's novel.[21] Other critics have understood the two parts of the novel as an opposition between realism and romance. Sarah Gates argues that George Eliot's *Daniel Deronda* demonstrates a loss of faith in the realist form.[22] Franco Moretti attributes what he perceives to be the flaws of the novel to the failure of the *Bildungsroman*, which he argues can no longer function as a symbolic form in the 'age of the masses'.[23] For Mikhal Dekel, *Daniel Deronda* shows the impossibility of creating a late-nineteenth century male Jewish *Bildungsroman* hero, since as soon as the Jew becomes particular he or she is also excluded from the British nation.[24]

Although Raphael and Sidney criticise *Daniel Deronda*'s accuracy, *Children of the Ghetto* explicitly dialogues with Eliot's novel, partly as a means to consider generic and formal approaches to representing the Anglo-Jewish community, one that privileges novelistic realism. The structure and characters in the novel loosely parallel *Daniel Deronda*, but with significant alterations so as to invoke and rework Eliot's book. Deronda's character is spread across Esther and Raphael in order to suggest the limitations of Raphael's middle-class and idealist perspective of Jewish life in contrast to the far more materialist experience of Esther.[25] Mordecai's character is omitted from the novel, and his absence is emphasised by the allusion in the title of Esther's novel, *Mordecai Josephs*.[26] Mordecai and his desire to pass on communal feelings through poetry are transformed into a materialist, realist novel written by a disaffected woman.

While *Children of the Ghetto* explicitly dialogues with Eliot's *Daniel Deronda*, I think it also responds to patterns of community developed in *Middlemarch*, foregrounding a subplot in Eliot's novel: Will Ladislaw's work as a newspaper editor. Ladislaw's editing of *The Pioneer* is refigured in Raphael Leon's work for *The Flag of Judah*, as both characters seek to allow for communal reforms but run into obstacles posed by the structural limitations of the newspaper. For Moretti, Ladislaw's failure of 'vocation' shows that the *Bildungsroman* can no longer achieve synthesis, sidelining this struggle to the periphery of the novel; by contrast, Daniel Deronda is able to achieve happiness and 'fulfil his vocation by firmly rooting himself in Jewish culture'.[27] Rather than being based in the everyday, as is *Middlemarch*, *Daniel Deronda* valorises 'a sense of identity and belonging, an ethnic continuity that transcends the individual'.[28] *Children of the Ghetto* restores the contradictions inherent to the *Bildung* to the Anglo-Jewish experience, amplifying that contradiction in the sense that the individual feels isolated not simply by one community but from multiple communities; moreover, the individual's desire for self-actualisation also mirrors the Anglo-Jewish community's desire for definition and inclusion. Late-nineteenth century Jewish newspapers reveal the problems of representing a coherent Anglo-Jewish population while simultaneously folding them into a larger national public. *Daniel Deronda* mostly evacuates the importance of the newspaper to the Anglo-Jewish community, but Israel Zangwill re-locates it to the core of the Jewish question in *Children of the Ghetto*.

Newspapers in *Children of the Ghetto* and *Middlemarch*

The Anglo-Jewish press partly emerged through the influence of early nineteenth-century Evangelical newspapers, as well as a European press fostered by the Jewish Enlightenment, or the Haskalah, a movement that sought to modernise Jewish life and encourage integration into contemporary society.[29] In 1841, Jacob Franklin founded the *Voice of Jacob*, which later merged with the *Jewish Chronicle*. These newspapers took on anti-Semitic representations of Jews in other newspapers and allowed for the creation of a Jewish public sphere. Like *The Times* and other mainstream, licensed newspapers, the *Jewish Chronicle* had to adapt to a new media environment after the 'taxes on knowledge' were abolished. The 1860s saw the founding of a penny newspaper, the *Jewish Recorder*, which imitated the style of the *Daily Telegraph*.

The *Jewish Chronicle* influenced middle-class Jews' perspectives on recent immigrants, deprecating religious and cultural practices that separated them from English-born Jews. In an 1881 editorial, the newspaper wrote,

> Our fair frame is bound up with theirs; the outside world is not capable of making minute discriminations between Jew and Jew, and forms its opinion of Jews in general as much, if not more, from them than from the anglicised portion of the community.[30]

The newspaper campaigned for anglicisation of recent Jewish immigrants and advocated for the use of philanthropy as a means to assimilate them into English society.[31] Indeed, *The Jewish Chronicle* provided a medium between British Jews and larger society, 'interpreting matters of Jewish interest (as understood by the paper), and offering a response that amounted, virtually, to the view of Anglo-Jewry'.[32] *The Jewish Chronicle* sought to maintain a consensual position and did not leave much room for dissension; it was pro-assimilationist and advocated centralised institutions to anglicise new immigrants in the East End. The newspaper 'helped [readers] to orientate themselves as Jews in relation to the dominant culture'.[33] The identity forged here, as well as elsewhere, relied upon readers' sense of how the non-Jewish perceived them and positioned the newspaper as the spokesperson for the community. *The Jewish Chronicle* thus indirectly reinforced the liminal position of Anglo-Jews, as it advocated for denationalisation of recent immigrants as a means of eradicating Jewish stereotypes.

Aside from *The Jewish Chronicle*, there were a variety of newspapers targeting different subsections of the Anglo-Jewish population. These other publications included the *Jewish Recorder*; the *Jewish World*, which covered East End crime in detail; and the *Jewish Standard*, an English-language Orthodox newspaper that Zangwill subedited. In addition to these publications, there were also Yiddish-language and Hebrew-language newspapers. While the more mainstream newspapers sought to accommodate readers and recent immigrants to English culture and also represent the Jewish community to the larger public, Jewish print culture more broadly was politically, culturally and linguistically diverse. In a sense, the *Jewish Chronicle*'s goal of depicting a unified and Anglicised Jewish community was at odds with the linguistic and cultural diversity of the population as a whole. This highlights the difficulty newspapers faced in constructing a sense of community when the lived experience of Anglo-Jews was far more varied and complex.

In light of the formative influence of the Jewish press on Anglo-Jewish identity, the newspaper's absence is marked in *Daniel Deronda*. When newspapers do appear, they are associated with tyrannical and repressive male characters, and a flawed universalism that lacks affective ties to individuals. For instance, Henleigh Mallinger Grandcourt's newspaper reading is associated with his aristocratic and passive 'inheritance of land'.[34]

> He glanced over the best newspaper columns on these topics [Schleswig-Holstein, the policy of Bismarck, trade-unions, household suffrage, or even the last commercial panic], and his views on them can hardly be said to have wanted breadth, since he embraced all Germans, all commercial men, and all voters liable to use the wrong kind of soap, under the general epithet of 'brutes'; but he took no action on these much agitated questions beyond looking from under his eyelids at any man who mentioned them, and retaining a silence which served to shake the opinions of timid thinkers.[35]

Grandcourt's newspaper reading reaffirms his sense of power and status, and it does so by eliminating nuance in favour of gross generalisation. Grandcourt positions himself as a weary and cynical man, who looks from under his eyelids in boredom and exerts his power through silence. But the narrator's searing satire undoes Grandcourt's cynical, all-knowing pose, emphasising that Grandcourt reads about the ridiculous and absurdly trivial, i.e. the voters who prefer the wrong kind of soap, as well as topics so general that they are evacuated of meaning. Grandcourt's practice of abstraction, drawn from the newspaper, invokes categories so general that they lack analytical meaning and instead simply suggest his social status. The only other major instance of a newspaper is in reference to Mirah's father. When Mrs Meyrick suggests the possibility of advertising in the newspaper for Mirah's lost mother and brother, Mirah is terrified: 'she was convinced that her father would see it – he saw everything in the papers'.[36] In both instances, the newspaper is associated with masculine authority and practices of surveillance.

Children of the Ghetto reveals a far more complex relationship between Jewish identity and the newspaper press, and in doing so, it dialogues with *Middlemarch* more than *Daniel Deronda*. Both *Children of the Ghetto* and *Middlemarch* include subplots about young male characters seeking to reform their communities by way of the newspaper. Raphael's experience at *The Flag of Judah* mirrors that of Will Ladislaw at the *Pioneer*, despite the fact that one is a provincial newspaper from the 1830s and the other an English-language Jewish newspaper of the 1880s. Both Raphael and Ladislaw aspire to inculcate reflective practices in their readers; Raphael seeks to cultivate a more self-conscious engagement with Judaism, and Ladislaw treats the newspaper as a soapbox for political reform in the lead up to the Reform Act 1832. The classical *Bildungsroman* – a la *Wilhelm Meister* – has been relegated in both novels to a subplot. In his analysis of the *Bildungsroman* and its nation-building impetus, Tobias Boes identifies 'cosmopolitan remainders' that disrupt nationalism's aim for closure in these novels.[37] Ladislaw and Raphael struggle to confront their relationship to community and nation via the newspaper, only to find that this impetus is at odds with their desires for self-actualisation.

Both Ladislaw and Raphael at first approach their respective newspapers with rose-tinted glasses. Ladislaw stands on the margins of Middlemarch society but envisions the newspaper as a means of getting closer to Dorothea, embedding himself in the community and facilitating local involvement in national reform. In this sense, Ladislaw sees the newspaper as a means of situating Middlemarch firmly within the vision of a democratising nation. Ladislaw is a rootless cosmopolitan who shares Deronda's ambiguous family history. Indeed, in 1958, Jerome Beaty argued that Ladislaw was an earlier version of Deronda.[38] Ladislaw's mother was an actress and his grandfather a pawnbroker, or as Mr Bulstrode suggests, 'a grafting ... Jew pawnbroker'. His grandmother – Mr Casaubon's Aunt Julia – was disinherited by her family for running away with a Polish musician. Ladislaw is an exile from Middlemarch's provincial community, a 'cosmopolitan remainder' by the very fact of his birth.

Ladislaw's experience reveals the newspaper to be both at the centre and the margins of communal identity making, particularly in the 1830s before its professionalisation. In a sense, the labour of editor metaphorises Ladislaw's ambiguous class position. When Mr Brooke decides to run for Parliament, he purchases the *Pioneer* and asks Ladislaw to take up the editorship. Middlemarch, however, is shocked that Ladislaw would take up the position of newspaper editor when he is related to a respectable member of the gentry. Chettam is outraged: 'What a character for anybody with decent connections to show himself in! – one of those newspaper fellows!'[39] Mr Hawley wonders whether 'this young fellow is some loose fish from London', to which Mr Hackbutt confirms, 'He is said to be of foreign extraction.'[40] Mr Hawley responds, 'I know the sort ... some emissary. He'll begin with flourishing about the Rights of Man and end with murdering a wench. That's the style.'[41] They associate him with the urban cosmopolitanism of London, conjecturing that he might be a foreign diplomat, a spy, a radical or a criminal. His place on the newspaper and his potentially Jewish background associate him with global forces; he represents the threat of modernity in this provincial community. The newspaper is an organ for potential political reform and nation building, yet it also firmly locates Ladislaw on the outskirts of communal respectability.

Yet Ladislaw envisions his role on the *Pioneer* as a means to bring political consciousness to Middlemarch, 'becoming more and more conscious of the national struggle for ... Reform'.[42] Ladislaw claims to speak on behalf of 'the people', a national abstraction in conflict with the gentry and Middlemarch's provincial order. He speaks of 'the country' and 'the public temper', figuring the reform movement as an unconscious but shared spirit that transcends individual voter or candidate. He argues that the election of the Reform candidate, the buffoonish Mr Brooke, will further the desires of 'the people'. He explains to Lydgate: '[Mr Brooke is] good enough for the occasion: when the people have made up their mind as they are making it up now, they don't want a man – they only want a vote.'[43] Mr Brooke's individual qualities – his lack of perception as well as his status as gentry – are neutralised in this logic. Ladislaw continues to use this rhetoric while editor of the *Pioneer*: He compares 'the public temper' to a 'cometary heat', saying 'things will grow and ripen as if it were a comet year'. He conceives of reform as a natural outcome of the People's innate desire for democratic representation. When Mr Brooke expresses reluctance to change 'the balance of the constitution', Ladislaw responds: 'But that is what the country wants. . . . And as to contending for a reform short of that, it is like asking for a bit of an avalanche which has already begun to thunder.'[44]

Ladislaw speaks on behalf of 'the country' as a voice for 'liberty and progress in general'.[45] His notion of 'the people' relies upon a shared contemporaneous spirit, a natural outgrowth that cannot be contravened, like a comet or an avalanche. Ladislaw offers a counterpoint to Trollope's Quintus Slide, as he holds onto a political conception of 'the people' independent of the marketplace and envisions the *Pioneer* as a reflection of this larger public sentiment. And contrary to *Daniel Deronda*, this is not a nationalism built upon shared ethnicity but rather one linked up with democratic ideals of representation and individual rights. This lofty ideal, however, quickly runs up against the partisan divisions and personal acrimony in Middlemarch. Rather than the voice of 'the people', Ladislaw becomes an 'understrapper of Brooke's', caught up within the rigid partisan structures of provincial politics and newspapers. Ladislaw forced to grapple with the distance between his abstract ideals and the material reality of Middlemarch society.[46]

Children of the Ghetto takes place nearly 50 years after *Middlemarch*, and Raphael Leon occupies a very different world from Will Ladislaw. Yet he too fails to self-actualise as the inexperienced editor of a new English-language Orthodox London newspaper called, *The Flag of Judah*. Raphael is something of a privileged, upper middle-class Don Quixote who knows nothing about newspapers, yet he takes on the editorship in the naïve belief that he can use it as a platform for philanthropy and Hebrew scholarship. The experience, however, proves to be a Sisyphean task, as Raphael runs up against the founding committee of the newspaper. *The Flag of Judah* was founded under the auspices of the Co-operative Kosher Society to advise its readers on kosher eating. Raphael's more lofty visions of Judaism's potential come into conflict with the committee's desire to give direction on the enactment of everyday Jewish rituals. The committee is outraged by Raphael's first leader, in which he portrays Judaism as 'a happy human compromise between an empty unpractical spiritualism and a choked-up over-practical formalism'.[47] The narrator characterises Raphael's approach as a 'rather unusual combination of rigid orthodoxy with a high spiritual tone'.[48] The committee wants the newspaper to be intensely Orthodox – which for them means discussing questions of food and ceremony – and they are worried that Raphael's leader will portray them as reform. They insist that

> the paper was founded to inculcate the inspection of cheese, the better supervision of the sale of meat, the construction of ladies' baths, and all the principles of true Judaism . . . and there's not one word about these things, but a great deal about spirituality and the significance of the ritual.[49]

Raphael envisions his leader as a means to rethink readers' relationship to Judaism; by contrast, the committee wants what amounts to a conduct book in order to retain a sense of religious stasis. They are disturbed by any detail that might not seem to reinforce proper Jewish living, anything that might encourage reflection and doubt. They fault Raphael for his use of Latin quotations, when he could easily have used Hebrew, and his assumption that every story in the Talmud may not be literally true.

In many ways, Raphael's editorial troubles mirror Zangwill's own experiences as a writer for late-Victorian Jewish newspapers.[50] While working for *The Jewish Standard*, Zangwill wrote a weekly column called 'Marour and Charouseth', which contained impressions of everyday encounters. Zangwill did not sign his own name but called himself the 'Marshallik', which means a jesting master of ceremonies. The column is generically varied – it contains retellings of biblical stories, rumours, news of interest and even poetry. Indeed, it mirrors the formal richness of *Children of the Ghetto* in its movement from one style to another. However, in one column Zangwill rants about his 'ignorant' readers:

> Alas! I was not long left in possession of my illusions. The inconceivable stupidity and impertinence to which my unselfish efforts for the good of the community have exposed me, are beyond all belief. My best-meant intentions have been distorted by foolish reflectors; my satire has been turned topsy-turvy . . . I have done a great deal of journalistic work in my time; but I can honestly say that the best work of this sort I have ever done has been done in *The Jewish Standard*. And I am very sorry for it.[51]

Zangwill characterises the work of journalism as one of misunderstanding and distortion. Readers fail to recognise satire and turn his writing upside down. He thus describes his newspaper career as one of disillusionment, as he comes to acknowledge the distance between his work and the capacity of his readers.

The labour involved in publishing a newspaper wears down Raphael's ethical and affective ties to his community. When first asked to be the editor of the newspaper Raphael worries about his ethical obligations to the various Jewish organisations and committees, since he would not be able to attend and report on every single meeting. The committee of the newspaper reassures him that such conscientiousness is not necessary: 'Oh, that will be all right. . . . We will leave out one and people will think it is unimportant. We are bringing out a paper for our own ends, not to report the speeches of busybodies.'[52] The subeditor Little Sampson adds that they can use the meeting agendas to pretend that they attended; otherwise they can 'fill up' a paper with reports of London, provincial sermons and foreign news. Sampson assures Raphael that

> There is never any dearth of foreign news. I translate a thing from the Italian *Vessillo Israelitico*, and the *Israelitische Nieuwsbode* copies it from us; *Der Israelit* then translates it into German, whence it gets into Hebrew, in *Hamagid*, thence into *L'Univers Israélite*, of Paris, and thence into the *American Hebrew*. When I see it in American, not having to translate it, it strikes me as fresh, and so I transfer it bodily to our columns, whence it gets translated into Italian, and so the merry-go-round goes eternally on.[53]

Little Sampson copies news reports from around the world to fill up the newspaper. As an experienced editor, he insists (and rightly so) that this liberal practice of borrowing and copying is a regular practice in journalism. This practice grows out of the pressure to generate news on a regular basis. It muddies the distinctions between foreign, national and communal, as 'foreign news' gets repurposed in each new publication. Little Sampson uses the words 'translate', 'copy', 'gets into' and 'transfer' interchangeably. This merry-go-round makes it impossible to trace the origin of the story, which in turn means that editors and readers are unable to evaluate its relevance to their own readership. Indeed, Little Sampson even admits to republishing the same story twice, for once he reads it in 'American', 'it strikes [him] as fresh'. This description transforms the newspaper from a linear, calendrical publication into a global cycle of borrowing and translation.

And it is no accident that Little Sampson is said to move foreign stories 'bodily' into his columns; *Children of the Ghetto* dramatises the bodily and mental labour involved in the everyday work of the newspaper. Raphael works sixteen hours per day, and he takes only one evening off per week. This laborious routine contributes to Raphael's loss of affective and moral integrity over the course of the novel, as he becomes lost within the timelessness of the newspaper's regular operation. When Joseph Strelitski comes to the newspaper office to enquire about Esther, who has been turned out of the Goldsmiths' house, Raphael initially can think only of news and copy. Strelitski's concern about Esther, however, snaps Raphael out of his journalistic coma into 'a sudden upwelling of tumultuous feeling'. The narrator explains:

> The ever-whirling wheel of journalism – that modern realization of the labour of Sisyphus – had carried him round without giving him even time to remember that time was flying. Day had slipped into week and week into month, without his moving an inch from his groove in search of the girl whose unhappiness was yet always at the back of his thoughts. Now he was shaken with astonished self-reproach at his having allowed her to drift perhaps irretrievably beyond his ken.[54]

The newspaper's regularity, and Raphael's production of that regularity, dulls his sensibility to the passage of time. Raphael is no longer connected to a community outside the newspaper office; rather, he is caught up within the newspaper's system of operations, which makes every day seem like the last. In this sense, the serial publication of the newspaper begins to look more like the film *Groundhog Day* than a linear temporal progression that enables an imagined community.

Eliot's *The Pioneer* and Zangwill's *The Flag of Judah* involve their editors in the mundane labour and petty politics of newspaper publishing. Both instances suggest the complications of speaking on behalf of a larger public via the newspaper. Ladislaw imagines himself to be forwarding the natural inclination of 'the people', while Raphael wants to reinvigorate readers' Jewishness; yet they both find themselves ground down by the production of the newspaper and the petty responses of their readers and colleagues. Both Raphael and Ladislaw grapple with conflict between the systemic operations of the newspaper and its imagined capacity to foster communal attachment. Zangwill's satirical depiction of *The Flag of Judah* demystifies the process of newspaper production and suggests its failure to represent the diverse and fractured Anglo-Jewish community.

Jewish Storytelling in Novelistic Form

Raphael's failed attempt to rejuvenate Judaism in *The Flag of Judah* stands in contrast to the methods practiced by Mordecai and his protégé, Daniel Deronda, in George Eliot's 1876 novel. Although Raphael resembles Deronda in temperament and background, *Children of the Ghetto* suggests the limitations of Deronda's and Mordecai's visions of an ethnic nationalism. Instead, Esther Ansell – who has experience living in both the anglicised middle-class community as well as among the more recent immigrants of Petticoat Lane and the Jewish East End – offers a more tangible model of nineteenth-century Jewish subjectivity than Mordecai's emphasis on Hebrew poetry and communal transmission.

As I have already suggested, the mainstream Anglo-Jewish press would have been a major source of communal cohesion for its readers (other than, of course, the synagogue). Yet, *Daniel Deronda* is almost completely devoid of newspapers. Instead, Cynthia Scheinberg has identified Deronda's propensity towards a 'poetic energy' as another source of national imagining, one that allows him to invigorate the everyday with a sense of the transcendent. For instance, when Deronda takes a walk in the Jewish neighbourhoods of London, the narrator writes:

> To glory in a prophetic vision of knowledge covering the earth, is an easier exercise of believing imagination than to see its beginning in newspaper placards, starting at you from a bridge beyond the corn-fields; and it might well happen to most of us dainty people that we were in the thick of the battle of Armageddon without being aware of anything more than the annoyance of a little explosive smoke and struggling in the ground immediately about us. It lay in Deronda's nature usually to contemn the feeble, fastidious sympathy which shrinks from the broad life of mankind . . . [55]

Drawing upon this excerpt, Scheinberg argues that Eliot offers an implicit connection between the treatment of Jewish identity in the novel and a heightened aesthetic sensibility. She traces Deronda's poetic sensibility – one that allows him to connect 'the everyday, actual, and often vulgar aspects of life to the great larger heroic, moral, and aesthetic questions of existence'[56] – to nineteenth-century arguments that lyric language is rooted in Jewish poetry and prophecy.[57] Deronda requires a heightened sensitivity and imagination to glimpse the hidden possibilities behind the newspaper placards and smoke. In this excerpt, the newspaper becomes yet another obscuring distraction from the 'prophetic' potential of the Jewish people.

Indeed, Mordecai's transmissions to both Jacob and Daniel are based in Hebrew poetry, much of it his own. Although deeply aware of the spiritual distance between the Cohens and himself, Mordecai seeks to educate young Jacob Cohen through poetic recitation. Mordecai sympathises with Jacob not because he is a specific individual but because of an 'idealising affection which merges the qualities of the individual child in the glory of childhood and the possibilities of a long future'.[58] Jacob's appeal dwells in both his particularity and his universality, suggesting the linkage between the mundane every day and the universal. Mordecai regularly distracts Jacob with a toy or some other mechanical device, at which point Mordecai recites a Hebrew poem and asks Jacob to repeat the lines after him. Mordecai invests these recitations with 'the fervor befitting a sacred occasion'.[59] Because he recites his own poetry, he is able to convey a sense of personal feeling in the moment of exchange. There is a sense of experience transmitted through this oral process of recitation lacking in print. And yet Mordecai imagines the action through the metaphor of print: 'The boy will get them engraved within him', thought Mordecai, 'it is a way of printing'.[60] He adds later, 'My words may rule him some day. Their meaning may flash out on him. It is so with a nation – after many days.'[61] To an external observer, this scene could look largely mundane: a consumptive man reciting poetry to a boy in a London pawnshop. But this mundane scene contains for Mordecai the possibility of a national past and future. The seemingly rote act of memorisation and recitation allows for Mordecai's feelings to influence Jacob and his relationship to Judaism. It also transmits meaning through Hebrew poetry to a future generation.

And yet, even as Scheinberg emphasises the importance of 'poetic energy' to *Daniel Deronda*, other critics warn against aligning Mordecai's vision of Jewish nationalism and racial destiny with Deronda. Amanda Anderson argues, for instance, that Deronda infuses Mordecai's nationalist fervour with his values for rational deliberation and civic pluralism. She calls this practice 'his conception of transformative dialogical interaction between races and nations, one that involves a delicate dialectic of detachment and engagement'.[62] This is why it is crucial that Deronda is raised an Englishman but is ethnically Jewish – in this sense, he is rather like the imagined 'Jewish Dickens' with which I began this chapter. Anderson argues that, via Daniel Deronda, Eliot 'advocates a form of cultural self-understanding that might best be called reflective dialogism: her model for one's relation to history, culture, and nationality becomes passionate argumentation, not simple embrace'.[63] This requires the ability to disengage from cultural norms and to see one's community with a reflective distance, a 'cultivated partiality' that allows for a 'reflective return to the cultural origins that one can no longer inhabit in any unthinking manner'.[64]

Esther's dialogical relationship to the Jewish East End reflects Anderson's account of Deronda's 'cultivated partiality' rather than Scheinberg's notion of Mordecai's 'poetic energy'. In part, *Children of the Ghetto* distributes Deronda's qualities across both Esther and Raphael. Esther is endowed with a unique reflective capacity as a result of her childhood in the Jewish East End. By contrast, Raphael shares Deronda's privileged upper-middle class background (he is born to rich parents and attends Harrow and Oxford) as well as Deronda's excessive sympathy. Anderson argues that Deronda's sympathy 'jeopardises his own moral development',[65] and this is similarly true for Raphael. When he participates in the foundation of the Holy Land League in Whitechapel, he admits to being 'moved to tears by enthusiasm'.[66] He is so overcome that he vibrates in response to others' suffering. Esther, however, is capable of detachment partly because of her familiarity with a broader swath of Anglo-Jewish society. She reflects later on in the novel:

> It seemed a part of the irony of things and the paradox of fate that Raphael, who had never known cold or hunger, should be so keenly sensitive to the sufferings of others, while she who had known both had come to regard them with philosophical tolerance.[67]

Esther shows here a reflective sympathy for Raphael in her capacity to recognise the intensity with which he experiences others' suffering; yet she also shows the role that her experience has played in helping her 'come to regard' suffering with tolerance. Esther's mingled attachment and detachment from her East End and West End worlds protects her from the incapacitating influence of excessive sensitivity to suffering.

Whereas Scheinberg argues that Deronda's alternation between detachment and engagement derives from his 'poetic energy', Esther is more grounded in material reality and the transcendent meanings and affective attachments that can be part of that materiality. Esther alternates between disgust for the 'wretchedness' of the East End and a sense of its 'intangible affinities' with her soul.[68] Despite his idealism, Raphael's newspaper gets bogged down in the mundane every day; Esther, on the contrary, is emotionally attuned to the spiritual meaningfulness of the apparently superficial. Zangwill privileges the female novelist over the male journalist, partly as a means to reflect on the form of his own Anglo-Jewish novel. *Children of the Ghetto* is able to convey Esther's alternating emotions towards the ghetto because of the possibilities of contrast and juxtaposition in novelistic realism. Like Esther and the experience of her *Bildung*, *Children of the Ghetto* presents apparently contradictory forms, discourses and experiences in one canvas. In particular, Zangwill's realist novel draws upon Yiddish literary and linguistic practices to develop a sense of community attentive to the unique pressures and changes experience by nineteenth-century Anglo-Jews.

'He Spoke Yiddish, Grown a Child Again': Yiddish Storytelling and Novelistic Form

In 1888, the American Jewish Publication Society conscripted Zangwill to write a 'Jewish *Robert Elsmere*'. Mrs Humphrey Ward's 1888 novel, *Robert Elsmere*, took Great Britain by storm; it features an Oxford clergyman who undergoes a spiritual transformation as he begins to doubt the doctrines of the Anglican Church. Zangwill's subsequent conscription suggests the extent to which the Jewish population, in both Britain and America, felt excluded, even alienated, by Ward's story of individual spiritual awakening. The result of this conscription was *Children of the Ghetto*, and yet it little resembles *Robert Elsmere*. Rather than focusing on individual rebirth and a life dedicated to charity, Zangwill depicts a whole cross-section of the Jewish East End and the erosion of their practices as a result of mainstream cultural pressure.[69] In the first half of the novel, Zangwill abandons the form of the *Bildungsroman* and depicts a loose web of characters yoked together by geography and community. The second half returns to the *Bildungsroman*, as we trace Esther's maturation as she leaves the East End for a West End education. This hybrid format intermingles English and Jewish storytelling practices, drawing upon a novelistic realism that represents the life of the mundane but also allows for a dialogical relationship between apparently contradictory discourses, languages and genres.

In a handwritten author's note on the novel's typescript, Zangwill wrote, '[T]he aim of this book is less to tell a story than to paint a community.'[70] This description aptly reflects the first half of the novel, which lacks a central narrative and is crowded with minor characters. Contemporary reviewers criticised Zangwill for his weak narrative even as they praised his realistic depiction of the East End. This first half, I argue, disavows a more linear narrative and instead paints the web of affective connections that link the East End community. In doing so, it mingles practices of Yiddish storytelling with the traditions of literary realism and sociological observation.

The novel itself, although written in English, echoes the conversational and associative structure of Yiddish. Many Yiddish texts are structured around what Benjamin Harshav calls 'associative talking', the most obvious example being *Tevye the Dairyman*:

> In this mode the small units of language and thematic motifs are not strung on a narrative string and made subordinate to the unfolding of plot or an architectonic structure, but are relatively independent and episodic ... At the same time, such a unit clashes with and relates to its discontinuous neighbors, creating mutual reinforcement, semantic density, stylistic play, and irony in this tangle.[71]

Harshav's account of associative talking reflects the structure of the first half of *Children of the Ghetto*, which tells a series of episodic stories that generate affect and irony through play, contrast and repetition. The novel moves associatively from one character sketch to another, following not a linear temporal trajectory but instead associations generated by connection or geographical proximity. For instance, the novel introduces the Belcovitch family when the young Esther's soup spills and leaks through the cracks of the floor into the apartment below. The reader follows the dribbling soup downwards to find Becky Belcovitch surrounded by her undesirable suitors. In this example, the narrative movement is not linear but spatial; the reader moves from one room to another in the small London tenement house. The scenes occur simultaneously, creating a sense of a shared East End community.[72]

This associative organisation mimics Zangwill's *Jewish Standard* column, 'Morour and Charouseth', which plays with generic boundaries to satirise middle-class Anglo-Jewish society, as contrasted with the hardship faced by immigrant Anglo-Jews. The column mingles reports about tensions between the mainstream Jewish community and socialists with humorous stories whose punch lines toy with Yiddish. In one column, he even playfully conceals his identity by speaking in third person about an author named 'I. Zangwill', an author so unknown to the public, he says, his name is constantly misremembered in the media. The column is divided up into short sections, and Zangwill develops his satire through contrast and contextualisation. He uses a similar practice of ironic juxtaposition in *Children of the Ghetto*, particularly a contrast of London geography and social class. This associative form relies on linguistic double meaning and the playful movement between different voices, genres and languages to convey satire, and it generates affective power when Zangwill uses it for his novel.

This associative structure is facilitated with the use of and reference to multiple languages in the novel, specifically English, Yiddish, Hebrew and sometimes even German. This stylistic interplay is contrasted to the homogenising force of modernisation and assimilation facing Jewish immigrant community, and also to the separatist preservation of an authentic Jewish culture. Zangwill highlights his characters' multilingualism, whether through the use of Yiddish or Hebrew words, or through syntactical signals in English. When the original publisher asked him to include a glossary of Yiddish terms, Zangwill resisted and acceded only for later editions, but still refused to write it himself. This resistance suggests that he thought that Yiddish could not be properly translated into English, and that the novel was playing with the possibilities and impossibilities of translation. According to Rochelson, Zangwill 'reproduces, celebrates and undercuts' Jewish forms of discourse. She writes, 'Yet when Yiddish is translated into English in the novel it is done literally, rather than idiomatically, making a rich and vital language sound archaic, almost reminiscent of the King James Version, yet allowing the occasional intrusion of vulgar metaphor.'[73] I contend that Zangwill represents Yiddish and Hebrew in three different modes: used directly and accompanied with a translation, used directly without a translation, or represented as that language yet written in English. Zangwill carefully signals when characters switch between languages, even if these languages are represented in the English language. As Rochelson mentions, Yiddish is often depicted in an English that uses Yiddish grammar and syntax. This English-Yiddish hybrid alienates both Yiddish and English-speaking readers, since the Yiddish grammar makes the dialogue sound archaic, particularly through the word 'thou'. I would add that Zangwill's refusal to anglicise Yiddish grammar in these English translations highlights the untranslatability of certain elements of language. Yiddish functions differently from Hebrew and English in the lived experience of Yiddish speakers. Zangwill maintains this linguistic contextualisation by retaining grammatical signifiers of each language. For instance, he mimics the characters' shift in languages by making changes in syntax: when Reb Shemuel's wife worries that he gave away all their money, she says:

> 'For thy salvation do I hope, O Lord,' murmured Simcha piously in Hebrew, adding excitedly in English, 'Ah, you'll kill yourself, Shemuel. . . . Here, you fool, you've been and done a fine thing this time! All your silver was in the coat you've given away!'
> 'Was it?' said Reb Shemuel, startled. Then the tranquil look returned to his brown eyes. 'No, I took it all out before I gave away the coat.'
> 'God be thanked!' said Simcha fervently in Yiddish. 'Where is it? I want a few shillings for grocery.'
> 'I gave it away before, I tell you!' . . .
> 'Here's the end of the week coming,' she sobbed, 'and I shall have no fish for *Shabbos*.'
> 'Do not blaspheme!' said Reb Shemuel, tugging a little angrily at his venerable beard. 'The Holy One, blessed be He, will provide for our *Shabbos*.'
> Simcha made a sceptical mouth, knowing that it was she and nobody else whose economies would provide for the due celebration of the Sabbath.[74]

Zangwill flags for the reader Simcha's shifts between Yiddish, Hebrew and English; but he also reflects the change in both the syntax of the sentences and the emotion Simcha expresses. Although the entire dialogue is conveyed in English, Zangwill mimics the syntax of Hebrew and Yiddish, so that Simcha's statements are missing articles and other grammatical elements necessary to English – for instance, 'a few shillings for grocery'. Simcha uses Hebrew to appeal to God on Reb Shemuel's behalf, then shifts to English to nag her husband, and finally falls into Yiddish to express her misplaced relief about the lost money. Similarly, Reb Shemuel's syntax suggests that he is speaking in Hebrew when he remonstrates his wife. The shift in language reveals a tension between the husband's idealising stance that God will provide and the wife's practical sense that *she* must provide. At one level, Simcha's shift between languages signals the tensions between supporting her family in the western world and still adhering to what Zangwill considers to be a separatist vision of Judaism, embodied particularly in Reb Shemuel. However, the movement between languages also signifies the everyday reality of most Yiddish speakers in this period.

Yiddish is traditionally a language used by multilingual speakers and contains various linguistic and historical references; it uses German, Hebrew and Aramaic components, although it also contains other influences. Harshav highlights that often two source languages clash in one utterance to create irony and multi-level meanings: 'This is what Yiddish is all about: the individual words may be very simple but their interaction – involving pieces of texts and divergent languages and cultural situations rather than mere lexical denotations – makes it rich, ironic, plurisignifying.'[75] The mingling of source languages and their traditional association enables a far richer means of expression than can be conveyed by a single language: 'In Yiddish, one can speak several languages in the same sentence.'[76] This spatial and stylistic juxtaposition mimics the imbrication of English, Yiddish, Hebrew and even implied German in the novel. In this excerpt, Reb Shemuel and Simcha speak several languages implied by the text's English, and their linguistic shifts signal additional levels of meaning to the reader.

This linguistic intermingling also suggests the complex relationship between language and nation. The novel reveals the sacrifice of meaning and community as multilingualism is replaced by the monolingual dominance of English language and culture, so often advocated by *The Jewish Chronicle*. It also examines the generational divide between the older generation of immigrants and their children, who seek to break from Jewish practices to become more English. The new generation accepts external portrayals of Jews as archaic and premodern, and they abandon many of the practices of Orthodox Judaism and the use of Yiddish. For them, they must become English in order to become modern. While a child, Esther becomes aware of her Jewish background because of the 'scoffing rhymes of Christian children', but she feels her Englishness more intensely:

> But far more vividly did she realise that she was an English girl; far keener than her pride in Judas Maccabaeus was her pride in Nelson and Wellington; she rejoiced to find that her ancestors had always beaten the French from the days of Cressy and Poictiers to the days of Waterloo, that Alfred the Great was the wisest of kings, and that Englishmen dominated the world and had planted colonies in every corner of it, that the English language was the noblest in the world and men speaking it had invented railway trains, steamships, telegraphs, and everything worth inventing. Esther absorbed these ideas from the school reading books.[77]

The language of this passage is full of superlatives, mimicking the patriotic and nationalist lessons Esther would have learned in school. Esther recognises her ancestors in medieval English battles rather than in Eastern Europe or Jerusalem. Zangwill ironically suggests the imaginary quality of historical and national background.

Through Esther, the novel depicts the competition between English modes of instruction and those of immigrant culture. Characters like Esther's aunt Malka oppose the English schools because 'it's English, not Judaism, they teach them in that godless school'.[78] Jacob Childers cites this same passage to argue the irreconcilable nature of English and Jewish identity in the novel. According to Childers, Esther can choose only one or the other, and here she chooses Englishness. However, this scene happens during Esther's childhood early in the novel, and her feelings about Judaism and Englishness transform over the course of the two halves. Although the novel satirises young Esther's schooled faith in her Englishness, it also satirises Malka's blind resistance to English influence. Zangwill contrasts Esther's schooling with another form of cultural and ideological storytelling: her father's stories.

Esther's father, Moses, offers an alternative history of the Jewish people through the practice of oral storytelling. Moses tells his children a story in Yiddish 'about the Emperor Nicholas [that] is not to be found in the official histories of Russia'.[79] In this story, Nicholas I threatens to drive the Jews out of their homes. When offers of reparation fail, the 'Masters of Cabalah' call upon the spirits of Abraham, Isaac, Jacob and Elijah the prophet, who 'took Nicholas the Emperor out of his warm bed and whipped him so soundly that he yelled for mercy'.[80] Nicholas finally annuls the edict for the Jews' expulsion after being repeatedly 'drubbed' by the spirits. By contradicting the official history of Russia, this story gives Moses and his children a sense of empowerment and historical longevity in the face of state power and cultural homogeneity. Zangwill's realist novel is able to convey the impression of an oral story and thereby preserve Jewish culture through novelistic realism. Sander Gilman has claimed that languages such as Yiddish and Hebrew marked Jews as different from mainstream Europe and therefore construed them as suspect; Zangwill, however, suggests the importance of Yiddish in allowing the Anglo-Jewish community to retain their identity while also participating in an English culture, in a way not possible in Jewish newspapers.

As characters become monolingual and anglicised, they are unable to participate in the world of the older generation. Zangwill depicts the poignancy of this generational gap by representing unspoken thought in the form of dialogue. The Hyamses, a family composed of an elderly couple and their adult children, show the misconceptions and communicative failures that inhibit their mutual understanding. Daniel Hyams knows he cannot marry the woman he loves because he must support his aging parents and thus refuses to attend a bar mitzvah where he would be forced to see his would be lover. But he disguises his reasons for declining the invitation when talking to his parents, claiming he simply has a conflicting obligation.

> It was a superfluous lie for so silent a man.
> 'He doesn't like to be seen with us,' Beenah Hyams thought. But she was silent.
> 'He has never forgiven my putting him to the fancy goods,' thought Mendel Hyams when told. But he was silent.[81]

Displayed as a dialogue, these misunderstandings are particularly moving because they are apparent only to the reader and are not communicated between characters. The inner isolation is expressed exactly at these moments when plot and spoken dialogue are suspended. This scene sets up a contrast to the richness of the Yiddish, Hebrew and English interaction between Reb Shemuel and Simcha. Where these characters communicate richly in ways that even they cannot understand, the Hyamses are silenced by their generational, linguistic and cultural difference.

Similarly, Esther's older brother, Benjamin Ansell, loses access to his personal history and childhood memories through his conversion to monolingualism. Forgetting most of his Yiddish while away at school, he is unable to communicate with the older members of his family when he visits home. Benjamin's inability to speak or understand Yiddish separates him from his family and from memories of his childhood, which the novel highlights as so important to Esther's formation as a character and a novelist herself: '[Yiddish] struck vague notes of old outgrown associations but called up no definite images'.[82] Father and son are also separated by a gulf in their understanding of Benjamin's future ambitions: Moses wants him to be a rabbi, and Benjamin wants to be an English writer more famous than Charles Dickens. When Benjamin becomes ill, he and his father are unable to communicate until Benjamin nears death and reverts to a childish state: 'He spoke Yiddish, grown a child again. Moses's face lit up with joy. His eldest born had returned to intelligibility. There was hope still then.'[83] As Rochelson has argued in her essay, 'Language, Gender, and Ethnic Anxiety', Benjamin is to some extent a double for Zangwill in his ambitions to become an author. However, Zangwill eliminates Benjamin because of his separation from his Jewish background, whereas Esther represents a fuller version of the Anglo-Jewish writer in her inability to forget her East End past. Very much a product of the realist novel, Esther is able to absorb both perspectives and discourses, that of the East End and that of the Jewish bourgeoisie.

But rather than creating a competition between these two nationalist and discursive outlooks, the novel fosters a hybridisation of them. The first half of the novel is an associative web of character sketches, cultural habits, and linguistic and stylistic mingling. It draws upon nineteenth-century sociological approaches to representative realism in its keen eye for everyday detail, but it moves into a more intimate register through the associative storytelling style and the affective ties fostered between characters. This web gives way to a *Bildungsroman* in the second half of the novel, as it traces Esther's maturation and her experience of crossing between the Jewish East and West Ends.

Esther, the *Bildungsroman* and Aestheticism

The novel's second half is organised as a *Bildungsroman* and follows Esther's growing cultural awareness and her cultivation of an affective connection to her East End roots. Zangwill mingles the *Bildungsroman* with other generic and discursive traditions in this part of the novel. By choosing a heroine, Zangwill taps into traditional ideas surrounding Jewish femininity and alludes to the Bible's Book of Esther. Not only is Esther Ansell a realist novelist, but she also becomes a potential saviour of her people.[84] Zangwill also draws upon and reworks practices in the newly emerging Yiddish literary tradition, including the common plot involving a character that travels from the *shtetl* to a big city to become enlightened. The plot echoes the homecoming that always follows in this Yiddish literary tradition, when the enlightened young Jewish man returns home and feels nostalgia for an imagined authentic Jewish space. *Children of the Ghetto* infuses novelistic realism with other discursive and generic practices so as to make Esther a mythic and modern heroine in her cultural intermingling. This hybridised novel weaves together these traditions in a way that reflects the experiences of the Anglo-Jewish community. The hybridising capacity of the novel is set up in opposition to the newspaper: it does not promise a unified and anglicised community, as does *The Jewish Chronicle*, nor does it get lost in the midst of the newspaper's systemic pressures, as does Raphael.

Zangwill borrows the use of symbolism in Yiddish storytelling throughout the novel, but none are so prominent as the name, Esther Ansell. Many of the characters have meaningful names – including Moses and Malka – and Esther's name, with its reference to the Bible's Book of Esther, imbues her with a mythic quality. The novel foregrounds this connection since many of the central scenes happen during Purim. In the Book of Esther, Xerxes, king of Persia, chooses Esther as a replacement for his disobedient wife. Concealing her Jewish background, Esther lives separately from the Jewish people until a prince convinces the king to order the destruction of all unassimilated Jews. At the behest of her cousin Mordecai, Esther reveals her background and implores the king to retract the order and kill the prince instead. Zangwill's decision to name Esther after this story is key in directing the reader what to take away from the novel. The biblical Esther does not immediately accept her duty to save the Jewish people; rather, she hesitates about her connection to a people she has not lived with for years. When her cousin Mordecai urges her to seek out the king, Esther responds that she has not been summoned by the king and that to go to the inner court without being summoned means almost certain death: 'I have not been summoned to go to the king these thirty days.'[85] As Michael Fox suggests, Esther initially worries more about her own wellbeing and feels that she could escape death since her Jewish identity is unknown.

Esther Ansell experiences a similar alienation from her Jewish background. As a child, she reads the New Testament and is drawn to the figure of Christ. As an adult, she lives with a middle-class family who yearns 'to approximate as much as possible to John Bull without merging in him'.[86] When Raphael celebrates the Jewish people, Esther responds, 'I was born in the Ghetto, and when you talk of the mission of Israel, silent, sardonic laughter goes through me as I think of the squalor and the misery.'[87] Dislocated from their childhood homes, both Esthers assimilate to the ways of their new abodes; in this case, Esther Ansell's residence at the Goldsmiths parallels Esther's position in Xerxes's household. However, just as the biblical Esther saves her people, Zangwill positions Esther Ansell as the potential hope for the Jewish people: that is, the hope of a modernised Jewish culture that neither assimilates nor separates. Like the biblical Esther, who is better able to serve her people as Jew *and* as Persian queen, Esther is importantly both English and Jewish. She is no longer part of the East End ghetto but has transcended it and returns to it as someone who is both inside and outside. When she returns to the ghetto after living with the Goldsmiths, she is at first shocked by both the lifestyle and poverty she encounters, but her feelings change as she spends more time there:

> [S]omething in Esther's breast seemed to stir with a strange sense of kinship. The race instinct awoke to consciousness of itself. Dulled by contact with cultured Jews, transformed almost to repulsion by the spectacle of the coarsely prosperous, it leaped into life at the appeal of squalor and misery.[88]

The East End imparts to Esther a sense of the community that has been lost by the middle-class West End Jews. Yet it is important that Esther is not quite one of them when she returns to the ghetto. Esther, for Zangwill, is the union of the East End immigrant and the educated bourgeoisie; she is representative of the potential for the Jewish community to become modernised and anglicised while still remaining Jewish. Unlike Daniel Deronda, who grew up English and subsequently discovers his Jewishness, Esther grows up in the East End and returns after she has developed a wider perspective.

Not only is *Children of the Ghetto* a reworking of the Book of Esther, it also borrows from tropes in Yiddish literature, particularly what Dan Miron has identified as the nostalgic idealisation of the shtctl. The mid to late nineteenth century saw what has been considered the birth of modern Yiddish literature. According to Miron, the archetypal fable of the native's return home can be found as early as eighteenth-century Yiddish dramas and was later featured in the nineteenth-century Yiddish novel.[89] Miron's examples include the first Yiddish novel, Aksenfeld's *Dos shterntikhl* ('The Headband') and the Hebrew novel, *Ayit tsavua* ('The Hypocrite'). In 1865, Sholem Yankev Abramovitsh published a Yiddish story called 'Dos vintshfingerl' ('The Magic Ring'), which was influenced by this homecoming trope and features a plot similar to the second half of Zangwill's novel. The main character leaves the shtetl to become an enlightened modern, and he returns at the end of the novel only to face the disintegration of his home. In 'The Magic Ring', the homecoming scene is darkened because no one recognises the hero. Abramovitsh later expanded this story into a longer work, which would span from the late 1830s to the early 1880s and 'throw light on Jewish life and discuss the most important problems we face nowadays'.[90]

Zangwill takes on this literary trope in the final pages of Esther's return to the East End. When Esther first returns to Whitechapel, her nostalgia is disrupted by a sense of change and foreignness: 'There was a sense of blankness in the wanderer's heart, of unfamiliarity in the midst of familiarity. What had she in common with all this mean wretchedness, with this semi-barbarous breed of beings?'[91] Her childhood memories of Whitechapel conflict with the poverty and dirt she faces as an adult returning to the neighbourhood. It also disrupts the timelessness that her nostalgia requires: 'She studies the posters and the shop-windows – all seemed as of yore. And yet here and there the hand of Time had traced new inscriptions.'[92] Esther's return both reinforces and disrupts the timeless ideal of the shtetl, in this case Whitechapel. And yet at the end of the paragraph, we're told that the ghetto itself has stayed the same while Esther has changed:

> It was hard to realise that Time's wheel had been whirling on, fashioning her to a woman; that, while she had been living and learning and seeing the manners of men and the cities, the Ghetto, unaffected by her experienced, had gone on in the same narrow rut. A new generation of children had arisen to suffer and sport in room of the old, and that was all.[93]

The depiction presents a divided portrayal of the East End, simultaneously timeless and changing. Zangwill echoes the division of Yiddish literature in its treatment of the shtetl, seeing it as a premodern lifestyle that needs to be supplanted by modernity and yet at the same time idealising it as a timeless space of authentic Jewishness. Miron has traced this tradition in his book, *The Image of the Shtetl*, which he calls the 'love-hate' relationship of Yiddish writers with the folkloric element of Eastern European Jewry.

Esther's confused nostalgia invokes the nostalgia that opens *Children of the Ghetto*. Zangwill begins with what he calls a 'Proem' that openly links the 'London Ghetto' with the shtetls of eastern Europe in a flowery, present-tense style notably different from the prose in the rest of the novel. Zangwill suggests that the everyday poverty and sordidness of the London Ghetto removes it from genres other than realism, but then he yokes this realism with romance:

> Natheless, this London Ghetto of ours is a region where, amid uncleanness and squalor, the rose of romance blows yet a little longer in the raw air of English reality; a world which hides beneath its stony and unlovely surface an inner world of dreams, fantastic and poetic as the mirage of the Orient where they were woven, of superstitions grotesque as the cathedral gargoyles of the Dark Ages in which they had birth.[94]

Zangwill crafts a romantic nostalgia around the idea of a London Jewish ghetto. Here, Zangwill suggests the persistence of an authentic

Jewish identity in the midst of pressures to assimilate. Zangwill metaphorically asks us to look for something in addition to the realism presented in the novel, an element of romance and fantasy.[95] Yiddish writers used realism as a means to convey modern values to what they perceived to be a poorly educated, separatist Jewish majority. The new literary movement emerged from the Haskalah, or the Jewish Enlightenment, which sought to modernise and liberalise the Jewish communities across Europe. Although Yiddish and realism were seen as aesthetically inferior, Yiddish writers strategically wrote in these modes as a way to reach a broader Jewish reading public. And yet in the midst of this realism, the writers articulated a romantic nostalgia for an imagined authentic Jewish shtetl.[96] To a certain extent, this divided approach to realism appears in Zangwill's novel in ways that mirror the budding Yiddish literary tradition. However, Zangwill also locates in nostalgia a protection against complete assimilation and anglicisation. Even as he represents the harsh reality of immigrant life in the East End, he highlights the sentimental importance of their daily material life. The novel invests the mundane and the material with mythic meaning, whether it be Esther's name or the 'pots and pans' of the East End tenement houses.

Esther's mythic quality, moreover, offers a counterexample to the alienated aesthetics of Sidney Graham. Whereas Esther is able to hybridise Englishness and Jewishness, Sidney abandons the Jewish people in his pursuit of an art isolated from the real world. The danger posed by this perspective is the loss of the Jewish people through assimilation (which Sidney predicts will happen). Towards the end of the novel, Zangwill deflects Sidney's position by marrying him off to Raphael's sister Addie, a resolution that is dissatisfying in its use of marriage to quash a larger political and social question. Years later, the figure of the Jewish aesthete arises more materially in the figure of Leopold Barstein, who reappears in stories throughout *Ghetto Comedies*, a series of stories published by Zangwill in 1907. The stories trace Barstein's development over the course of the collection, bringing him to a stronger awareness of his Jewish origin. In the first story, 'The Jewish Trinity', Barstein is described as 'a Jewish native of that thriving British centre, [who] should have felt proud and happy. But Barstein was young and a sculptor, fresh from the Paris schools and Salon triumphs. He had long parted company with Jews and Judaism'.[97] When Barstein meets a Jewish MP whom he believes to be a devout Jew, 'a racial pride he had not known latent in him surged up through all his cosmopolitanism'.[98] He comes to this internal awakening through imagining Sir Asher carefully enacting Jewish rituals: 'There came to him a touch of new and artistic interest in this prosy, provincial ex-M.P., who, environed by powdered footmen, sat at the end of his glittering dinner-table uttering the language of the ancient prophets.'[99] His awakening remains despite his discovery that the MP is a hypocrite and embodies what Barstein calls the 'Jewish trinity': 'The Briton, the Jew, and the anti-Semite – three-in-one and one-in-three.'[100] Barstein is inspired to leave off his cosmopolitan and aesthetic perspective in order to become an artist in touch with a Judaic past and a Zionist future. Zangwill suggests that even as the aesthete claims to disown the real, he is actually abandoning his community.

Zangwill published *Children of the Ghetto* just two years after Oscar Wilde's *The Picture of Dorian Gray*. One of the preeminent works of aestheticism, *Dorian Gray* provides a stark, one-dimensional portrayal of the East End and its Jewish population. *Children of the Ghetto* is in part a response to Wilde's only novel, and it centrally thematises aestheticism in order to suggest its shortfalls in relation to the problems encountered by Anglo-Jews. Sidney Graham inverts Dorian Gray's double life. Dorian Gray lives his respectable existence in London's West End and then revels in debauchery in the East. He begins his double life when he visits a playhouse in the East End, where he meets a Jewish stage manager and a young Jewish actress with whom he falls in love and later abandons. The Jewish stage manager, Isaacs, is a stock melodramatic figure and is described by Dorian as a 'monster' and as the most 'hideous Jew, in the most amazing waistcoat I ever beheld in my life'.[101] In contrast, Sidney seeks the West End for his second life, where he denies his Jewish heritage and is engaged to a Christian woman unbeknownst to his family.[102]

In Wilde's novel, the East End becomes a place of sexual license, where Dorian Gray can conceal his identity.[103] Whereas for Wilde the East End is an indeterminate space of sexual freedom, Zangwill highlights and idealises the centrality of the space of the ghetto to retaining Jewish identity in a modern world. His 'Proem' compares the London ghetto to 'the olden Ghetto of the Eternal City'. Despite the ethnic variety of Victorian London's East End, Zangwill portrays it as a 'Ghetto' that is almost purely Jewish. Rather than being disrupted by non-Jewish residents, the London ghetto passes away because its Jewish inhabitants slowly leave and disperse into a greater world: 'For better or for worse, or for both, the Ghetto will be gradually abandoned, till at last it becomes only a swarming place for the poor and the ignorant, huddling together for social warmth'.[104] Zangwill's proem expresses nostalgia for the separate life that he imagines the

London ghetto formerly offered and increasingly does not. He misses the days when the Jewish upper class lived in the same neighbourhood as 'aristocrats of the Ghetto' and gave charity in 'the same Oriental, unscientific, informal spirit in which the *Dayanim*, those cadis of the East End, administered justice'.[105] Zangwill imagines a past when England's Jewish community was self-supportive and coherent within the East End, when the wealthy happily supported the poor, in contrast to the realist text that then follows this proem. Zangwill importantly here mingles nostalgia and realism. Zangwill responds to Wilde's murky depiction of the East End with an idealised version of his own that, as I already suggested, draws upon eastern European representations of the shtetl. This juxtaposition suggests the limited perspective of the cosmopolitan aesthete and Wilde's relegation of the East End and the Jews to melodrama and crime.

The implicit dialogue of the novel with *Dorian Gray* also contrasts the novel's East End with its frequent depiction in the press. When Dorian visits the theatre in the East End, Isaacs – whom Dorian calls, 'the horrid old Jew' – asks if he writes for the newspapers. The implication is that Isaacs associates outsiders with newspaper writers and reviewers; it highlights that Dorian does not belong in the East End theatre. Dorian, meanwhile, is enchanted by Sybil Vane's acting because it is so completely at odds with the poverty surrounding her: as he says to Hallward and Lord Henry, 'I left her in the forest of Arden; I shall find her in an orchard in Verona.' Not long after he jilts her, however, Dorian learns that the morning papers have reported her death. Because no one at the theatre knows his name, Dorian is able to disappear and disengage from any connection to the 'scandal'. Sibyl Vane's death, as reported by the morning newspapers, becomes a tragedy for Dorian, 'like a wonderful ending to a wonderful play', and Lord Henry treats her as a disposable girl who lacks uniqueness unto herself. He assures Dorian that her death saved them from an 'absolute failure' of a marriage and that

> If you had married this girl, you would have been wretched. . . . [S]he would have soon found out that you were absolutely indifferent to her. And when a woman finds that out about her husband, she either becomes dowdy, or wears very smart bonnets that some other woman's husband has to pay for.

Sibyl seems no longer to have the value of human life but rather to be one among many such girls from the East End. The result of this scene is Dorian's realisation that her death 'does not affect [him] as it should'. In *The Picture of Dorian Gray*, the impersonal report of Sybil Vane's death affirms her distance from Dorian, both in her relegation to a melodramatic East End and her association with art and make-believe. Dorian appreciates the aesthetic quality of his brief relationship with Sibyl but does not feel pain over her loss.

Conclusion

When contemporary critics claimed to admire the realism in the novel, they meant its sociological observations of the East End. In her introduction to the Wayne State University edition of the novel, Rochelson traces the range of contemporary responses to the novel, with positive reviews lauding its realistic rendering of the ghetto and for providing a 'panopticon of Ghetto scenes and characters'.[106] However, the realism in the novel goes beyond this encyclopaedic account of everyday immigrant life, as it fosters a stylistic intermingling of various discourses, forms and genres. In doing so, *Children of the Ghetto* contrasts itself with Raphael's newspaper and with Jewish newspapers more broadly. The novel offers a broader critique of Jewish newspapers, particularly *The Jewish Chronicle;* by advocating for the anglicisation of recent immigrants, newspapers like the *Chronicle* inadvertently render themselves outsiders, requiring an erosion of their Jewish particularity before they can become part of the national public. Newspapers like *The Jewish Chronicle* require the appearance of communal coherence when speaking to English readers.

In *Children of the Ghetto*, Raphael is unable to reflect seriously on Judaism and the state of the Anglo-Jewish population; the pressures of the continual demands to make copy mean that he becomes more preoccupied with filling up the columns than in reflecting on what he is writing. Part of the problem is the system of operations of the newspaper; even an idealist like Raphael gets caught up in the machine of the newspaper, worn down by the labour of regularly producing a newspaper. Previously so sensitive to others' suffering, Raphael finds 'his moral fibre . . . weakened. It is impossible to touch print and not be defiled'.[107] Raphael is burdened by the pressure to generate news and to satisfy the demands of his collaborators and readers; by contrast, Esther's novel is her own. When Raphael rereads

Mordecai Josephs after learning of her authorship, he is amazed he failed to recognise her in it before:

> Esther stared at him from every page. She was the heroine of her own book; yes, and the hero, too, for he was but another side of herself translated into the masculine. The whole book was Esther, the whole Esther and nothing but Esther, for even the satirical descriptions were but the revolt of Esther's soul against means and evil things.[108]

This realistic and satirical depiction of middle-class Anglo-Jewish life is deeply embedded in Esther's character. Her relationship to this minority community and the British nation more broadly is one based on her individual experience and development over the course of the novel. Not only does her novel require its readers to critique the superficiality of middle-class society, it also startles Raphael into suddenly realising the depth of his affection for Esther. Her novel thus generates reflective and affective feeling at both the communal and intimate registers.

However, Esther's example is not the only alternative to *The Flag of Judah* in Zangwill's novel: another is, ironically, the *London Journal*. *The London Journal; and Weekly Record of Literature, Science and Art* (1845–1928) was a penny illustrated fiction weekly central to the development of a nineteenth-century cheap press. Originally edited by George W. M. Reynolds, the paper was known for publishing long serial melodramatic novels.[109] Zangwill's treatment of the *London Journal* does not focus on its production but rather its consumption, a scene of deeply affective intimacy between two marginalised female characters. While still a child, Esther befriends a girl who lives in a second-floor backroom of her family's tenement house; this girl, named Dutch Debby, is a social outcast disowned by her family for giving birth to a short-lived illegitimate child. Debby keeps old issues of the *London Journal* under her bed, and Esther and Debby become close friends by reading and rereading these issues together. As Debby explains to Esther, she used to pay a penny a week for the paper until she realised she had a bad memory and never remembered what she read. Instead of buying new issues, Debby reads the back issues and then starts over again every two weeks. Esther grows to relish these 'treasures' and regularly visits Debby to read aloud to her:

> ... in an atmosphere laden with whiffs from a neighbouring dairyman's stables, Esther lost herself in wild tales of passion and romance. She frequently read them aloud for the benefit of the sallow-faced

needle-woman, who had found romance square so sadly with the realities of her own existence. And so all a summer afternoon, Dutch Debby and Esther would be rapt away to a world of brave men and women, a world of fine linen and purple, of champagne and wickedness and cigarettes, a world where nobody worked or washed shirts, or was hungry or had holes in boots, a world utterly ignorant of Judaism and the heinousness of eating meat with butter.[110]

This reading ceremony creates a very different kind of community than the one described by Benedict Anderson. Although both Esther and Debby participate in a regular ceremony of reading, they do so with old newspapers and melodramatic stories distant from their immediate reality. By dreaming of a world beyond their own, they are able to share thoughts and feelings triggered by the content of their reading. It is a shared experience of fanciful reading and imagination that offers an escape from the hard realities of their lives but also is firmly grounded in that small room smelling of 'a neighboring dairyman's stables'. This reading practice remakes the *London Journal* into a repetitive ceremony capable of developing an emotional connection between two marginalised characters. The affective connection between Debby and Esther is so important that, when Esther returns to the East End at the end of the novel, the first familiar person she visits is Debby. This scene is in sharp contrast to Mordecai's recitation of Hebrew poetry for Jacob in *Daniel Deronda*. It is not a scene of reading led by a teacher but rather one that fosters a spontaneous sense of intimacy. Whereas Mordecai hopes that Jacob will remember the words and later attach more national feeling to them than he does now, the reading of the *London Journal* relies upon Debby's ability to forget and enter into yet another reading session with her young friend. Rather than a more expansive platform like the newspaper, or a transmission passed down from an authority to the next generation, *Children of the Ghetto* privileges these affective encounters between individual characters and multiplies them over the course of the novel. Esther's relationship with Debby is what continues to connect her to the ghetto, even after she has adapted to middle-class life. *Children of the Ghetto* is a compendium of mundane yet intimate, and at times mythic, encounters that add up to a sense of communal belonging.

Notes

1. Part of Chapter 4 first appeared as 'How to Write Yiddish in English, or Israel Zangwill and Multilingualism in *Children of the Ghetto*' in *Studies in the Novel*, Volume 46, Issue 3, 2014, pp. 215–334.

2. 'Jews in Fiction', p. 3.
3. This article was among a handful of late-nineteenth-century essays addressing depictions of Jews in fiction. For instance, in an 1886 edition of *The Jewish Chronicle*, Amy Levy published 'The Jew in Fiction', in which she criticised the binary approach to Jews in British fiction exemplified by Charles Dickens, who created the corrupt Fagin of *Oliver Twist* and the impossibly good Riah of *Our Mutual Friend*. Another such article includes Rabbi David Phillipson's 'The Jew in English Fiction', published in 1889. Bernstein, 'Mongrel Words', pp. 135–56.
4. In a loose sense, this alternate Dickens resembles George Eliot's Daniel Deronda, who, according to Cynthia Scheinberg, is both Jew and non-Jew and therefore equipped with the aesthetic capacity to hold onto both the 'decayed and sublime aspects of his Jewish experience'. Scheinberg, 'The beloved ideas made flesh', p. 822.
5. For more information on Judaism and the problems of liberalism, see Anderson, 'Trollope's Modernity', p. 39.
6. For instance, Zangwill is referred to as 'The Dickens of the Ghetto' in an 1895 column in *The San Francisco Call*. Elzas, 'Israel Zangwill – A Sketch'.
7. Zangwill was a transatlantic celebrity in his time and a political activist in the international Jewish community. He has, however, been largely marginalised in the twentieth and twenty-first centuries, arguably because of his opposition to a Jewish state in Palestine. Meri-Jane Rochelson has worked to correct misconceptions about Zangwill and to make him a central figure of Victorian studies. In her book, *A Jew in the Public Arena*, Rochelson critiques scholars like Joseph Udelson who reduce Zangwill's worldview to one divided between assimilation in the West and Orthodoxy elsewhere. She also critiques readings of Zangwill's tensions and inconsistencies as evidence of self-divided ambivalence about his Jewish identity. Instead, she sees these inconsistencies as a pragmatic response to lived situations: she writes, 'By insisting upon both sides of his identity, his Jewishness and his Englishness, Zangwill made choices that are indeed emblematic of those faced by many in his generation and later . . . '. In this chapter, I agree with Rochelson's reluctance to read Zangwill's tensions around Jewish and English identity as representative of some psychological ambivalence about his status as an Anglo-Jew. Instead, I consider the generic, formal and linguistic elements of Zangwill's relationship to identity, in particular his movement between Yiddish, Hebrew and English language and literary traditions. Rochelson, *A Jew in the Public Arena*, p. 4.
8. Childers, 'At Home in Empire', p. 222.
9. Bryan Cheyette and Nadia Valman have argued that the 1890s saw a rejection of Enlightenment values alongside a racial science that replaced universal brotherhood of man. Cheyette and Valman, 'Introduction', p. 12.

10. Zangwill uses a nostalgic realism in the novel's first book and *Bildung* in the second book as means of representing the problem of Jewish representation. Zangwill provides a central character, Esther Ansell, who is able to forge a sense of liberal individuality in tandem with her obligations to the Jewish community.
11. According to Rochelson, Esther's character and circumstances were loosely based on Amy Levy, who was criticised for her portrayal of the Jewish middle class in her 1888 novella, *Reuben Sachs*. Rochelson, 'A Religion of Pots and Pans', p. 121.
12. Zangwill, *Children of the Ghetto*, p. 329.
13. Ibid. p. 390.
14. Williams, 'The Anti-Semitism of Tolerance'.
15. For more information on this topic, see the following: Bar-Yosef and Valman, eds, *'The Jew' in Late-Victorian and Edwardian Culture*; Cheyette, 'Englishness and Extraterritoriality'; Cheyette, *Constructions of 'the Jew'*; and Cheyette and Valman, *Image of the Jew*.
16. Bar-Yosef, Introduction, *The Jew' in Late-Victorian and Edwardian Culture*, p. 3.
17. In her discussion of *Dracula*, Melissa Olson emphasises that Victorians used phrenology to justify anti-Semitic stereotypes. Phrenology and physiognomy were used to link Jewish features with hereditary criminality and degeneration. Olson, 'Dracula the Anti-Christ', p. 32.
18. As Daniel Boyarin, Daniel Itzkovitz and Ann Pelegrini write, 'Longstanding stereotypes of Jewish gender difference were thus translated into signs of racial difference.' Boyarin, Itzkovitz and Pelegrini, *Queer Theory and the Jewish Question*, p. 2.
19. Zangwill, *Children of the Ghetto*, p. 331. These critiques echo Christina Crosby's argument that *Daniel Deronda*'s representation of Judaism requires that 'the specificity and materiality of the Jews and Judaism must be radically disavowed', Crosby, *The Ends of History*, p. 14.
20. For more information on representation of Jews in English novels, see Wisse, *The Modern Jewish Canon*.
21. Ironically, Eastern European Jews excised the Gwendolen plot in translations of *Daniel Deronda*. According to Mikhal Dekel, the 1893 Hebrew translation omitted significant portions of the so-called English half. As part of the Hebrew Renaissance, Dekel argues that Deronda came to embody 'the universal-particular male subject at the core of the liberal nation-state' as writers sought to transform the Jewish man into a universal man. Dekel writes, '[T]he story of *Deronda*'s absorption into the Hebrew canon is ultimately a story of national identity: what may be included? What must be expelled? Who controls it?' Dekel, 'Who Taught This Foreign Woman', p. 785.
22. She writes, 'Whereas in Eliot's earlier fiction the force of realism acts as a kind of demystification of the energies produced by, for example, romance or pastoral in order to rein them in to the stable domestic

closures that constitute the transcendent endings traditional to English realism, in *Deronda* Eliot adds the weightier energies of epic and tragedy to the kinds of romance that have directed so many of the stories in her earlier works, and so doing stretches that force beyond its capacity to perform this demystifying and domesticating function.' Gates, 'A Difference of Native Language', p. 699.
23. For Moretti, the *Bildungsroman* believes in the individual's ability to develop according to his own nature; in contrast, the collectivist nature of Eliot's sympathy to Jewish nationalism requires a split with the realist novel's valorisation of individualism. Moretti, *Way of the World*, p. 227.
24. Mikhal Dekel argues that the plot line of the novel traces a shift in British liberal thought from individualism to collectivism. According to Dekel, *Daniel Deronda* suggests the impossibility of *Bildungsroman* for a male Jewish hero, 'once he is faced with the collapse of Enlightenment liberal "national" discourse and the rise of the "Jewish question?"' Dekel, *Universal Jew*, pp. 41–3.
25. In this sense, the novel engages with the Evangelical critique of Jewish ritualism.
26. Centrally, the question interrogates how to represent Anglo-Jews, both in the media and political life. Many contemporaries viewed Judaism as incompatible with modern English liberalism, because of alleged Jewish separatism. In English literary and political culture Jews were depicted as overdetermined extremes, perceived simultaneously as premodern figures incapable of enlightenment and as ultra-modern cosmopolitan wanderers. As a result, racialised constructions of Jews and other 'races' were at the heart of domestic liberalism and its self-definition. Because of its tradition of liberalism, England largely tolerated the Jewish minority and absorbed them into the nation. As David Cesarani argues, Anglo-Jews were pressured by this tolerant ambivalence to transcend their cultural differences and conform to a homogeneous Britishness. Many Englishmen refused the possibility that Jews could be English, since their alleged separatism and outside interests incapacitated them to become the disinterested and self-reliant liberal subjects required by an English nation. Thus, at the core of the Jewish question is a tension between the particular and the general. Cesarani, The Jewish Chronicle and Anglo-Jewry. For more on the novel, liberalism and the Jewish question, see Irene Tucker, *A Probable State*.
27. Moretti, *Way of the World*, p. 225.
28. Ibid.
29. For more on the Haskalah and Anglo-Jews, see Feldman, *Englishmen and Jews*.
30. Cesarani, *The Jewish Chronicle*, p. 76.
31. Israel Finestein argues that the denationalization of the Jews was seen as part of political reform and liberal individualism.

32. Cesarani, *The Jewish Chronicle*, X.
33. Ibid. p. 45.
34. Eliot, *Daniel Deronda*, p. 584.
35. Ibid.
36. Ibid. p. 223.
37. Boes, *Formative Fictions*.
38. Beaty, 'The Forgotten Past of Will Ladislaw', pp. 159–63.
39. Eliot, *Middlemarch*, p. 379.
40. Ibid. p. 358.
41. Ibid.
42. Ibid. p. 465.
43. Ibid.
44. Ibid. p. 460.
45. Ibid. p. 461.
46. Ladislaw would not have been alone in writing and editing the *Pioneer*, yet *Middlemarch* seems to portray the newspaper as a one-person venture. Staffing and daily operations of provincial daily newspapers would have varied widely. It is important that *Middlemarch* effaces the manpower behind Ladislaw's newspaper.
47. Zangwill, *Children of the Ghetto*, p. 366.
48. Ibid. p. 366.
49. Ibid. p. 367.
50. When editing *Ariel*, a comic paper started in 1890, Zangwill said he had 'sunk entirely into the slough of journalism with a heavy heart'. Leftwich, *Israel Zangwill*, p. 53.
51. Zangwill, 'Morour and Charouseth', p. 10.
52. Zangwill, *Children of the Ghetto*, p. 357.
53. Ibid. p. 359.
54. Ibid. p. 471.
55. Eliot, *Daniel Deronda*, p. 381. As Mark E. Wohlfarth points out, Deronda's sympathy proves limiting in the beginning of the novel. Deronda requires the sense of national belonging to redirect his sympathy in more productive ways. Early in the novel, Deronda faces 'a dizzying array of life possibilities. Any continuity of life is thus dispersed'. Wohlfarth argues that the discovery of his ethnic origin allows him to make sense of his life as a sequence and unity. He writes, 'The function of art and of an aesthetic education must be moral, and within the larger nationalist argument of *Daniel Deronda* that means that art needs to draw sustenance from and rest its meaning on a national(ist) center, a core of collective spirit.' Wohlfarth, 'Daniel Deronda and the Politics of Nationalism', p. 194, p. 205.
56. Ibid. p. 827.
57. Citing 1829 writer Henry Hart Milman, Scheinberg emphasises Deronda's 'poetic faculty', which she defines as his ability to see both the potential for sublime glory and permanent decay in the scenes around him.

58. Eliot, *Daniel Deronda*, p. 471.
59. Ibid. p. 476.
60. Ibid.
61. Ibid.
62. Anderson, *Powers of Distance*, p. 132.
63. Ibid. p. 121.
64. Ibid. According to Bryan Cheyette and Nadia Valman, 'Deronda's nationalism persistently moves toward the universalist civic model of nationality often associated with John Stuart Mill and built on the principle of democratic debate, while Mordecai's follows the collectivist-romantic model of a unified national will and a projected national destiny.' Cheyette and Valman, *Image of the Jew*, p. 210.
65. Anderson, *Powers of Distance*, p. 129.
66. Ibid. p. 346.
67. Zangwill, *Children of the Ghetto*, p. 425.
68. Ibid. p. 336.
69. In fact, Naomi Hetherington argues, '*Children of the Ghetto* does not promote a new Jewish faith in the way that *Robert Elsmere* reinvents Christianity with the hero's founding of the New Brotherhood of Christ.' She also points out, however, that Zangwill appropriates the language and forms of the Christian majority, particularly the conversion plot. Hetherington, 'A Jewish *Robert Elsmere*', p. 191.
70. Rochelson, *A Jew in the Public Arena*, p. 69.
71. Harshav, 'The Semiotics of Yiddish Communication', p. 147. For more information, also see Wisse, 'Two Jews Talking', p. 132.
72. Yet although Zangwill borrows associative organisation from Yiddish literature, particularly for his first book in the novel, he differs in one important aspect: an impersonal narrator describes the East End, whereas *Tevye the Dairyman* is narrated by a character using associative storytelling.
73. Rochelson, 'Religion of Pots and Pans', p. 123.
74. Zangwill, *Children of the Ghetto*, p. 133.
75. Harshav, *The Meaning of Yiddish*, p. 36.
76. Caplan, *How Strange the Change*, p. 9.
77. Ibid. p. 152.
78. Ibid. pp. 101–3.
79. Ibid. p. 158.
80. Ibid.
81. Ibid. p. 169.
82. Ibid. p. 202.
83. Ibid. p. 275.
84. Zangwill's use of Esther as a hybrid ideal draws upon stereotypical nineteenth-century portrayals of Jewish women as more susceptible to reform than their male counterparts. Zangwill uses the conversion discourse surrounding the Jewess to substantiate Esther's elevation to an ideal. Ragussis, *Figures of Conversion*.

85. Fox, *Character and Ideology*, p. 61.
86. Zangwill, *Children of the Ghetto*, p. 331.
87. Ibid. p. 344.
88. Ibid. p. 453.
89. Miron, *The Traveler Disguised*, p. 90.
90. Miron, *The Image of the Shtetl*.
91. Zangwill, *Children of the Ghetto*, p. 424.
92. Ibid. p. 435.
93. Ibid. p. 436.
94. Ibid. p. 61.
95. It is worth noting that this reflects Dickens's early valorisation of fancy in *Household Words*.
96. Examples of Yiddish writers who idealise the shtetl and represent it as a purely Jewish space include Sholem Aleichem and his fictional town Kasrilevke as well as Y. L. Peretz and his towns in *Bilder fun a provints rayze*. Miron, *The Image of the Shtetl*, p. 4.
97. Zangwill, *Ghetto Comedies*, p. 105.
98. Ibid. p. 110.
99. Ibid. p. 109.
100. Ibid. p. 135.
101. Wilde, *The Picture of Dorian Gray*, pp. 47–8.
102. S. I. Salamensky questions to what extent we can ascribe the anti-Semitic descriptions of Isaacs to Wilde, suggesting that the 'Jew serves as a fixture of the picturesque landscape of decadence.' And yet Isaacs is also the wrong kind of decadent for Wilde, threatening to 'corrode, pervert, and, as it were, degrade decadence by yoking fashion to flash and high art to the crass vernacular'. Salamensky, 'Oscar Wilde's "Jewish Problem"', p. 203, p. 208.
103. By the end of the nineteenth century, slumming had become a common practice, whether it was done to experience sexual and social freedom or for philanthropic purposes. The space of the East End operates much like the variable figure of the Jew, serving as an empty container for anything opposed to the West End. Many scholars, such as Judith Walkowitz and Seth Koven, have highlighted the extent to which the East End was exoticised as an imperial outpost within the domestic city. Zangwill counters this interpretation by a marked focus on place in the structure of his novel, evidenced even in its title. As I argued earlier in this paper, Zangwill allows the narrative to move more spatially than temporally, as his narrator guides the reader around the East End and offers glimpses of the Petticoat Lane market and the tenement houses. Walkowitz, *City of Dreadful Delight*; Koven, *Slumming*.
104. Zangwill, *Children of the Ghetto*, p. 62.
105. Ibid.
106. See Rochelson, 'Introduction', p. 12. Rochelson is quoting from '*Children of the Ghetto*': First Notice, *Jewish World* 14 October 1892: Howells, 'Life and Letters', p. 508.

107. Zangwill, *Children of the Ghetto*, p. 413.
108. Ibid. p. 429.
109. Reynolds edited the journal until 1847. For more information, see 'London Journal', *Dictionary of Nineteenth-Century Journalism*, p. 374.
110. Zangwill, *Children of the Ghetto*, p. 161.

Postscript

Children of the Ghetto was published in 1892, just one year after George Gissing's *New Grub Street* (1891) and five years before Bram Stoker's *Dracula* (1897). These contemporaneous novels offer widely divergent accounts of the newspaper and emerging new media. *New Grub Street* presents a stark portrayal of the 1880s literary marketplace, where hack writers flourish at the expense of serious literature. The capitalist marketplace and literary production are so intermingled that characters are warped by the pressure to generate literary outputs. Marian Yule, for instance, describes the constant production of text as a 'desert of print', one that robs her of personhood and the potential for self-actualisation. The literary marketplace renders publishers, writers and readers into bits and pieces valued only for their use value. People become fragments of text, rather like the short blurbs that the fictional *Chit Chat* – based on the weekly magazine *Tit-Bits* founded in 1881 – supplies for the 'reading multitude'. Published just a few years later, *Dracula*, by contrast, presents the potential for an integrated information system. Mina collects and collates journals, newspaper clippings, letters and phonograph recordings to craft a readily accessible portfolio of information about Dracula, thereby enabling the group to collaborate on the best way to defeat him. In Mina Harker, *Dracula* conceives the writer not as an artist but as a collator of information. Her transcriptions draw upon a wide array of text and new media, such that the novel invokes a larger information system crossing national boundaries. She memorises information, including European train times, to enable the group's pursuit of the vampire. *Dracula* envisions the world as an interconnected system of trade, information and media.[1]

Thus, *Dracula* suggests the possibility of a modern information system connecting the globe while also fostering a British, European and American alliance, while *New Grub Street* emphasises the capacity of the print media to divide, impoverish and fracture individuals and their communities.

These three novels, published in the same decade, reveal widely divergent visions of print and new media. *Plotting the News* has argued that nineteenth-century novels responded to changes in the newspaper press through its incorporation into narrative, metaphor and other formal qualities. *Children of the Ghetto* parallels the production of the newspaper to the endless labour of Sisyphus and *New Grub Street* to an all-consuming 'desert of print', while *Dracula* – expanding to include non-textual media – more optimistically imagines an information system that can be tracked, collated and interpreted by an intrepid woman. These conflicting yet contemporaneous metaphors suggest the difficulty of making sense of diversifying media at the end of the century. Jewish newspapers interlink an expansive Jewish diaspora, but the Anglo-Jewish iterations are caught in between their own communities and the larger nation. Esther is able to communicate feeling only through the realist novel. By contrast, *New Grub Street* suggests the literary marketplace has made literary community impossible, while *Dracula* worries about the threat of immigration and foreign influence on western culture, cultivating a cosmopolitanism that is limited to Western Europe, Britain and the United States.

In all these cases, novels grapple with the newspaper and new media's visions of community through formal experimentation. *Children of the Ghetto* hybridises novelistic realism and the *Bildungsroman*, while also representing other aesthetic modes, including Yiddish storytelling, the newspaper, the novel and painting. *Dracula* shapes itself according to Mina's collection of material fragments, an embodiment of the larger information system. These novelistic aesthetics reveal experimentation with text's influence on social formations, one that allows for 'an exploration of politics through culture and of culture through politics'.[2] Rather than figuring aesthetic and social forms as inherent or rigid structures, these novels explore their potentialities through the process of formation.

As a result, this monograph rethinks Caroline Levine's understanding of form as a concept that spans the aesthetic, the social and the political. Levine draws upon a concept from design theory – affordances – that describes 'the potential uses or actions latent in materials and designs'.[3] For Levine, this concept

> allows us to grasp both the specificity and the generality of forms – both the particular constraints and possibilities that different forms afford, and the fact that those patterns and arrangements carry their

affordances with them as they move across time and space. What is a walled enclosure or a rhyming couplet *capable* of doing? Each shape or pattern, social or literary, lays claim to a limited range of potentialities.[4]

It is telling that Levine uses the word 'grasp'. She draws upon a design term – affordance – that is used to describe the latent uses of an object, but she applies it instead to abstract concepts and literary form. For Levine, a sonnet or a network have a limited set of latent potentialities implied by their very form. Form thus operates beyond the category of the aesthetic, extending in parallel ways to the social and political. While she acknowledges that forms sometimes act in unexpected ways, her account largely ascribes a limited set of potentialities to particular forms and concepts.

The novels in this monograph reveal the ways that the nineteenth-century novel was in formation alongside developing cultural understandings of the newspaper and the press. While at times ascribing particular sets of potentialities to literary forms, the novels more broadly reveal a playful and adaptive experimentation with the ways that form can work. They all imagine that literary and textual forms have real social resonance in ways unique to their potentialities, but these visions also reveal processes of aesthetic formation and shifting metaphors for the ways that society can be rendered in art. Rather than exploring the extant affordances of a form, these novels erect and dismantle, imagine and re-imagine varying means of creating communities in and from texts.

Notes

1. Some have argued that Dracula represents Jewish immigration, thereby directly in conversation with *Children of the Ghetto*.
2. Armstrong, *Novel Politics*, p. 209.
3. Levine, *Forms*, p. 6.
4. Ibid.

Bibliography

Collections

Berg Collection, New York Public Library
Gale British Library Newspapers
Morris L. Parrish Collection of Victorian Novelists, Princeton University Library
Robert H. Taylor Collection, Princeton University Library

Periodicals

Athenaeum
Bradford Observer
Caledonian Mercury
Cornhill
The Derby Mercury
Edinburgh Review
Household Words
The Jewish Chronicle
The Jewish Standard
The John Bull and Britannia
Lloyd's Weekly Newspaper
Pall Mall Gazette
Reynolds's Newspaper
The Times

Books

Alfano, Veronica, and Andrew Stauffer (eds), *Virtual Victorians: Networks, Connections, Technologies* (Basingstoke: Palgrave Macmillan, 2015).

Altick, Richard D., *English Common Reader: A Social History of the Mass Reading Public, 1800–1900* (Chicago: University of Chicago Press, 1957).

—, *Deadly Encounters: Two Victorian Sensations* (Philadelphia: University of Pennsylvania Press, 1986).

—, *The Presence of the Present: Topics of the Day in the Victorian Novel* (Columbus: Ohio State University Press, 1991).

Anderson, Amanda, 'Trollope's Modernity', *ELH* 74:3 (Fall 2007), pp. 509–34.

—, *The Powers of Distance: Cosmopolitanism and the Cultivation of Detachment* (Princeton: Princeton University Press, 2011).

Anderson, Benedict, *The Spectre of Comparisons: Nationalism, Southeast Asia, and the World* (New York: Verso, 1998).

—, *Imagined Communities: Reflections on the Origin and Spread of Nationalism* (New York: Verso, 2006).

Armstrong, Isobel, *The Radical Aesthetic* (Hoboken, NJ: Wiley-Blackwell, 2000).

—, *Novel Politics: Democratic Imaginations in Nineteenth-Century Fiction* (Oxford: Oxford University Press, 2016).

Armstrong, Nancy, *Desire and Domestic Fiction: A Political History of the Novel* (Oxford: Oxford University Press, 1990).

Armstrong, Nancy, and Leonard Tennenhouse, 'Novels before Nations: How Early U.S. Novels Imagined Community', *Canadian Review of Comparative Literature* 42.4 (2015), pp. 353–69.

—, *Novels in the Time of Democratic Writing: The American Example* (Philadelphia: University of Pennsylvania Press, 2017).

Auerbach, Erich, *Mimesis: The Representation of Reality in Western Literature*, trans. Willard R. Trask (Princeton: Princeton University Press, 1968).

Bachman, Marie K. and Don Richard Cox (eds), *Reality's Dark Light: The Sensational Wilkie Collins* (Knoxville: The University of Tennessee Press, 2003).

Bagehot, Walter, *Literary Studies* (New York: Longman, Green, and Co., 1891).

Barker, Hannah, *Newspapers, Politics and English Society, 1695–1855* (London: Routledge, 2014).

Bar-Yosef, Eitan and Nadia Valman,*'The Jew' in Late-Victorian and Edwardian Culture Between the East End and East Africa* (Basingstoke: Palgrave Macmillan, 2013).

Beaty, Jerome, 'The Forgotten Past of Will Ladislaw', *Nineteenth-Century Fiction* 13:2 (1958), pp. 159–63.

Beetham, Margaret, 'Towards a Theory of the Periodical as a Publishing Genre', *Investigating Victorian Journalism*, ed. Laurel Brake (London: Palgrave Macmillan, 1990), pp. 19–32.

Benjamin, Walter, 'The Storyteller', *Theory of the Novel: A Historical Approach*, ed. Michael McKeon (Baltimore: The Johns Hopkins University Press, 2000), pp. 77–93.

Bernstein, Susan David, 'Introduction', *Reuben Sachs: a Sketch* (New York: Broadview Press, 2006).

—, '"Mongrel Words": Amy Levy's Jewish Vulgarity', *Amy Levy: Critical Essays*, ed. Naomi Hetherington and Nadia Valman (Athens: Ohio University Press, 2010), pp. 135–56.

Boes, Tobias, *Formative Fictions: Nationalism, Cosmopolitanism, and the Bildungsroman* (Ithaca: Cornell University Press, 2012).

Bourdieu, Pierre, *On Television*, 1996, trans. Priscilla Parkhurst Ferguson (New York: The New Press, 1998).

Boyarin, Daniel, Daniel Itzkovitz and Ann Pelegrini (eds), *Queer Theory and the Jewish Question* (New York: Columbia University Press, 2003).

Boyle, Thomas, *Black Swine in the Sewers of Hampstead: Beneath the Surface of Victorian Sensationalism* (New York: Viking, 1989).

Braddon, Mary Elizabeth, *Eleanor's Victory* (London: Tinsley Brothers, 1863).

—, *Lady Audley's Secret* [1862] (Oxford: Oxford University Press, 1998).

—, *Aurora Floyd* [1863] (Germany: Jazzybee Verlag Jurgen Beck, 2014).

Brake, Laurel (ed.), *Investigating Victorian Journalism* (Basingstoke: Palgrave Macmillan, 1990).

—, *Subjugated Knowledges: Journalism, Gender and Literature in the Nineteenth Century* (New York: New York University Press, 1994).

—, *Print in Transition: Studies in Media and Book History* (Basingstoke: Palgrave Macmillan, 2014).

Brake, Laurel, Bill Bell and David Finkelstein, *Nineteenth-Century Media and the Construction of Identities* (Basingstoke: Palgrave Macmillan, 2000).

Brake, Laurel, and Julie Codell (eds), *Encounters in the Victorian Press: Editors, Authors, Readers* (Basingstoke: Palgrave Macmillan, 2005).

Brake, Laurel and Marysa Demoor (eds), *Dictionary of Nineteenth Century Journalism in Great Britain and Ireland* (London: Academia Press, 2009).

Brantlinger, Patrick, *The Reading Lesson: The Threat of Mass Literacy in Nineteenth-Century British Fiction* (Indianapolis: Indiana University Press, 1998).

—, 'What is "Sensational" about the "Sensation Novel"', *Nineteenth-Century Fiction*, 37.1 (1982), pp. 1–28.

Brennan, James R., 'International News in the Age of Empire', *Making News: The Political Economy of Journalism in Britain and America from the Glorious Revolution to the Internet*, ed. Richard R. John and Jonathan Silberstein-Loeb (Oxford: Oxford University Press, 2015).

Brennan, Timothy, 'The National Longing for Form', *Nation and Narration*, ed. Homi K. Bhabha (London: Routledge, 1990), pp. 107–32.

Brooks, Peter, *The Melodramatic Imagination: Balzac, Henry James, Melodrama, and the Mode of Excess* (New Haven: Yale University Press, 1976).

—, *Reading for the Plot: Design and Intention in Narrative* (Cambridge, MA: Harvard University Press, 1984).

Brown, Daniel, 'Realism and Sensation Fiction', *A Companion to Sensation Fiction*, ed. Pamela Gilbert (Hoboken, NJ: Blackwell, 2011).

Brown, Lucy, *Victorian News and Newspapers* (Oxford: Clarendon Press, 1985).

Buzard, James, *Disorienting Fiction: The Autoethnographic Work of Nineteenth-Century British Novels* (Princeton: Princeton University Press, 2005).

Caplan, Marc, *How Strange the Change: Language, Temporality, and Narrative Form in Peripheral Modernisms* (Palo Alto: Stanford University Press, 2011).

Carlyle, Thomas, *On Heroes, Hero-Worship, and the Heroic in History* (Middlesex: Echo Library, 2007).

Cesarani, David, *The Jewish Chronicle and Anglo-Jewry, 1841–1991* (Cambridge: Cambridge University Press, 1994).

Cheyette, Bryan, *Constructions of 'the Jew' in English Literature and Society: Racial Representations 1875–1945* (Cambridge: Cambridge University Press, 1993).

—, 'Englishness and Extraterritoriality: British-Jewish Writing and Diaspora Culture', *Literary Strategies: Jewish Texts and Contexts. Studies in Contemporary Jewry*, ed. Ezra Mendelsohn (Oxford: Oxford University Press, 1996).

Childers, Joseph, 'At Home in Empire', *Homes and Homelessness in the Victorian Imagination*, ed. Murray Baumgarten and Hillel Matthew Daleski (New York: AMS Press, 1998), pp. 215–26.

Clemm, Sabine, *Dickens, Journalism, and Nationhood: Mapping the World in Household Words* (New York: Routledge, 2009).

Cohn, Dorrit, *The Distinction of Fiction* (Baltimore: The Johns Hopkins University Press, 2000).

Colby, Robert A, '"Into the Blue Water": The First Year of "Cornhill Magazine" under Thackeray', *Victorian Periodicals Review*, 32:3 (1999), pp. 209–22.

Collini, Stefan, *Public Moralists: Political Thought and Intellectual Life in Britain, 1850–1930* (Oxford: Clarendon Press, 1993).

Collins, Wilkie, *Basil* [1852] (Oxford: Oxford University Press, 1990).
—, *Armadale* [1866] (New York: Penguin, 1995).
—, *The Moonstone* [1868] (New York: Penguin, 1998).
—, *The Law and the Lady* [1875] (New York: Penguin, 2004).
Costantini, Mariaconcetta,'Wo/Men of Letters: Writing and Identity in *Armadale*', *Armadale: Wilkie Collins and the Dark Threads of Life*, ed. Mariaconcetta Costantini (Rome: Aracne, 2009).
Crosby, Christina, *The Ends of History: Victorians and 'the Woman Question'* (Abingdon: Routledge, 1991).
Culler, Jonathan, 'Anderson and the Novel', *Diacritics* 29 (1999), pp. 19–39.
Curtis, L. Perry, Jr., *Jack the Ripper and the London Press* (New Haven: Yale University Press, 2001).
Daly, Nicholas, 'Railway Novels: Sensation Fiction and the Modernization of the Sense', *ELH* 66.2 (1999), pp. 461–87.
Dames, Nicholas, *The Physiology of the Novel* (Oxford: Oxford University Press, 2007).
David, Deirdre, 'Writing about America', *The Cambridge History of Victorian Literature*, ed. Kate Flint (Cambridge: Cambridge University Press, 2012).
Davis, Lennard J., *Factual Fictions: The Origins of the English Novel* (Philadelphia: University of Pennsylvania Press, 1996).
Dekel, Mikhal, '"Who Taught This Foreign Woman About the Ways and Lives of the Jews?": George Eliot and the Hebrew Renaissance', *ELH*, 74.4 (2007), pp. 783–98.
—, *Universal Jew: Masculinity, Modernity, and the Zionist Movement* (Chicago: Northwestern University Press, 2011).
Delany, Paul, *Literature, Money and the Market: From Trollope to Amis* (Basingstoke: Palgrave Macmillan, 2002).
Deleuze, Gilles, and Felix Guattari, *Kafka: Toward a Minor Literature*, trans. Dana Polan (Minneapolis: University of Minnesota Press, 1986).
Dickens, Charles, *Martin Chuzzlewit* [1844] (Oxford: Oxford University Press 2009).
—, *Our Mutual Friend* [1865] (New York: Penguin Classics, 1998).
Dowling, William C., *Ricoeur on Time and Narrative* (Chapel Hill: University of Notre Dame Press, 2011).
Drew, John M. L., *Dickens the Journalist* (Basingstoke: Palgrave Macmillan, 2004).
Eigner, Edwin M., *The Dickens Pantomime* (Berkeley: University of California Press, 1989).
Eliot, George., *Middlemarch* [1871] (New York: Penguin Classics, 1994).
—, *Daniel Deronda* [1876] (New York: Penguin Classics, 2003).

—, *Adam Bede* [1859] (New York: Penguin Classics, 2008).

Farina, Jonathan V, '"A Certain Shadow": Personified Abstractions and the Form of *Household Words*', *Victorian Periodicals Review* 42 (Winter 2009), pp. 392–415.

Felber, Lynette, 'Trollope's Phineas Diptych as Sequel and Sequence Novel', *Part Two: Reflections on the Sequel*, ed. Paul Budra and Betty A. Schellenberg (Buffalo: University of Toronto Press, 1998).

Feldman, David, *Englishmen and Jews: Social Relations and Political Culture, 1840–1914* (New Haven: Yale University Press, 1994).

Feltes, N. N., *Modes of Production of Victorian Novels* (Chicago: University of Chicago Press, 1986).

Fenton, Laurence, *Palmerston and the Times: Foreign Policy, the Press and Public Opinion in Mid-Victorian Britain* (London: I. B. Tauris, 2012).

Ferguson, Frances, 'Jane Austen, *Emma*, and the Impact of Form', *Modern Language Quarterly* 61.1 (2000), pp. 157–80.

—, *Pornography, the Theory: What Utilitarianism Did to Action* (Chicago: The University of Chicago Press, 2004).

Figes, Orlando, *The Crimean War: A History* (New York: Metropolitan Books, 2011).

Finch, Casey, and Peter Bowen, '"The Tittle-Tattle of Highbury": Gossip and Free Indirect Style in *Emma*', *Representations*, 31 (Summer 1990), pp. 1–18.

Finestein, Israel, *Anglo-Jewry in Changing Times: Studies in Diversity, 1840–1914* (London: Vallentine Mitchell, 1999).

Fiske, Shanyn, *Heretical Hellenism: Women Writers, Ancient Greece, and the Victorian Popular Imagination* (Athens: Ohio University Press, 2008).

Fox, Michael, *Character and Ideology in the Book of Esther* (Eugene: Wipf and Stock, 2010).

Frank, Catherine O, 'Trial Separations: Divorce, Disestablishment, and Home Rule in *Phineas Redux*', *College Literature*, 35.3 (2008), pp. 30–56.

Fyfe, Paul, 'An Archaeology of Victorian Newspapers', *Victorian Periodicals Review* 49:4 (Winter 2016), pp. 546–77.

Gallagher, Catherine, *Nobody's Story: The Vanishing Acts of Women Writers in the Marketplace, 1670–1820* (Berkeley: University of California Press, 1994).

Galvan, Jill, *The Sympathetic Medium: Feminine Channeling, the Occult, and Communication Technologies, 1859–1919* (Ithaca: Cornell University Press, 2011).

Garrett, James M., *Wordsworth and the Writing of the Nation* (Abingdon: Ashgate, 2008).

Gaskell, Elizabeth., *Wives and Daughters* [1864–66] (New York: Penguin Books, 1986).

Gaskill, Nicholas, 'The Close and the Concrete: Aesthetic Formalism in Context', *New Literary History*, 47.4 (2016), pp. 505–24.

Gates, Sarah, '"A Difference of Native Language": Gender, Genre, and Realism in *Daniel Deronda*', *ELH*, 68.3 (2001), pp. 699–724.

Gattrell, V. A. C., *The Hanging Tree: Execution and the English People 1770–1868* (New York: Oxford University Press, 1994).

Gegeef, 'Our National Press', Michael Sadleir Collection of Ephemera, The Lilly Library, Indiana University, *London Low Life: Street Culture, Social Reform and the Victorian Underworld*.

Gilbert, Pamela, *Disease, Desire and the Body in Victorian Women's Popular Novels* (Cambridge: Cambridge University Press, 1997).

Gilman, Sander L, *Inscribing the Other* (Lincoln: University of Nebraska Press, 1991).

Gissing, George, *New Grub Street* [1891], ed. John Goode (Oxford: Oxford University Press, 1998).

Glover, David, 'Imperial Zion: Israel Zangwill and the English Origins of Territorialism', *The Jew in Late-Victorian and Edwardian Culture: Between the East End and East Africa*, ed. Eitan Bar-Yosef and Nadia Valman (Basingstoke: Palgrave Macmillan, 2009).

GoGwilt, Christopher, *The Fiction of Geopolitics: Afterimages of Culture, from Wilkie Collins to Alfred Hitchcock* (Stanford: Stanford University Press, 2000).

Goode, Mike, 'The Public and the Limits of Persuasion in the Age of Caricature', *The Efflorescence of Caricature, 1759–1838*, ed. Todd Porterfield and Ersy Contogouris (Abingdon: Routledge, 2011).

Goodlad, Lauren, *Victorian Literature and the Victorian State: Character and Governance in a Liberal Society* (Baltimore: The Johns Hopkins University Press, 2003).

—, *The Victorian Geopolitical Aesthetic: Realism, Sovereignty, and Transnational Experience* (Oxford: Oxford University Press, 2015).

Goodlad, Lauren, and Frederik Van Dam, 'Trollope and Politics', *The Routledge Research Companion to Anthony Trollope*, ed. Deborah Denenholz Morse, Margaret Marwick and Mark Turner (Abingdon: Routledge, 2017), pp. 15–34.

Griffiths, Andrew, *The New Journalism, the New Imperialism and the Fiction of Empire, 1870–1900* (Basingstoke: Palgrave Macmillan, 2015).

Habermas, Jürgen, *The Structural Transformation of the Public Sphere*, trans. Thomas Burger (Boston, MA: MIT Press, 1991).

Hadley, Elaine, *Living Liberalism: Practical Citizenship in Mid-Victorian Britain* (Chicago: University of Chicago, 2010).

—, *Melodramatic Tactics: Theatricalized Dissent in the English Marketplace* (Stanford: Stanford University Press, 1995).

—, 'No Representation Without Mediation: Revisioning Politics in Victorian Britain', in 'Victorian Politics and Media Networks' at North American Victorian Studies Association, 29 Sept. 2012.

Hall, N. John, *Trollope: A Biography* (Oxford: Oxford University Press, 1991).

Halperin, John, *Trollope and Politics: A Study of the Pallisers and Others* (London: Harper and Row Publishers, 1977).

—, 'Trollope's Phineas Finn and History', *English Studies* 59.2 (1978), pp. 121–37.

Hamer, Mary, *Writing by Numbers: Trollope's Serial Fiction* (New York: Cambridge University Press, 1987).

Hampton, Mark, *Visions of the Press in Britain* (Champaign: University of Illinois Press, 2004).

Harshav, Benjamin, *The Meaning of Yiddish* (Palo Alto: Stanford University Press, 1999).

—, 'The Semiotics of Yiddish Communication', *What is Jewish Literature*, ed. Hana Wirth-Nesher (Philadelphia: The Jewish Publication Society, 1994).

Hauser, Helen, 'Form and Reform: The "Miscellany Novel"', *Victorian Literature and Culture* 41 (2013), pp. 21–40.

Haywood, Ian, *Faking It: Art and the Politics of Forgery* (Brighton: The Harvester Press, 1987)

—, 'George W. M. Reynolds and "The Trafalgar Square Revolution: Radicalism, the Carnivalesque and Popular Culture in mid-Victorian England"', *Journal of Victorian Culture,* 7:1 (2002), pp. 23–59.

—, *The Revolution in Popular Literature: Print, Politics and the People, 1790–1860* (Cambridge: Cambridge University Press, 2004).

Hensley, Nathan K, '*Armadale* and the Logic of Liberalism', *Victorian Studies*, 51.4 (2009), pp. 607–32.

Hetherington, Naomi. '"A Jewish *Robert Elsmere?*": Amy Levy, Israel Zangwill, and the Postemancipation Jewish Novel', *Amy Levy: Critical Essays*, ed. Nadia Valman and Naomi Hetherington (Athens: Ohio University Press, 2010).

Hewitt, Martin, *The Dawn of the Cheap Press in Victorian Britain: The End of the 'Taxes on Knowledge', 1849–1869* (London: Bloomsbury, 2018).

Hobbs, Andrew, *A Fleet Street in Every Town: The Provincial Press in England, 1855–1900* (Cambridge: Open Book Publishers, 2018).

House, Madeline, Graham Storey, and Kathleen Tillotson (eds), *The Letters of Charles Dickens* (Oxford: Clarendon Press, 1965).

Huett, Lorna, 'Among the Unknown Public: *Household Words, All the Year Round* and the Mass-Market Weekly Periodical in the Mid-Nineteenth Century', *Victorian Periodicals Review*, 38 (Spring 2005), pp. 61–82.

Hughes, Linda K. and Michael Lund, *The Victorian Serial* (Charlottesville: University of Virginia Press, 1991).

Hughes, Winifred, *The Maniac in the Cellar: Sensation Novels of the 1860s* (Princeton: Princeton University Press, 1981).

Humpherys, Anne, 'Generic Strands and Urban Twists: The Victorian Mysteries Novel', *Victorian Studies*, 34.4 (Summer 1991), pp. 455–72.

James, Louis, 'From Egan to Reynolds: The Shaping of Urban "Mysteries" in England and France, 1821–48', *European Journal of English Studies*, 14.2 (2010), pp. 95–106.

Jameson, Fredric, 'Afterword', *A Concise Companion to Realism*, ed. Mathew Beaumont (Oxford: Verso Books, 1998), pp. 279–89.

—, *The Antinomies of Realism* (London: Verso Books, 2013).

Jones, Aled, 'Local Journalism in Victorian Political Culture', *Investigating Victorian Journalism*, ed. Laurel Brake (London: Macmillan Press, 1990).

—, *Powers of the Press: Newspapers, Power and the Public in Nineteenth-Century England* (Aldershot: Scolar Press, 1996).

Jordan, John O., and Robert L. Patten, *Literature in the Marketplace: Nineteenth-Century Publishing and Reading Practices* (Cambridge: Cambridge University Press, 1995).

Joyce, Patrick, *Democratic Subjects: The Self and the Social in Nineteenth-Century England* (Cambridge: Cambridge University Press, 1994).

Kendrick, Walter M., *The Novel-Machine: The Theory and Fiction of Anthony Trollope* (Baltimore: The Johns Hopkins University Press, 1980).

Kent, Christopher, 'Probability, Reality and Sensation in the Novels of Wilkie Collins', *Wilkie Collins to the Forefront: Some Reassessments* (New York: AMS Press, 1995).

King, Andrew, and John Plunkett, *Victorian Print Media: A Reader* (Oxford: Oxford University Press, 2005).

Klancher, Jon P., *The Making of English Reading Audiences, 1790–1832* (Madison: The University of Wisconsin Press, 1987).

Kornbluh, Anna, *Realizing Capital: Financial and Psychic Economies in Victorian Form* (New York: Fordham University Press, 2014).

Koven, Seth, *Slumming: Social and Sexual Politics in Victorian London* (Princeton: Princeton University Press, 2004).

Kreilkamp, Ivan, *Voice and the Victorian Storyteller* (Cambridge: Cambridge University Press, 2005).

Krouse, Richard W, 'Two Concepts of Democratic Representation: James and John Stuart Mill', *The Journal of Politics*, 44.2 (1982), pp. 509–37.

Ledger, Sally, *Dickens and the Popular Radical Imagination* (Cambridge: Cambridge University Press, 2007).

Leftwich, Joseph, *Israel Zangwill* (New York: Thomas Yoseloff Inc., 1957).

Levine, Caroline, *The Serious Pleasures of Suspense: Victorian Realism and Narrative Doubt* (Charlottesville: University of Virginia Press, 2003).

—, *Forms: Whole, Rhythm, Hierarchy, Network* (Princeton: Princeton University Press, 2015).

Levine, George, *The Realistic Imagination: English Fiction from Frankenstein to Lady Chatterley* (Chicago: University of Chicago Press, 1983).

Levy, Amy, *The Complete Novels and Selected Writings of Amy Levy, 1861–1889*, ed. Melvyn New (Gainesville: University Press of Florida, 1993).

Liddle, Dallas, *The Dynamics of Genre: Journalism and the Practice of Literature in Mid-Victorian Britain* (Charlottesville: University of Virginia Press, 2009).

Loesberg, Jonathan, 'The Ideology of Narrative Form in Sensation Fiction', *Representations*, 13 (1986), pp. 115–38.

—, *A Return to Aesthetics: Autonomy, Indifference, and Postmodernism* (Stanford: Stanford University Press, 2005).

Lonergan, Patrick, 'The Representation of Phineas Finn: Anthony Trollope's Palliser Series and Victorian Ireland', *Victorian Literature and Culture*, 32.1 (2004), pp. 147–58.

Lonoff, Sue, *Wilkie Collins and His Victorian Readers: A Study in the Rhetoric of Authorship* (New York: AMS Press, 1982).

Luhmann, Niklas, *The Reality of the Mass Media*, trans. Kathleen Cross (Stanford: Stanford University Press, 2000).

Lukács, Georg, *The Historical Novel*, trans. Hannah Mitchell and Stanley Mitchell (Lincoln: University of Nebraska Press, 1983).

—, *Theory of the Novel: A Historico-Philosophical Essay on the Forms of Great Epic Literature*, trans. Anna Bostock (Boston, MA: MIT Press, 1971).

MacGowan, Douglas, *The Strange Affair of Madeleine Smith: Victorian Scotland's Trial of the Century* (Edinburgh: Mercat Press, 2007).

Magee, Gary B. and Andrew S. Thompson, *Empire and Globalisation: Networks of People, Goods and Capital in the British Word* [c. 1850–1914] (Cambridge: Cambridge University Press, 2010).

Markovits, Stefanie, 'Rushing into Print: "Participatory Journalism" During the Crimean War', *Victorian Studies* 50:4 (2008).

Markwick, Margaret, *New Men in Trollope's Novels: Rewriting the Victorian Male* (Aldershot: Ashgate, 2007).

McKeon, Michael, *Origins of the English Novel, 1600–1740* (Baltimore: The Johns Hopkins University Press, 1987).

McLuhan, Marshal, *Understanding Media: The Extensions of Man* (Boston, MA: MIT Press, 1994).

McWilliam, Rohan, 'Melodrama and the Historians', *Radical History Review* 78 (2000), pp. 57–84.

Menke, Richard, *Telegraphic Realism: Victorian Fiction and Other Information Systems* (Palo Alto: Stanford University Press, 2008).

Michie, Helena, 'Rethinking Marriage: Trollope's Internal Revision', *The Routledge Research Companion to Anthony Trollope*, ed. Deborah Denenholz Morse, Margaret Markwick and Mark W. Turner (London: Routledge, 2017).

Mill, John Stuart, *On Liberty and Other Essays*, ed. John Gray (Oxford: Oxford University Press, 2008).

Miller, Andrew, 'Lived Unled in Realist Fiction', *Representations*, 98.1 (2007), pp. 118–34.

Miller, D. A., *The Novel and the Police* (Berkeley: University of California Press, 1988).

Miron, Dan, *The Image of the Shtetl and Other Studies of Modern Jewish Literary Imagination* (Syracuse: Syracuse University Press, 2001).

—, Introduction to *Tevye the Dairyman and Motl the Cantor's Son* (New York: Penguin Classics, 2009).

—, *A Traveler Disguised: A Study in the Rise of Modern Yiddish Fiction in the Nineteenth Century* (New York: Shocken Books, 1973).

Moretti, Franco, *The Way of the World: The Bildungsroman in European Culture* (New York: Verso, 1987).

Morse, Deborah Denenholz, *Reforming Trollope: Race, Gender, and Englishness in the Novels of Anthony Trollope* (Abingdon: Routledge, 2016).

—, 'The Way He Thought Then: Modernity and the Retreat of the Public Liberal in Anthony Trollope's *The Way We Live Now*, 1873', *BRANCH: Britain, Representation and Nineteenth-Century History*, ed. Dino Franco Fellugo. Extension of *Romanticism and Victorianism on the Net*, Web (July 2019).

Mundhenk, Rosemary, 'The Education of the Reader in *Our Mutual Friend*', *Nineteenth-Century Fiction*, 34 (Spring 1979), pp. 41–58.

Mussell, James, 'Cohering Knowledge in the Nineteenth Century: Form, Genre and Periodical Studies', *Victorian Periodicals Review*, 42:1 (2009), pp. 151–67.

—, 'Repetition: Or, "In Our Last"', *Victorian Periodicals Review*, 48:3 (2015), pp. 343–58.

Nahshon, Edna, *From the Ghetto to the Melting Pot: Israel Zangwill's Jewish Plays* (Detroit: Wayne State University Press, 2006).

Nemesvari, Richard, '"Judged by a Purely Literary Standard": Sensation Fiction, Horizons of Expectation, and the Generic Construction of Victorian Realism', *Victorian Sensations: Essays on a Scandalous Genre*, ed. Kimberly Harrison and Richard Fantina (Columbus: Ohio State University Press, 2006).

Niles, Lisa, 'Owning "the dreadful truth"; Or, Is Thirty-Five Too Old?: Age and the Marriageable Body in Wilkie Collins's *Armadale*', *Nineteenth-Century Literature* 65:1 (2010), pp. 65–92.

Olson, Melissa, 'Dracula the Anti-Christ: New Resurrection of an Immortal Prejudice', *Images of the Modern Vampire: The Hip and the Atavistic*, ed. Barbara Brodman and James E. Doan (Lanham: Rowman & Littlefield, 2013).

Pal-Lapinksi, Piya, 'Chemical Seductions: Exoticism, Toxicology, and the Female Poisoner in *Armadale*', *Reality's Dark Light: The Sensational Wilkie Collins*, ed. Maria K. Bachman and Don Richard Cox (Knoxville: University of Tennessee Press, 2003).

—, *The Exotic Woman in Nineteenth-Century British Fiction and Culture: A Reconsideration* (Amherst: University of New Hampshire Press, 2004).

Parrinder, Patrick, *Nation and Novel: The English Novel from its Origins to the Present Day* (Oxford: Oxford University Press, 2008).

Parry, Jonathan, *The Rise and Fall of Liberal Government in Victorian Britain* (New Haven: Yale University Press, 1996).

Patten, Robert L., *Charles Dickens and 'Boz': The Birth of the Industrial-Age Author* (Cambridge: Cambridge University Press, 2012).

Pettitt, Clare, *Patent Inventions: Intellectual Property and the Victorian Novel* (Oxford: Oxford University Press, 2004).

—, 'Dickens and the Form of the Historic Present', *Dickens and Style*, ed. Daniel Tyler (Cambridge: Cambridge University Press, 2013), pp. 110–36.

Phelan, James, 'Rhetoric, Ethics, Aesthetics, and Probability in Fiction and Nonfiction: *Pride and Prejudice* and *The Year of Magical Thinking*', *Reception* 2 (2009).

Plunkett, John, and Andrew King (eds), *Victorian Print Media: A Reader* (Oxford: Oxford University Press, 2006).

Poovey, Mary, *Uneven Developments: The Ideological Work of Gender in Mid-Victorian England* (Chicago: University of Chicago Press, 1988).

—. *Making the Social Body: British Cultural Formation, 1830–1864* (Chicago: University of Chicago Press, 1995).

Potter, Simon, *News and the British World: The Emergence of an Imperial Press System* (Oxford: Oxford University Press, 2003).

Pykett, Lyn, 'Reading the Victorian Periodical Press: Text and Context', *Victorian Periodicals Review*, 22 (1989), pp. 100–8.

—, *The Nineteenth-Century Sensation Novel* (Tavistock: Northcote House Publishers, 2011).

Rader, Ralph, 'Defoe, Richardson, Joyce, and the Concept of Form in the Novel', *Fact, Fiction, and Form: Selected Essays*, ed. James Phelan and David H. Richter (Columbus: Ohio State University Press, 2011).

Ragussis, Michael, *Figures of Conversion: 'The Jewish Question' and English National Identity* (Durham: Duke University Press, 1995).

Rance, Nicholas, *Wilkie Collins and Other Sensation Novelists: Walking the Moral Hospital* (Madison: Farleigh Dickinson University Press, 1991).

Reynolds, George W. M., *Master Timothy's Book-case, or The Magic Lanthorn of the World* (London: Paget & Co., 1843).

—, *The Mysteries of London*, Vol. I (London: G Vickers, 1849).

—, *Pickwick Abroad; or, The Tour in France* (London: Henry G. Bohn, 1864).

Ricoeur, Paul, *Time and Narrative*, trans. Kathleen McLaughlin and David Pellauer (Chicago: University of Chicago Press, 1990).

Rochelson, Meri-Jane, 'Language, Gender, and Ethnic Anxiety in Zangwill's *Children of the Ghetto*', *English Literature in Transition, 1880–1920*, 31.4 (1988), pp. 399–412.

—, '*The Big Bow Mystery*: Jewish Identity and the English Detective Novel', *Victorian Review*, 17.2 (1991), pp. 11–20.

—, *A Jew in the Public Arena: The Career of Israel Zangwill* (Detroit: Wayne State University Press, 2008).

—, '"Religion of Pots and Pans": Jewish Materialism and Spiritual Materiality in Israel Zangwill's *Children of the Ghetto*', *Victorian Vulgarity: Taste in Verbal and Visual Culture*, ed. Susan David Bernstein and Elsie B. Michie (Burlington: Ashgate, 2009), pp. 119–35.

—, 'Zionism, Territorialism, Race, and Nation in the Thought and Politics of Israel Zangwill', *The Jew in Late-Victorian and Edwardian Culture Between the East End and East Africa*, ed. Eitan Bar-Yosef and Nadia Valman (Basingstoke: Palgrave Macmillan, 2009).

Rosenthal, Jesse, *Good Form: The Ethical Experience of the Victorian Novel* (Princeton: Princeton University Press, 2016).

Rubery, Matthew, *The Novelty of Newspapers: Victorian Fiction After the Invention of News* (New York: Oxford University Press, 2009).

Russett, Margaret, *Fictions and Fakes: Forging Romantic Authenticity, 1760–1845* (Cambridge: Cambridge University Press, 2006).

Sachs, Joe, 'Introduction', *Aristotle's Metaphysics* (Sante Fe: Green Lion Press, 2002).

Salamensky, S. I. 'Oscar Wilde's "Jewish Problem": Salome, the Ancient Hebrew and the Modern Jewess', *Modern Drama*, 55:2 (Summer 2012), pp. 197–215.

Scheinberg, Cynthia, '"The beloved ideas made flesh": *Daniel Deronda* and Jewish Poetics', *ELH* ,77.3 (2010), pp. 813–39.

Seys, Madeleine C., *Fashion and Narrative in Victorian Popular Literature: Double Threads* (New York: Routledge, 2018).

Shattock, Joanne, and Michael Wolff, *The Victorian Periodical Press: Samplings and Soundings* (Toronto: University of Toronto Press, 1982).

Sinnema, Peter W., *Dynamics of the Printed Page: Representing the Nation in the* Illustrated London News (Brookfield: Ashgate, 1998).

Sommer, Doris, *Foundational Fictions: The National Romances of Latin America* (Berkeley: University of California Press, 1993).

Stoker, Bram., *Dracula*, 1897, ed. Maurice Hindle (New York: Penguin Classics, 2003).

Storey, Graham, and K. J. Fielding (eds), *The Letters of Charles Dickens*, Vol. V (Oxford: Oxford University Press, 1980).

Sullivan, Anne, 'Animating Flames: Recovering Fire-Gazing as Moving-Image Technology', *Interdisciplinary Studies of Fire in Nineteenth-Century British Culture* 25 (2017), pp. 1–21.

—, and Kate Flint, 'Introduction: Technologies of Fire in Nineteenth-Century British Culture', *Interdisciplinary Studies in the Long Nineteenth Century* 25 (2017).

Sumpter, Caroline, *The Victorian Press and the Fairy Tale* (Basingstoke: Palgrave Macmillan, 2008).

Taylor, Jenny Bourne, 'Introduction', *Cambridge Companion to Wilkie Collins*, ed. Jenny Bourne Taylor (Cambridge: Cambridge University Press, 2006).

—, *In the Secret Theatre of Home: Wilkie Collins, Sensation Narrative, and Nineteenth-Century Psychology* (London and New York: Routledge, 1988).

Terdiman, Richard, *Discourse/Counter-Discourse: The Theory and Practice of Symbolic Resistance in Nineteenth-Century France* (Ithaca: Cornell University Press, 1985).

Teukolsky, Rachel, 'Novels, Newspapers, and Global War: New Realisms in the 1850s', *Novel: A Forum on Fiction*. 45:1 (2012), pp. 31–55.

Tierney-Hynes, Rebecca, *Novel Minds: Philosophers and Romance Readers, 1680–1740* (Basingstoke: Palgrave Macmillan, 2012).

Tillotson, Kathleen, 'Introduction', *The Woman in White* (Boston: Houghton Mifflin, 1969).

Trollope, Anthony, *Barchester Towers* [1857] (New York: Penguin Classics, 1983).

—, *The Prime Minister* [1876] (New York: Penguin Classics, 1994).

—, *He Knew He Was Right* [1869] (New York: Penguin, 1996).

—, *Can You Forgive Her?* [1864] (New York: Penguin Classics, 2004).

—, *Phineas Finn* [1868] (Oxford: Oxford University Press, 2008).

—, *Phineas Redux* [1873] (Oxford: Oxford University Press, 2008).

—, *An Autobiography* [1883] (Oxford: Oxford University Press, 2008).

—, *Orley Farm* [1861] (Oxford: Oxford University Press, 2009).

—, *The Warden* [1855] (New York: Penguin Books, 2012).

Trumpener, Katie, *Bardic Nationalism: The Romantic Novel and the British Empire* (Princeton: Princeton University Press, 1997).

Tucker, Irene, *A Probable State; The Novel, the Contract, and the Jews* (Chicago: The University of Chicago Press, 2000).

Turner, Mark, *Trollope and the Magazines: Gendered Issues in Mid-Victorian Britain* (Basingstoke: Palgrave Macmillan Press Ltd., 2000).

Udelson, Joseph, *Dreamer of the Ghetto: The Life and Works of Israel Zangwill* (Tuscaloosa: University of Alabama Press, 1990).

Valdez, Jessica R., 'Dickens's "Pious Fraud": The Popular Press and Narrative's Potential for Social Control', *Victorian Periodicals Review*, 44.4 (Winter 2012), pp. 377–400.

—. 'How to Write Yiddish in English, or Israel Zangwill and Multilingualism in *Children of the Ghetto*', *Studies in the Novel*, 46.3 (Fall 2014), pp. 315–34.

Valman, Nadia, *The Jewess in Nineteenth-Century British Literary Culture* (Cambridge: Cambridge University Press, 2007).

Vanden Bossche, Chris R., 'The Value of Literature: Representations of Print Culture in the Copyright Debate of 1837–1842', *Victorian Studies* (Autumn 1994), pp. 41–68.

—, *Reform Acts: Chartism, Social Agency, and the Victorian Novel, 1832–1867* (Baltimore: The Johns Hopkins University Press, 2014).

Vermeulen, Peter, 'Community and Literary Experience in (between) Benedict Anderson and Jean-Luc Nancy', *Mosaic*, 42.4 (2009), pp. 95–111.

Waldron, Jeremy, 'Mill and the Value of Moral Distress', *Political Studies*, 35.3 (1987), pp. 410–23.

Walkowitz, Judith, *City of Dreadful Delight: Narratives of Sexual Danger in Late-Victorian London* (Chicago: Chicago University Press, 1992).

Watt, Ian, *The Rise of the Novel: Studies in Defoe, Richardson and Fielding* (London and New York: Penguin Books, 1957).

Welsh, Alexander, *George Eliot and Blackmail* (Cambridge, MA: Harvard University Press, 1985).

White, Hayden, *Metahistory: The Historical Imagination in Nineteenth-Century Europe* (Baltimore: The Johns Hopkins University Press, 1975).

Wilde, Oscar, *The Picture of Dorian Gray* [1890] (New York: W. W. Norton & Company, 2006).

Williams, Bill, 'The Anti-Semitism of Tolerance: Middle-class Manchester and the Jews', *City, Class and Culture: Studies of Social Policy and Cultural*

Production in Victorian Manchester, ed. A. J. Kidd and K. W. Roberts (Manchester: Manchester University Press, 1985).

Williams, Kevin, *Read All About It!: A History of the British Newspaper* (New York: Routledge, 2001).

Wisse, Ruth, *The Modern Jewish Canon: A Journey through Language and Culture* (New York: The Free Press, 2000).

Index

Page numbers in *italics* refer to illustrations and those followed by n are notes

aestheticism, 150–7, 160n, 169
alienation, 59
All the Year Round, 58n
Altick, Richard, 61, 62, 95
American Jewish Publication Society, 143
American press, 31–2, 53n
Anderson, Amanda, 89n, 125, 141–2
Anderson, Benedict
  caricatures, 82
  Imagined Communities, 3–6, 69
  literature and the newspaper, 22n
  'mass reading ceremony', 8, 159
  national community, 21n, 93
  post office, 26–7
  premodern time, 105
Anglo-Jews, 124–66, 162n
'appetite for news', 28–32
Armstrong, Isobel, 21n
  Novel Politics, 21n, 22n
  The Radical Aesthetic, 21n
Armstrong, Nancy, 21n

Arnold, Matthew, 11
'associative talking', 144
Athenaeum, 105–6

'bad infinity', 59, 68–78
Bagehot, Walter, 28
Balzac, Honoré de, 119n
Barrell, John, 10
Beaty, Jerome, 134
Beetham, Margaret, 8
Benjamin, Walter, 29, 55–6n, 105
Bentley, Richard, 31
Bentley's Miscellany, 31
Bernstein, Susan David, 130
bibliomancy, 105
Bildung, 59, 60, 68–78, 143, 161n
Bildungsroman
  Children of the Ghetto, 168
  Esther Ansell (character), 127–8, 143, 150–7
  historical novel, 68–9
  and Jewish hero, 126, 130–1, 162n
  social pressures, 88n
  as subplot, 134

Boes, Tobias, 134
Bossche, Chris R. Vanden, 46
Bourdieu, Pierre, 5–6, 63
Boyarin, Daniel, 161n
Braddon, Mary Elizabeth, 95, 96
  Aurora Floyd, 95, 96–9, 117
  Bell's Life (fictional newspaper), 97, 99, 117
  Lady Audley's Secret, 1
The Bradford Observer, 16
Brantlinger, Patrick, 22n, 36, 45
Briggs, Thomas, 40–2
British Parliament represented in novels, 61, 64
British press and the nation, 9–16
Britishness, 24n, 125, 162n
Brooks, Peter, 94, 96, 105, 115, 119n
Brown, Daniel, 23n
Brown, Lucy, 62
  Victorian News and Newspapers, 24n
Burke, Edmund, 10

Caledonian Mercury, 106, 120n
Carlyle, Thomas, 10, 71
Cesarani, David, 162n
characterisation of the press, 59–92
Chartists, 46–7
cheap press, 23n, 29–30
Cheyette, Bryan, 160n, 164n
Childers, Joseph, 126–7
Christianity, 164n
Chronicle, 11
Church of England represented in novels, 61, 64–5, 71, 84

Clemm, Sabine, 31
Collins, Wilkie
  Armadale, 93–5, 100–15, 117, 119–20n, 119n, 120–1n, 122n
  Basil, 115–16
  female characters, 119n
  The Law and the Lady, 116
  Lydia Gwilt (character), 18, 20, 95, 99–117, 119–20n, 119n, 120–1n, 122n
  melodrama, 122n
  modernity, 96, 118–19n
  The Moonstone, 105, 123n
  'unknown public', 10, 91n
Copyright Amendment Act 1842, 45–6
copyright debate, 45–6
Cornhill Magazine, 95, 100, 109–12, 112
Costantini, Mariaconcetta, 113, 122n
crime news, 94–5
Crimean War (1853–56), 73–4, 90n
Crosby, Christina, 161n
Culler, Jonathan, 4
Curtis, L. Perry, 41

Daily News, 11, 12–13, 117
daily press, 26–7
Daily Record, 83–4
Daily Telegraph, 13–15, 132
Daly, Nicholas, 117n
Dames, Nicholas, 87n
Davis, Lennard, 8, 22n, 23n
'deception', 99–100
Defoe, Daniel
  Moll Flanders, 121n
  Robinson Crusoe, 105
Dekel, Mikhal, 126, 130, 161n, 162n

The Derby Mercury, 107
diary, 112–15
Dickens, Charles, 26–58
  Bleak House, 58n, 110
  Bradley Headstone (character), 34–6, 40–1, 42–3, 54–5n
  David Copperfield, 37, 63
  Dombey and Son, 39, 50
  Eugene Wrayburn (character), 34–6, 40–1, 42–3
  John Harmon (character), 1, 34, 36–41, 51–2, 55–6n
  Lizzie Hexham (character), 34–6, 43, 52
  'magician's wand', 124–5
  Martin Chuzzlewit, 31–2, 44–5, 51–2
  Master Humphrey's Clock, 31, 49
  modernity, 118–19n
  Oliver Twist, 58n, 160n
  Our Mutual Friend, 1, 27, 32, 33–44, 160n
  Pickwick Papers, 44, 47
  as reporter, 26–7
  representation of Jews, 160n
  Rowdy Journal (fictional), 31–2
  satirised in *The Warden*, 71
  striking Imitation of Boz, 44–50
  tyrannical press, 16
Disraeli, Benjamin, *Sidonia*, 124
domestic community, 30–1
domestic romance, 105–9
Drew, John M. L., *Dickens the Journalist*, 28
The Dublin Pilot, 47
Duncan, Ian, 69

East End, 124–66, 165n
educational systems, 54n
Eigner, Edwin, *The Dickens Pantomime*, 37
Eliot, George
  Adam Bede, 90n
  Daniel Deronda, 122n, 124, 126–7, 130–6, 140–2, 152, 159, 160–4n
  Middlemarch, 110, 122n, 127, 131, 132–9, 163n
  Pioneer (fictional newspaper), 131, 134, 135–6, 139, 163n
Express, 11

factuality, 8–9
Farina, Jonathan V., 53–4n
Ferguson, Frances, 79–80
Finestein, Israel, 162n
Flint, Kate, *Interdisciplinary Studies in the Long Nineteenth Century*, 21n
'fourth estate', 10, 83
Frank, Catherine O., 64, 87n, 88n
Franklin, Jacob, 132
fraud, 49–50
free press, 10, 15
French press, 53n

Gallagher, Catherine, *Nobody's Story*, 22n
Gaskell, Elizabeth, *Wives and Daughters*, 95, 109–10
Gates, Sarah, 130, 161–2n
Gegeef, 'Our National Press', 12–15, *14*
ghettos, 19, 68, 126–8, 143, 150–6, 157

Gissing, George
  Chit Chat (fictional magazine), 167
  New Grub Street, 60, 167–8
Glasgow Herald, 107
Globe, 11, 13
GoGwilt, Christopher, 123n
Goode, Mike, 81–2
Goodlad, Lauren, 87n, 90n
Goodman, Kevin, 39
Gothic sensibility, 95, 118n
The Graphic, 61, 86n

Habermas, Jürgen, 5–6, 12, 23n, 79, 94
Hadley, Elaine, 10–11, 59, 83, 85n, 91n, 115, 118n
Hamer, Mary, 87n
Hampton, Mark, *Visions of the Press in Britain*, 23–4n
Hariman, John, 120n
Harshav, Benjamin, 144
Hauser, Helen, 57–8n
Haywood, Ian, 48
  Faking It, 22n
Hebrew translations, 161n
Hensley, Nathan, 119n
Herald, 11
Hetherington, Naomi, 164n
historical novels, 68–9
historical present tense, 23n, 39–40
Household Words
  'The Appetite for News', 11–12, 13
  'appetite for news', 28–32
  family-oriented, 10
  fictional narrative in, 53–4n
  imagination in, 51
  narrator, 26–7
  'A Paris Newspaper', 53n
  'A Preliminary Word', 29–30, 53n
Huett, Lorna, 29–30
Hughes, Linda K., 87n, 122–3n

immediacy, 8
'imperial press system', 24n
information technology, 118n, 167–8
Itzkovitz, Daniel, 161n

James, Louis, 48
Jameson, Frederic, 115, 122n, 123n
Jewish Chronicle, 132–3, 147, 150, 157
'The Jew in Fiction', 160n
Jewish community, 128–31
Jewish Recorder, 132, 133
The Jewish Standard, 133
'Jews in Fiction', 124–5
  'Morour and Chrouseth', 125–6, 137–8, 144–5
Jewish storytelling, 140–3; *see also* Yiddish storytelling
Jewish World, 133
John Bull and Britannia, 106, 120n
journalism and the novel, 16
  adaptation of journalistic form, 61–8
  American and French, 53n
  caricatures, 81
  commercial, 91n
  Dickens and, 27–8, 50
  fickle public, 25n
  immediacy, 39
  Jupiter (fictional newspaper), 89n

journalism and the novel (*cont.*)
  liberalism, 88n
  realism, 90n, 129
  Rubery, 56n
  self-reflexivity, 3
  Trollope, 60–6, 84
  virtues, 23n
  Zangwill, 137–9, 163n

Kendrick, Walter M., 63
Klancher, Jon, 118n
Knight, Charles, 23n
Knight Hunt, Frederick, *The Fourth Estate*, 10
Koven, Seth, 165n
Kreilkamp, Ivan, 10

Leavis, F. R., 130
Ledger, Sally, 10, 79
Leicester Chronicle, 23n
Levine, Caroline, 168–9
  The Serious Pleasures of Suspense, 7
Levine, George, 9
Levy, Amy, 161n
  'The Jew in Fiction', 160n
liberalism, 59–60, 85n, 88n, 89n, 91n, 162n
Liddle, Dallas, 5–6, 15
literary value, 45–6
Lloyd's Weekly Newspaper, 41–2, 44
Loesberg, Jonathan, 123n
The London Journal, 47, 158–9
Lonoff, Sue, 119n, 122n
Luhmann, Niklas, 8–9, 99–100, 109
Lukács, Georg, 59
  Theory of the Novel, 69
Lund, Michael, 87n

Mahon, Lord, 45
Manse, H. L., 94–5

McKeon, Michael, 121n
McLuhan, Marshall, 86n
McWilliam, Rohan, 120n, 122n
melodrama
  Armadale, 94–5, 120–1n
  Balzac, 119n
  and character, 105–9
  Eliot, 122–3n
  imagination, 105
  modernity, 118n
  realism, 123n
  self-reflexivity, 115
  sensation novel, 96–9, 122n
Messianic time, 105
Michie, Helena, 88–9n
Mill, John Stuart, 11, 76, 164n
Miller, Andrew, 50
Miller, D. A., 51, 79
minority communities, 124–66
Miron, Dan, 152
  The Image of the Shtetl, 153
Mitchell, Charles, 16
  The Newspaper Press Director, 25n
Mitchell, William Woods, 16
modernism, 123n
modernity, 94, 118–19n
Moretti, Franco, 3, 126, 130, 162n
Morning Post, 11
Müller, Franz, 40–2, 43–4, 56n
Mundhenk, Rosemary, 55n

national community, 3–6, 21n, 69, 93–4
national press, 23–4n
Nemesvari, Richard, 123n
news, form of, 6–9
news agents, 24n
'the Newspaper Novel', 94–5
newspaper target audiences, 10–12
Niles, Lisa, 119–20

'norm violator', 109
nostalgic realism, 19, 126–7, 150–6, 161n; *see also* realism

O'Connor, Fergus, 83
Olson, Melissa, 'Dracula and the Anti-Christ', 161n

The Pall Mall Gazette, 25n
Pal-Lipinski, Piya, 122n
Patten, Robert, 45
Pelegrini, Ann, 161n
Penny Magazine, 23n
penny newspapers, 15–16, 57n, 91n
'people's friend', 78–83
periodical press, 8
Pettitt, Clare, 39–40, 48
Phelan, James, 86–7n
phrenology, 161n
'pious fraud', 37–8, 50–1, 54n, 55n
'poetic energy', 140–2, 163n
political caricature, 81–3
The Political Register, 23n
Poovey, Mary, 23n
post office, 26–7
Potter, Simon, 24n
'presence of the present', 61–8
Press Association, 24n
providential plot, 99–105
'public', 10–11
public opinion, 78–83
Pyket, Lyn, 119n

Rader, Ralph, 7, 9, 22n, 99, 116, 121n, 123n
Rance, Nicholas, 118n, 122n
realism
  Armadale, 112–15
  Armstrong, 22n
  Children of the Ghetto, 126, 128–9, 168
  Daniel Deronda, 130
  definitions of, 6–9
  Eliot, 161–2n
  Jameson, 123n
  Levine, 23n
  'narratives of the real', 2
  national community, 3
  nostalgic realism, 19, 126–7, 150–6, 161n
  sensation novel, 115–16
  Wives and Daughters, 109–10
  Yiddish storytelling, 143, 154
  Zangwill, 156
Reform Act 1832, 15, 91n, 134
Reform Act 1867, 61
Reuters, 24n
Reynolds, George W. M., 46–50, 57–8n
  The London Journal, 158
  Master Timothy's Book-case, 49–50, 57n
  Mysteries of London, 46–7, 48–9
  Mysteries of the Court of London, 48
  Pickwick Abroad; or, The Tour in France, 47–8
Reynold's Miscellany, 47
Reynolds's Weekly, 47
Reynolds Weekly, 42
Richardson, Samuel, *Pamela*, 112–15, 121n
Ricoeur, Paul, 53n
Rochelson, Meri-Jane, 145, 157, 161n
  A Jew in the Public Arena, 160n
romantic British periodical, 118n
Rosenthal, Jesse, 53n

Rubery, Matthew, 56n, 77, 89n
Russell, William Howard, 90n

Saint Pauls Magazine, 61
Salamensky, S. I., 165n
scandal and gossip, 22n
Scheinberg, Cynthia, 140–1, 142, 160n, 163n
Scott, Sir Walter, *Isaac of York*, 124
self-reflexivity, 6–7, 71, 95, 96, 115
Semarang Hitam, 4–5
sensation novel, 93–23, 117n, 118n, 122n, 122–3n
serial form, 87n
shtetl, 150, 152–6, 165n
Smith, Madeleine, 95, 106–7, 120n
Society for the Diffusion of Useful Knowledge, 23n, 57n
Soyer, Alexis, 11–12
The Spectator, 106, 119–20
Standard, 11
Star, 15
Stoker, Bram, *Dracula*, 167–8
Sullivan, Anne, *Interdisciplinary Studies in the Long Nineteenth Century*, 21n
Sunday Times, 47

Talfourd, Thomas Noon, 45–6
'taxes on knowledge', 12, 15–16, 24n, 132
Taylor, Jenny Bourne, 118–19n
Tennenhouse, Leonard, 21n
Terdiman, Richard, 39
Teukolsky, Rachel, 90n

Thackeray, William Makepeace, 109
Tierney-Hynes, Rebecca, 121n
Tillotson, Kathleen, 118n
The Times
   Armadale, 93, 104–5
   Collins, 117
   Crimean War (1853–56), 73–4
   Müller, 41
   target audiences, 11
   'taxes on knowledge', 15, 132
   Trollope, Anthony, 91n
Tit-Bits, 167
Trollope, Anthony, 59–92
   An Autobiography, 62–3
   Barchester Towers, 73, 80
   Mr Harding (character), 69–74, 89n
   He Knew He Was Right, 83–5
   Jupiter (fictional newspaper), 69–74, 78, 89n, 91n
   Palliser novels, 59, 60, 61–8, 79, 86n, 91n
   The People's Banner (fictional newspaper), 66, 75–7, 80–1, 91n
   Phineas Finn, 1, 61, 62, 78–9, 80, 82–3, 91n
   Phineas Finn (character), 59, 60, 63–8, 77–8, 79, 80–1
   Phineas Redux, 61, 63–4, 67–8, 77–8, 80, 87n
   Plantagenet Palliser (character), 59, 60, 63, 67, 75–8, 80–1
   The Prime Minister, 63, 74–7, 80–1
tyrannical press, 16
The Warden, 69–74, 76–7, 78, 80, 83–4, 89n

true crime stories, 18, 95, 123n
tyrannical press, 16

Udelson, Joseph, 160n
'unknown public', 10, 45, 91n
Utilitarians, 23n

Valman, Nadia, 160n, 164n
Van Dam, Frederik, 87n, 90n
Vermeulen, Pieter, 22n
Voice of Jacob, 132

Walkowitz, Judith, 165n
Ward, Mrs Humphrey, *Robert Elsmere*, 143, 164n
Welsh, Alexander, 118n
Wilde, Oscar, *The Picture of Dorian Gray*, 155–7, 165n
Wills, W. H., 28

Wohlfarth, Mark E., 163n
Woloch, Alex, 114
Wynne, Deborah, 95

Yiddish storytelling, 126–7, 143–50, 150–1, 152, 164n, 168
Yule, Marian, 167

Zangwill, Israel
  Children of the Ghetto, 16, 124–66, 167–8
  Esther Ansell (character), 66: 124–166, 161n, 164n
  The Flag of Judah (fictional newspaper), 19, 131, 134, 136, 139, 140, 158
  Ghetto Comedies, 154–5
  as Jewish celebrity, 160n
  'the Jewish Dickens', 124–66
  'Jewish *Robert Elsmere*', 143

EU representative:
Easy Access System Europe
Mustamäe tee 50, 10621 Tallinn, Estonia
Gpsr.requests@easproject.com

www.ingramcontent.com/pod-product-compliance
Lightning Source LLC
Chambersburg PA
CBHW070356240426
43671CB00013BA/2531